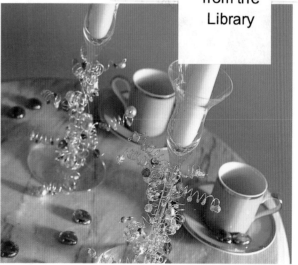

THE ILLUSTRATED GUIDE TO CRAFTING WITH
TIN, WIRE & FOIL

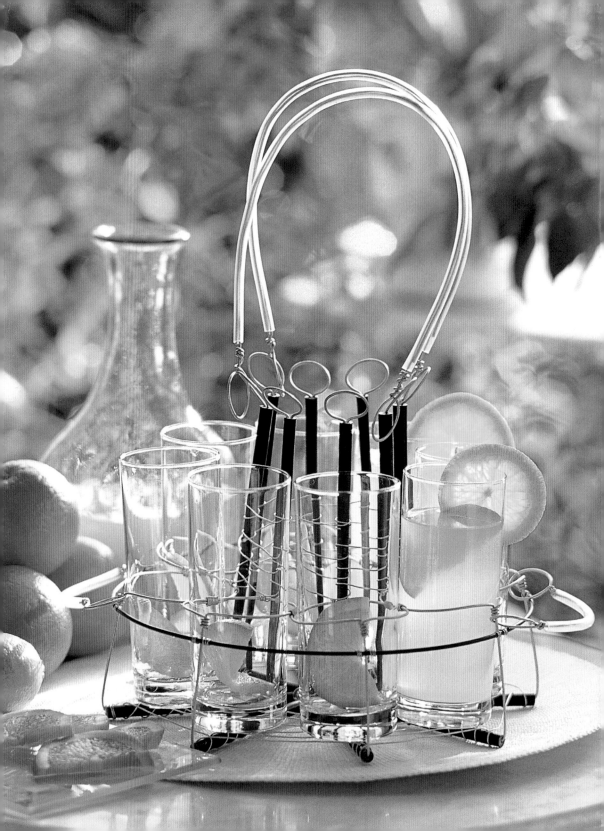

THE ILLUSTRATED GUIDE TO CRAFTING WITH
TIN, WIRE & FOIL

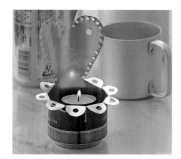

MAKE STUNNING GIFTS AND DECORATIVE
ITEMS FOR THE HOME AND GARDEN
WITH 100 STEP-BY-STEP PROJECTS

SIMONA HILL

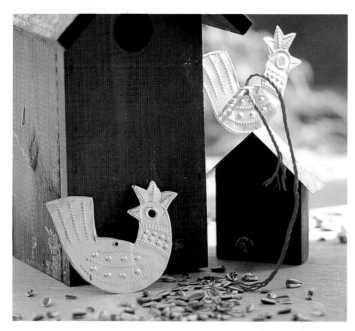

southwater

This edition is published by Southwater, an imprint of
Anness Publishing Ltd, Hermes House, 88–89 Blackfriars Road,
London SE1 8HA; tel. 020 7401 2077; fax 020 7633 9499

www.southwaterbooks.com; www.annesspublishing.com

If you like the images in this book and would like to investigate using
them for publishing, promotions or advertising, please visit our website
www.practicalpictures.com for more information.

UK agent: The Manning Partnership Ltd; tel. 01225 478444;
fax 01225 478440; sales@manning-partnership.co.uk
UK distributor: Grantham Book Services Ltd; tel. 01476 541080;
fax 01476 541061; orders@gbs.tbs-ltd.co.uk
North American agent/distributor: National Book Network;
tel. 301 459 3366; fax 301 429 5746; www.nbnbooks.com
Australian agent/distributor: Pan Macmillan Australia; tel. 1300 135 113;
fax 1300 135 103; customer.service@macmillan.com.au
New Zealand agent/distributor: David Bateman Ltd; tel. (09) 415 7664;
fax (09) 415 8892

Publisher: Joanna Lorenz
Managing Editor: Helen Sudell
Project Editor: Simona Hill
Photographers and Stylists: Deena Beverley, Stephanie Donaldson, Rodney
Forte, Michelle Garrett, Janine Hosegood, Rose Jones, Leean Mackenzie,
Lizzie Orme, Debbie Patterson, Graham Rae, Russel Sadur, Lucinda Symons
and Mark Wood
Designer: Nigel Partridge
Editorial Reader: Jonathan Marshall
Production Controller: Wendy Lawson

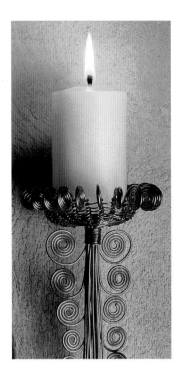

ETHICAL TRADING POLICY
Because of our ongoing ecological investment programme, you, as our
customer, can have the pleasure and reassurance of knowing that a tree is
being cultivated on your behalf to naturally replace the materials used to
make the book you are holding. For further information about this scheme,
go to www.annesspublishing.com/trees

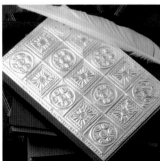

A CIP catalogue record for this book is available from the British Library.

Previously published as *Decorative Tin & Wirework*

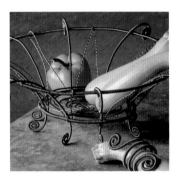

SAFETY NOTE
Working with tin and wire is great fun and can fill many rewarding
hours. For safety, protective gloves should be worn when using wire
and tin that has sharp ends.

Contents

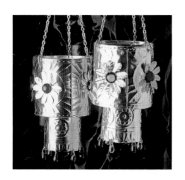

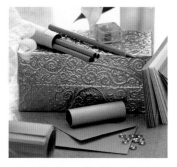

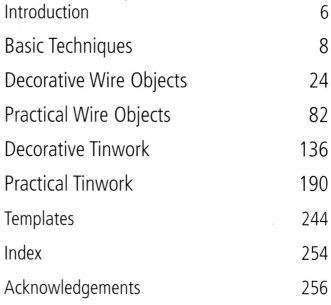

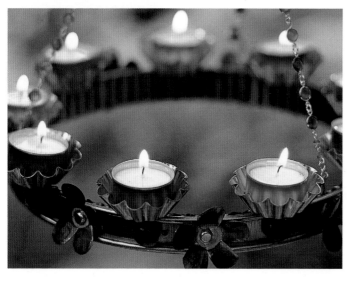

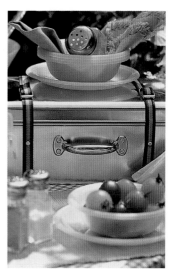

Introduction

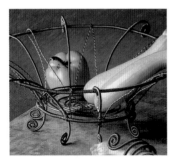

Decorating with wire and tin is fun to do and can be immensely satisfying. There is a host of lovely pieces you can make, both practical and decorative, for your home. As well as explaining and illustrating the different techniques involved in working with wire and metal, this book contains over 100 step-by-step projects, ranging from simple to complex and from small to large.

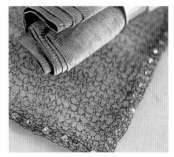

You can begin with a cheerful wire necklace or an embossed metal greetings card and progress to more ambitious projects such as chandeliers, bird chimes and even a barbecue. All involve skills such as wrapping, coiling and weaving wire, and punching, riveting and soldering metal, and even metal mosaic. Follow the symbols that indicate which of the projects are easy or more time-consuming. The symbol ⚇ indicates that a

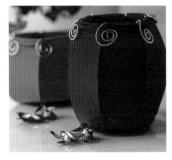

project is relatively straightforward to do and that a complete beginner could tackle it with ease. Projects with the symbol ⚇⚇⚇⚇⚇ indicate that an advanced level of skill and knowledge is required to complete the project.

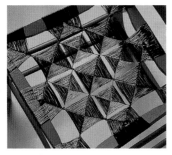

Many of the designs require you to draw a motif or pattern. If you are artistic, you may want to draw your own designs freehand, but if not, there are plenty of templates to trace or enlarge to the size required. Some of the most striking designs are the simplest: for example, geometric ruled lines can be used decoratively to create a castellated metal border for a shelf, or simple twisted spirals can be woven together into all sorts of durable, decorative and practical objects.

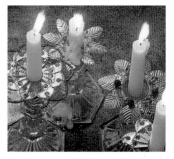

It is wise to practise all the techniques first so that you get the feel of how to bend and twist wire or hammer metal. That way you will get a more professional finish to your work. You will soon find

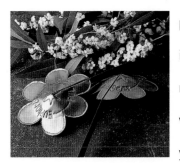

it becomes second nature to use round-nosed (snug-nosed) pliers and hide hammers in just such a way without the material snapping or denting. With your new-found skills, you will soon be filling your home with innovative, practical and decorative pieces of sculptural artwork that are sure to become a talking point.

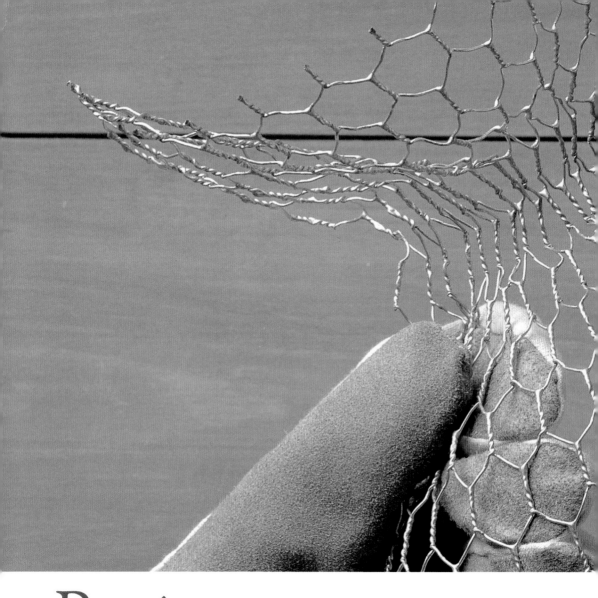

Basic

Techniques

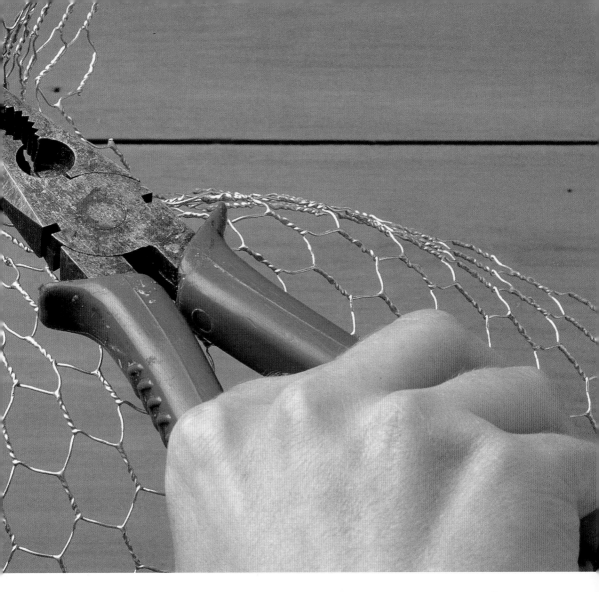

Before beginning any wire- or tinwork project, it is important to have an understanding of the basic techniques. In wirework, these include twisting, wrapping, coiling and weaving wire, and sculpting with chicken wire. In metalwork, basic techniques include cutting, filing, punching, embossing and soldering. Once these skills are acquired, you will be able to attempt any of the projects that follow in this book, and even create some of your own.

You can buy wire from good jewellery, craft and sculpture suppliers, as well as some hardware stores. There are also specialist wire suppliers, and electrical stores may also stock the materials you need.

Wirework Materials

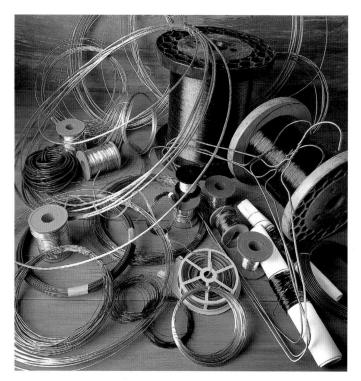

ideal for outdoor use. Galvanized wire is hard, so does not bend easily. This wire is springy, so needs to be used with caution. Available in five gauges.

Garden wire

This is easy to manipulate as it is plastic-coated. It is perfect for kitchen or bathroom accessories because it is waterproof, long-lasting and colourful.

Pipe cleaners and paper clips (fasteners)

These less obvious wirework materials are great fun to work with.

Silver-plated copper wire

This wire is particularly well suited to jewellery making and fine wirework.

Straining wire

This strong, textured wire is made of strands of galvanized wire twisted together. Take care when using it.

Tinned copper wire

This is shiny and does not tarnish, so it is suitable for kitchenware.

Twisty wire tape

This thin, flat tape with a wire core comes in green for gardening and blue and white for household use.

Wire coat hangers

These are cheap and widely available.

Aluminium wire

This is a dull blue-grey colour. It is the easiest to work with because it is so soft and easy to bend.

Chicken wire

This is made from galvanized steel wire. Usually used for fencing and for animal pens, it comes with different-sized holes and in a range of widths. The projects in the book call for the smallest gauge. Chicken wire is easy to manipulate and inexpensive.

Copper wire

This has a warm colour and comes in different tempers (hardnesses). Soft copper wire is easy to work with and is available in a broad range of gauges.

Enamelled copper wire

Used in the electronics industry, this is available in a wide range of colours.

Galvanized wire

This is zinc-coated steel wire. The zinc coating prevents rusting, making it

The most important tools for wirework are a good pair of wire cutters and some pliers. General-purpose pliers will be sufficient for some projects, although round-nosed pliers are a worthwhile investment.

Wirework Equipment

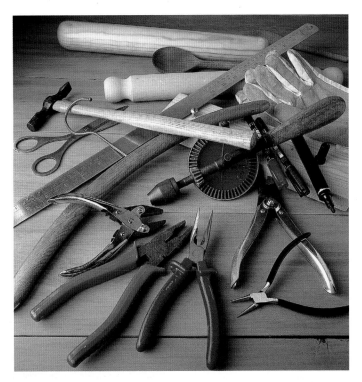

Parallel (channel-type) pliers – These are suitable for straightening bent wire and for bending angles.

Round-nosed pliers – Also known as snug-nosed jewellery pliers, these can be used for many different crafts, as well as for repairing broken jewellery. Use to bend wire into tiny circles.

Rolling pin, wooden spoon, pencil, broom handle

Many household objects are useful to coil wire around.

Ruler or tape measure

Many projects require very accurate measurements to ensure a good result.

Scissors

Use to cut through thin wire.

Wire cutters

Choose cutters with good leverage and long handles.

Wooden coat hangers

These can be used to twist galvanized wire together. Make sure the handle is secure and will not unscrew.

Wooden form

To bend strong wire into small circles use a wooden mould. Drill a screw into a piece of wood, but leave the head protruding from the wood. Bend the wire around the screw.

Gardening gloves and goggles

These protect your skin when working with scratchy wire. Wear goggles when manipulating long lengths of wire, especially if the wire you are using is under tension.

Hammer

A hammer is useful for flattening the ends of cut lengths of wire.

Hand drills

Useful for twisting soft wires together.

Permanent marker pens

Use to mark measurements on wire.

Pliers

General-purpose pliers – These often have serrated jaws to give a strong grip. Place a piece of leather between the pliers and the wire to prevent any marking.

Needle-nosed pliers – These are very useful for reaching into difficult places and are the best pliers for working with chicken wire.

These instructions will help you with the basic wirework techniques used to make the projects in this book. Try to familiarize yourself with this section before embarking on any of the projects.

Wire Techniques

Twisting Wire   This is a simple and effective way of joining two or more wires to add strength and texture to a design. Soft wires, such as copper, are easiest to twist, and using a hand drill speeds up the process. The harder wires, such as galvanized wire, require more effort. If you use a coat hanger to twist wires, choose the wooden type with a wire hook that revolves, ensuring that the handle is securely attached and will not unscrew.

Twisting Hard Wire

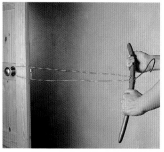

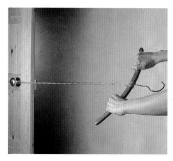

1 Cut a piece of wire three times as long as the required twisted length. Double the length of wire and loop it around a door handle or other secure point. Wrap the loose ends on one side of the coat hanger hook. Make sure you hold the wire horizontally, otherwise you may get an uneven twist.

2 Keeping the wire taut, begin turning the coat hanger. Do not relax your grip as this may cause an uneven texture. Twist the wire to the degree required, taking care not to overtwist as the wire may snap.

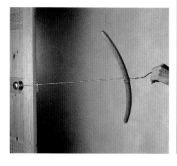

▶ **3** To release the tension in the wire, hold the hanger firmly in one hand and grip its hook in the other. Quickly release your hold on the hanger, which will spin around a bit. Remove the wire from the handle and cut off the ends.

Twisting Soft Wire

1 Double the lengths of wire to be twisted, by folding it in the middle. Two lengths have been used here, and you can use wires with different finishes. Loop the wires around a door handle and wrap the other ends with masking tape before securing them into the hand-drill chuck.

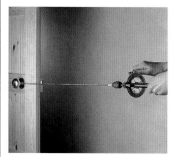

2 Keeping the wire taut, rotate the drill to twist the wire to the degree required. Start slowly at first so that you can gauge the tension. With soft wires there is no need to release the tension in the wire before removing them from the drill bit and trimming the ends.

Wrapping Wire   When wrapping wire, ideally the core wire should be both thicker and harder than the wrapping wire. Copper wire is the most suitable to use to wrap around a core. When cutting the core wire, remember to allow an excess length of at least 6.5cm/2½in to form a winding loop. The long lengths of soft wire used in wrapping can be unmanageable, so coil the wire first, as described in method B.

Method A	Method B	Tips for Wrapping Wire

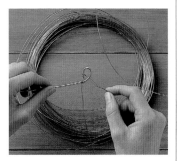

1 Using round-nosed (snug-nosed) pliers, make a loop at the end of the core wire. Neatly attach the wrapping wire to this loop.

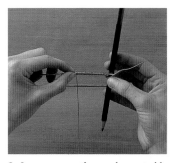

2 Insert a pencil or other suitable object into the loop and use it as a winder. While winding, hold your thumb and index finger right up against the coil to ensure that the wire is closely wrapped.

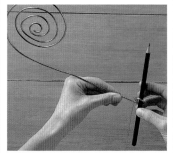

1 Using round-nosed (snug-nosed) pliers, make a loop at the end of the core wire and bend the wire into the desired shape along half its length. Form a loop at the other end of the core wire and secure the wrapping wire to the loop. Insert a pencil into the loop and use it as a winder.

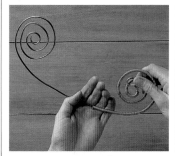

2 Wrap part of the wire, remove the pencil and coil the wire that has been wrapped. Now use this section as the winder. Use your hand to support the core wire from beneath, with the wrapping wire running between your fingers and thumb.

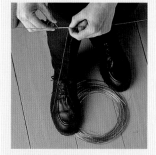

When using wire from a skein, keep it on the floor with your foot holding it in place. This will help you achieve the necessary tension for wrapping the wire and prevent the wire skein from unravelling and knotting.

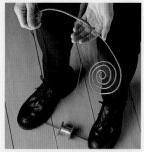

When using wire from a spool, it is easier if you insert a long stick through it and hold it in place with your feet. This will allow the spool to unwind quite freely while keeping the wire sufficiently taut.

Making Coils Coils are probably the most commonly used decorative device in wirework. They also have a practical use as they neaten and make safe what would otherwise be sharp ends. The flattened extended coil is a common structural and decorative device used in wirework. It is a quick and easy way to make the side walls of a container, for instance.

Open Coils

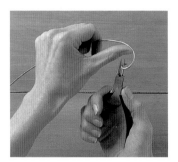

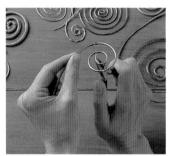

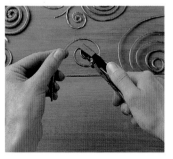

1 Using round-nosed (snug-nosed) pliers, make a small loop at the end of the wire. Hold the loop in the pliers, place your thumb against the wire and draw the wire across it to form a curve. Use your thumb to supply the tension.

2 Use your eye to judge the space left between the rings of the coil. If the wire is thicker, you will need more tension to make the curve and it will be more difficult to make the curve evenly spaced.

3 Finally, carefully flatten the coil with parallel (channel-type) pliers. Bend the coil into shape carefully.

Closed Coils

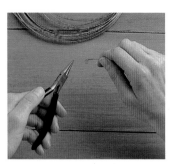

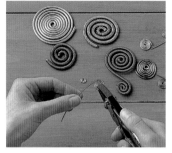

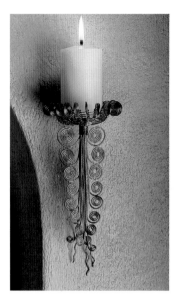

1 Using round-nosed (snug-nosed) pliers, make a small loop at the end of the wire.

2 Hold the loop securely with parallel (channel-type) pliers. Bend the wire around the loop until you have a coil of the size required. Keep adjusting the position of the pliers as you work.

Right: Ornate and stylish, wirework coils are surprisingly simple to make.

Flattened Extended Coils

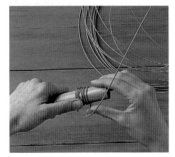

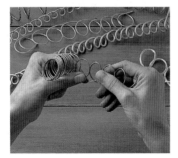

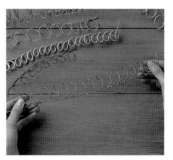

1 Wrap the wire several times around a broomstick or other cylindrical object to give you a coil. If using galvanized wire, you need to brace your thumb firmly against it.

2 After removing the coil from the broomstick, splay out the loops one by one, holding them firmly between your fingers and thumbs.

3 Keep splaying out the loops until the whole coil has been flattened. The loops will now look more oval than round. You can stretch the coil further to open the loops if you wish.

Weaving Many basketwork and textile techniques can be applied to wirework. Knitting and lacemaking techniques can also be employed with great success. Fine enamelled copper wire is especially suitable for weaving as it is soft and pliable and comes in a wide range of colours. Of the techniques described here, methods B and C will give a more closely woven and tidier finish than method A. Method A is the simplest.

Method A

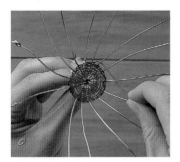

The quickest and easiest way to weave is to wind the wire in and out of the struts to create an open texture.

Method B

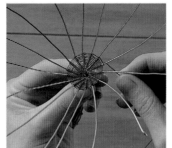

Pass the wire under each strut before looping it around the strut to create ridges in the weave.

Method C

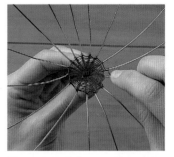

Weave around the struts by passing the wire over each strut and looping it around the wire to create a smooth, closely woven surface. This result is similar to method B but the rib will be on the outside.

Chicken Wire Techniques

Chicken wire is malleable and light, making it ideal for creating large structures. For ease of explanation, the instructions refer to struts (the horizontal, twisted wires in the hexagons) and strands (the single wires). Wear gloves when you work. Finish off any project by tucking away all the sharp ends.

Binding Wire – Method A

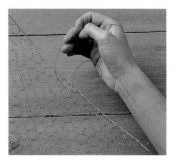

Place a length of wire along the edge of the chicken wire. Using a thinner wire, bind the length of wire and the chicken wire together.

Binding Wire – Method B

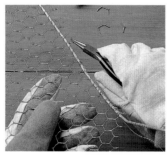

When binding diagonally, bind along the diagonal strands of the chicken wire. Bind evenly, taking in each strut as you come to it.

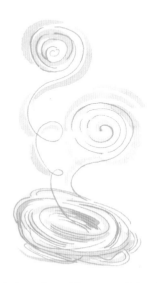

Transforming Hole Shapes

Hexagonal hole shapes give chicken wire lots of moulding potential and the shapes are easy to make.

Hearts

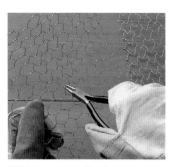

Hold the centre of each strut in turn with round-nosed (snug-nosed) pliers and twist up the wire to each side to create a cleft in the centre. When this process is repeated a pattern of heart shapes will emerge.

Brick Wall

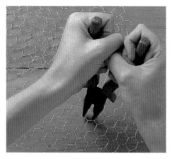

Insert pliers into the holes in the wire so that the sides of the pliers are up against the struts. Pull the handles gently apart to transform each into a rectangle shape. Work carefully to keep the mesh from buckling.

Fishing Net

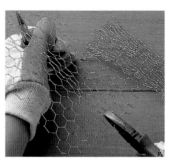

Hold the wire secure with small pliers and then pull it with general-purpose pliers to elongate the holes. You could hook the chicken wire over some nails hammered into a piece of wood if you were stretching a larger area.

Joining Chicken Wire

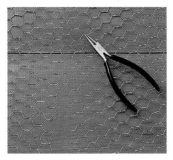

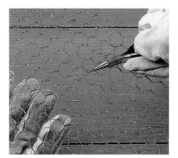

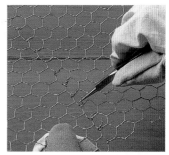

1 Cut the chicken wire at the point just before the wire strands twist into struts so that one of the edges is a row of projecting double strands and the other is a row of projecting struts.

2 Place the projecting struts on top of the other piece so that they overlap slightly. Using round-nosed (snug-nosed) pliers, carefully wrap each of the projecting strands around the corresponding strand on the upper-most piece of chicken wire.

3 Twist the overlapping struts firmly together using round-nosed pliers.

Shaping Chicken Wire

Chicken wire can be shaped into any number of shapes. For extra strength, work with the struts running horizontally and for a more elegant shape, work with the struts running vertically.

Shaping with Vertical Struts

Shaping with Horizontal Struts

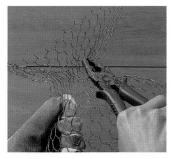

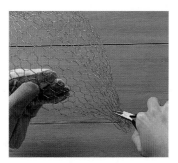

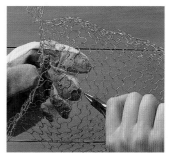

1 Using general-purpose pliers, squeeze the struts together to form the neck, pulling all the time to elongate the wires. To make the bulge, stretch out the holes by inserting general-purpose pliers as described for the brick wall effect, but only stretch them a little for a more elegant shape.

2 Using round-nosed (snug-nosed) pliers, squeeze the struts together to make the bottom tip, pulling again to elongate the wires.

Make the hexagons heart-shaped. Squash the cleft in each heart with round-nosed pliers. Mould with your thumbs. To make the bulge, mould with your fingers from inside, pulling out with pliers. To make the bottom tip, squash the clefts, contracting them to form a tight core.

For tin plate, metal foils and sheet metals, purchase materials from a specialist hardware store, or for recycled materials, a metal merchant or scrap yard. Always wear protective gloves, a work shirt and goggles.

Tinwork Materials

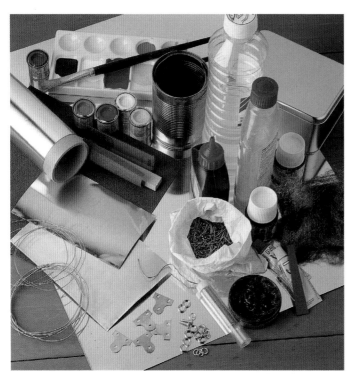

Silicon carbide (wet & dry) paper

This is abrasive. Fine-grade paper, when dampened, is useful for finishing off filed edges. Clamp the item in a bench vice and wrap the paper around a small wooden block.

S-joiners and jump rings

Use to join sections of an object together and to attach lengths of chain. They are very strong, and pliers are used to open and close the links.

Solder

This is an alloy, or mixture, of metals. Solder is a liquid metal filler that is melted, then used to join two pieces of metal together. Always use a solder that has a lower melting point than the metals to be joined. Follow the manufacturer's instructions.

Tin plate

This is a mild sheet steel that has been coated with tin. The plating will not tarnish in the open air or in humid conditions. Sheet metals are made in different thicknesses, or gauges. The higher the gauge, the thinner the metal. At 30 gauge (approximately 0.2mm/$\frac{1}{125}$in), tin plate can be cut by hand with tin snips and shears.

Biscuit tins

A good source of tin. Some tins have a plastic sheen so scrub with wire (steel) wool, if you intend to solder them.

Epoxy resin glue

This glue comes in two parts. Mix up as much glue as you need at one time. Once it has set the join is strong.

Flux

Used during soldering to make the area to be soldered chemically clean.

As the flux is heated, it runs along the metal preparing the surface. This helps the solder to flow and adhere.

Metal foils

These thin sheet metals usually come on rolls. Metal foil is so thin that it can be cut with household scissors. A variety of metal foils is available, and includes brass, aluminium and copper. The foil's thinness makes it very soft and it is easy to draw designs into the surface.

Zinc sheet

Thin zinc sheet has a dull matt surface and is fairly soft and easy to cut.

You may already have most of the basic tinwork tools. The more specialist items, such as punches, snips and shears, are available from good hardware stores.

Tinwork Equipment

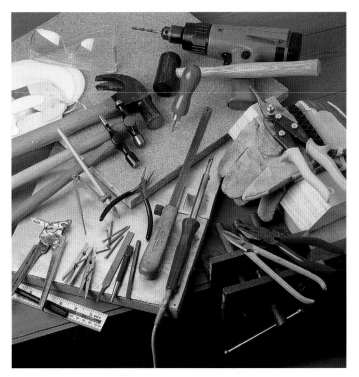

Hide mallet
This is made from leather. It has a soft head so will not mark the tin.

Pliers
Use to hold tin when you are cutting it and for turning over edges. Round-nosed (snug-nosed) pliers are good for making small circles of wire.

Soldering iron
This is used to heat the solder that joins two pieces of metal together.

Soldering mats
Various fireproof soldering mats are available and may be purchased from good hardware stores and metal supply shops.

Tin shears
These are very strong scissors used for cutting sheet metal. Shears come with straight blades to cut a straight line, or blades curved to the left or right to cut circles and curves.

Tin snips
These are good for cutting small shapes from tin.

Wooden blocks
It is useful to have a wooden block with 90° edges and another with a 45° edge when turning over the sides of a piece of tin.

Bench vice
Use to clamp metal shapes when filing, sanding, and hammering edges.

Bradawl (awl)
Use to make holes in metal.

Centre punch, chisel, nails
Use to punch decorative patterns.

Chipboard
This is used as a work surface when punching tin and embossing foil.

Hammers
A variety of hammers are used. A medium-sized ball head hammer is used with nails or a punch to make a pattern in tin. A tack hammer is used to knock panel pins (tacks) into wood. A heavy hammer is used with a chisel to make decorative holes.

Hand file
Use to remove any burrs of metal from the tin after a shape has been cut out.

Only a few basic techniques are required for making simple tinwork items. Read through this section before embarking on the projects in this book.

Tinwork Techniques

Cutting Tin   It is not difficult to cut through thin sheets of tin plate or tin cans. It is important to get used to cutting smoothly to avoid making jagged edges, so practise first on scraps of tin. Cutting tin produces small shards of metal that are razor-sharp, so collect scraps as you cut and keep them together until you can dispose of them safely.

Cutting a Section from a Sheet

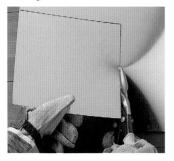

To cut a section of tin from a large sheet, use tin shears. To avoid creating a dangerous jagged edge when cutting, never close the blades of the shears completely. Instead, make a cut almost the length of the blades each time, open the shears, then guide the metal back into the blades and continue. Keep the blades in the cut, without removing them until the line of the cut is complete. If you are cutting a straight-sided shape, don't try to turn the shears around once you have reached a corner. Instead, remove the shears and cut across to the corner from the edge of the sheet of metal.

Cutting a Small Shape from a Section of Tin

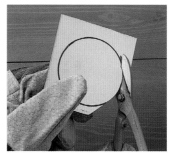

Use tin snips rather than shears to cut small shapes. They are easier to manipulate and control, especially if you are cutting an intricate shape. Again, don't attempt to turn the snips around in the metal; cut as much as you can, then remove the snips and turn the metal so that you can follow the cutting line more easily.

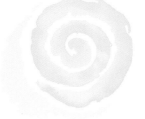

Safety Advice
• Always wear a heavy work shirt and protective leather gloves when you are handling metal pieces or uncut sheet metal.
• Tin shears and snips are very powerful, being strong enough to cut through fairly heavy metal, and very sharp. They should be handled with respect and, like all tools, should always be kept in a safe place away from children.
• A protective face mask and goggles should always be worn during soldering as the hot metal, solder and flux give off fumes. Work should be carried out on a soldering mat and the iron put on a metal rest when not in use.
• All soldering should be carried out in a properly ventilated area and frequent breaks should be taken when working. Don't lean too near your work to avoid close contact with the fumes. Wear protective gloves when you are soldering as the metal is hot.

Cutting Metal from an Oil Drum

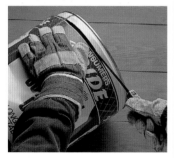

1 The metal found in oil drums is very often thin and springy, and so care must be taken when cutting out panels from a drum. Protect your eyes with goggles for extra safety. To remove the top of the drum, make a cut in the side using a hacksaw blade. Open the cut slightly, then insert the blades of a pair of tin shears into the space and cut around the drum, removing the top.

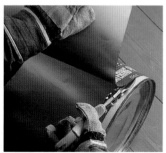

2 Carefully cut down a side to within 18mm/¾in of the drum base using tin shears. Gently snip around the base of the drum, pushing back the panel as it is freed from the base. Once you have removed the panel, it may be used in the same way as a sheet of tin plate. Mop up any oil residue on the surface of the tin using tissue paper.

Finishing the Edges

All tin items should be considered unfinished and unsuitable for use until all the edges have been smoothed or turned over. This should be done immediately to avoid any accidents. Long, straight edges may be folded and flattened with the aid of a hammer and wooden blocks with measured 90° and 45° edges. Irregularly shaped items may be finished with a hand file and silicon carbide (wet and dry) paper for complete smoothness. Tin cans should always be filed smooth around the rims before use to remove any jagged edges.

Filing Cut Metal

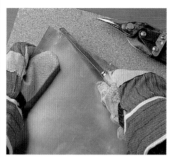

The raw, cut edges of a piece of tin plate are very sharp, and should be smoothed or finished immediately to prevent them causing harm to yourself or anyone else. Small shapes should be smoothed with a hand file while being firmly clamped in a vice. The file should be moved forwards at a right angle to the metal in one light stroke, then lifted and returned. This will remove most of the rough edges.

Using Silicon Carbide Paper

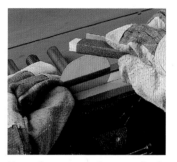

To make a cut edge completely smooth after filing, finish with fine-grade silicon carbide (wet and dry) paper. This is dampened and wrapped around a small wooden block like sandpaper (glasspaper). Sanding with this paper removes any remaining rough edges and leaves the metal smooth to the touch.

Turning Over Cut Edges

The cut edges of straight-sided pieces of tin plate should be turned over immediately after cutting to avoid accidents. Mechanically made baking tins and boxes have their edges bent over to an angle of 45° by a folding machine. The edges are then pressed flat and made safe. It is simple to replicate this process at home using two blocks of wood.

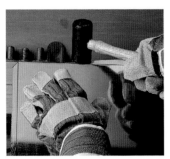

1 Clamp a thick block of wood with an accurately measured 90° edge firmly in a bench vice. Draw a border around the cut edges of the tin plate. Place the piece of tin on the block with the borderline lying along the edge of the block. Strike the edge of the tin with a hide hammer to mould around the edge of the block.

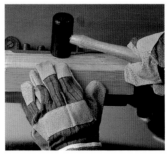

2 Turn the piece of tin over and place a block of wood with a 45° edge inside the fold. Keep the wooden block firm with one hand while hammering down on the folded edge of tin with a hide hammer.

3 Once the metal has been folded over to this angle, remove the block then hammer the edge completely flat using a hide hammer. Fold each side of the piece of tin in turn and once all its edges have been hammered flat, file the corners to smooth any sharp edges. Straight edges should always be finished in this way to avoid accidents, even if the panel is to be set into a recess, for example in the case of a punched panel cabinet.

Soldering

Sections of metal may be joined together by soldering. It is essential that both surfaces to be joined are clean before they are soldered. Rubbing both areas with wire (steel) wool will help to remove any dirt and grease. All soldering should be done on a soldering mat, wearing protective gloves, masks and goggles, and the soldering iron should be placed on a metal stand when not in use.

1 Place together the two sections to be joined. Hold them in place with wooden pegs (pins) or masking tape. Smear the joint with flux. This is essential, as when the metal is heated, an oxide forms on the surface that may inhibit the adhesion of the solder. The flux prevents the oxide from forming on the metal.

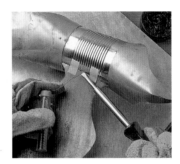

◄ **2** The hot soldering iron heats the metal, which causes the flux to melt. Pick up a small amount of solder on the end of the iron. It will start to melt. The iron is drawn down the joint and the solder flows with it, and displaces the flux. The solder then cools and solidifies, joining the two pieces of metal together.

Punching Tin   Tin may be decorated in a variety of ways. Punching, when a pattern of indentations is beaten into the surface of the metal, is one of the most common methods. A centre punch or nail, plus a ball hammer, are used to produce the knobbly patterns, either on the front or back of the tin. Small chisels and metal stamps are also used. Opaque and translucent enamel paints are suitable for decorating tin plate and other metals. Thin metal foils, such as aluminium foil, are so soft that a design may be drawn on to the surface to leave a raised or "embossed" pattern.

Getting the Design Right

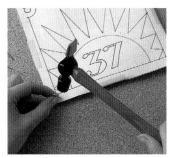

Nails or punches can be used to make indentations and holes in tin. If you want a sophisticated pattern, draw the design first on to a sheet of graph paper and punch through the paper into the tin following the lines. The paper should be taped to the tin, and the tin attached to chipboard using panel pins (tacks) to keep it steady as you punch.

Punching Tin from the Front

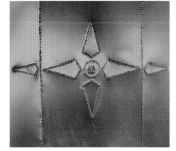

A design punched from the front will have an indented pattern. If an area of tin is punched from the front, and the indentations are made very close together, the punched area recedes and the unpunched area becomes slightly raised. This is one form of "chasing", where decorative patterns are punched into metal from the front and stand out in low relief.

Punching Tin from the Back

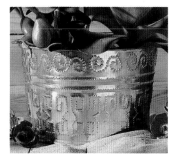

A design punched from the back will have a raised pattern and a pleasing knobbly effect on the surface. Patterns can be applied with nails of different sizes or punches to make a dotty texture. Short lines can be made by using a small chisel. It is also possible to buy decorative punches with designs engraved into the tip.

Embossing Aluminium Foil   ▶

Aluminium foil is very soft thin metal. It can be cut with household scissors and bent or folded as desired. It is especially useful for cladding frames, books, boxes and other small items. Its softness makes it easy to emboss. This is done by drawing on to the back of the foil using a dry or empty ballpoint pen, which leaves a raised surface on the other side.

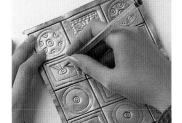

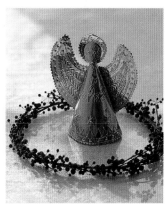

Right: *Many projects combine a range of decorating techniques.*

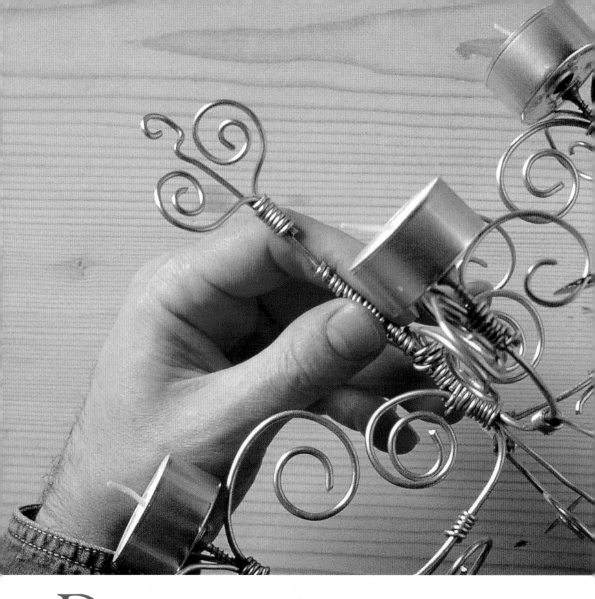

Decorative

Wire Objects

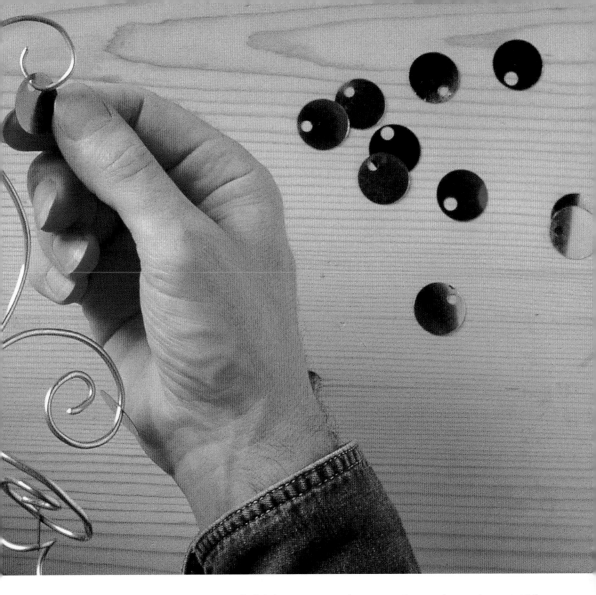

Wire is available in a variety of thicknesses and strengths and can be used in a multitude of ways to create imaginative and decorative items for the home. You can make fabulous jewellery, charming ornaments, unusual greetings cards and picture frames, elegant candle sconces and candlesticks, and even mesh tablemats, to name just a few. Be bold and explore the decorative potential of wire.

Twist and Sculpt

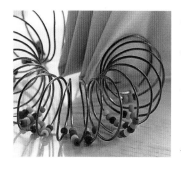

Once you have mastered the skill of using pliers, working with wire is easy, though labour intensive, and the results can be quite spectacular.

There are many types of wire, in a variety of thicknesses and colours. All wires, however, possess the same quality of malleability, enabling you to bend, coil, shape and sculpt them. Pipe cleaners come in a whole range of vivid colours, and are easy to use – you don't even need pliers – making them ideal wires for children to experiment with. Another wire that is commonly used in wirework is galvanized wire.

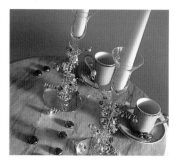

This doesn't rust, so it's a good material to use to make projects for the garden. Other lightweight wires used in these projects include enamelled copper wire and aluminium wire. You can also use coat hangers, which are

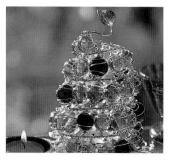

good for sculpting unusual shapes, and even wires from inside telephone cabling.

The instinctive thing to do with wire is to bend it into decorative motifs. Stars, flowers, hearts and circles are a few easy shapes you could try. Once you

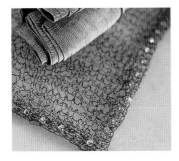

feel proficient try small-scale sculptures, perhaps using gold, or silver-plated wire for hanging ornaments, or motifs for a greetings card. In addition to bending wire, you can also twist two different types of wire together to create unusual

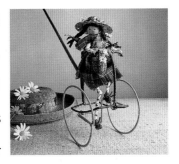

textures and subtle colours. Twisted or plaited (braided) wire can be used decoratively. Alternatively, coiling wire around a cylindrical object such as a broom handle or pen, gives spirals of wire, which can be used as edging, as springs or to provide delicate decoration. Amazingly, lightweight wire can be knitted to create a mesh-like effect, or woven to make a basket.

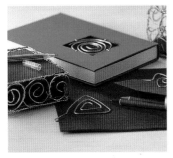

Wire is often used as a framework in a project, to which more elaborate wire decorations are added. For larger and more complicated projects, you can create separate parts of an item, and then solder the units together. For extra sparkle, glass beads can be threaded on to wire coils, or you can also spray-paint galvanized wire with metallic paints to inject more colour into the finished piece.

Fan-shaped panels of opaque polypropylene are the perfect foil for the light, silvery wire framework around this pot. The wire stitching used to attach the plastic to the framework makes an interesting feature.

Panelled Flower Pot Cover

you will need

flower pot base, circumference 33cm/13in, height 15cm/6in

paper

soft pencil

ruler

scissors

polypropylene sheet

long-nosed pliers

galvanized wire, 2mm/¹⁄₁₃in, 1mm/¹⁄₂₅in and 3mm/¹⁄₈in thick

wire cutters

cutting mat

bradawl (awl)

soldering iron, solder and flux

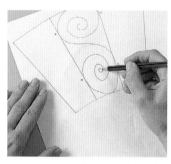

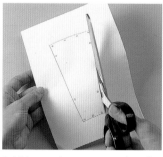

1 Using the template provided at the back of the book, make a pattern to fit around the outside of your flower pot. If your pot is not the specified size, adjust the template to fit by scaling it up or down on a photocopier.

2 Make another paper template that shows just one of the opaque panels of the pot cover. Mark on this the stitching holes for the panels. Cut around the edge of the shape carefully.

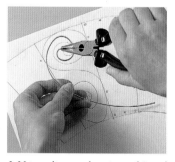

3 Using a soft pencil, trace around the second template on to the sheet of polypropylene. Cut out four pieces. Use different colours, if you like.

4 Using pliers, curl a piece of 2mm/ ¹⁄₁₃in wire to match the S-shape design. Repeat to make four matching S-shapes.

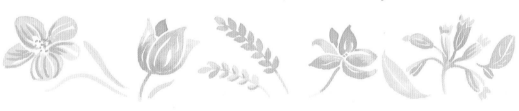

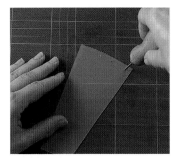

5 Working on a cutting mat and using a bradawl (awl), pierce small holes around the edges of the plastic panels where indicated on the template.

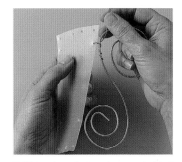

6 Using 1mm/¹/₂₅in wire, neatly bind the S-shapes to the plastic sections. Join all four of the plastic sections together in this way with a wire shape between each one. Trim any untidy wire ends.

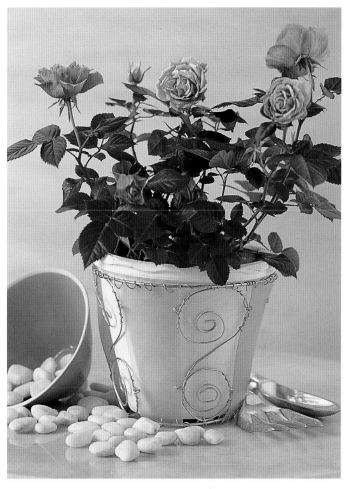

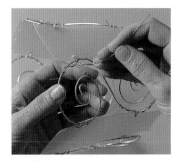

7 Bind the last wire shape and panel together to complete the pot shape. Bend any panels that have become mis-shapen back into shape.

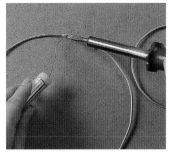

8 Cut two lengths of 3mm/¹/₈in wire to fit around the top and the base of the pot cover. Solder the ends of each length together.

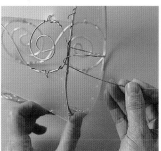

9 Bind the top and bottom rings to the pot cover using the 1mm/¹/₂₅in galvanized wire. Trim the ends neatly. Place the flower pot in the cover.

Galvanized wire is ideal for the garden, as it will not rust when exposed to the elements. Use this pretty repeating heart to edge a window box, or even to add an orderly edging to an unruly garden border.

Window Box Edging

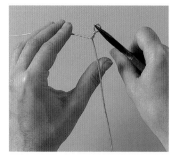

1 Scale up the template at the back of the book to a height of 15cm/6in, as a guide for bending the wire. Cut a 43cm/17in length of galvanized wire and bend it in half. Hold the centre point with pliers and twist the two ends around each other twice.

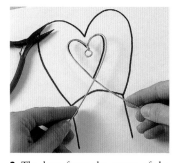

2 The loop forms the centre of the heart. Bend the two tail ends around the loop to form a small heart shape, using the scaled-up template as a guide. Cross the wires at the bottom of the heart. Try to make the heart shape symmetrical.

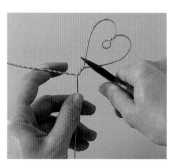

3 Hold the heart with pliers just above the crossing point and twist the two free ends around three times.

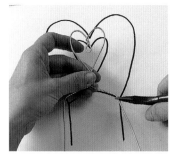

4 Use the pliers to bend the two free ends out and down, following the template.

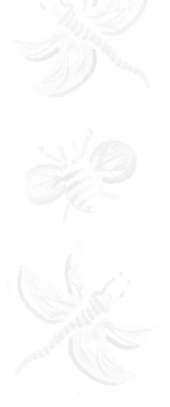

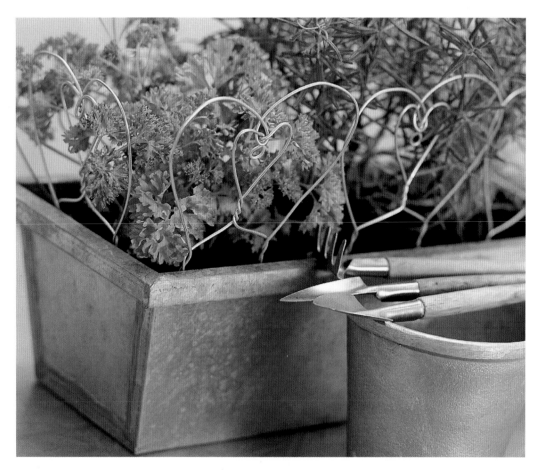

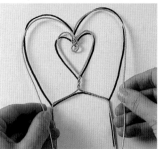

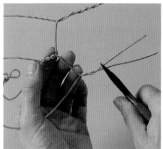

5 Cut a 48cm/19in length of wire, bend it in half as before and loop the central point over the twisted loop in the small heart. Use pliers to flatten the loop, then bend the wires down following the template.

6 Align the wire ends from the small and large hearts on each side, and twist them tightly together. Use the wire cutters to even up the wire at the bottom of the twists. Ensure the ends are long enough to add stability.

These necklaces are great fun to create and are the perfect project to make with children. You could also make matching accessories using clip-on earring backs and headband bases.

Happy Hippy Necklace

you will need
round-nosed (snug-nosed) pliers
plain, furry and thick, bumpy
pipe cleaners
coloured paper clips (fasteners)
twisty wire tape
wire cutters

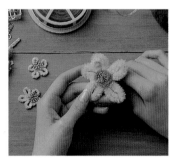

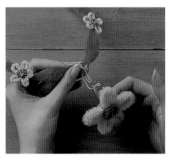

1 Using round-nosed (snug-nosed) pliers, make small flowers from plain pipe cleaners. Make the flower centres by straightening paper clips (fasteners) and coiling them into spirals. Bend a furry pipe cleaner into a five-petalled flower. Twist the ends together.

2 Coil a plain pipe cleaner and striped paper clip into tight, neat spirals to make the centre of the largest flower. Cut a length of twisty wire tape and tie a knot in it. Thread it neatly through the flower centre so that the knot sits at the front.

3 Bend a thick, bumpy pipe cleaner to form the necklace. Bind the small flowers to the pipe cleaner necklace with the twisty tape, tucking in the tape ends behind the flowers. Bind the large flower to a paper clip and clip on to the pipe cleaner necklace.

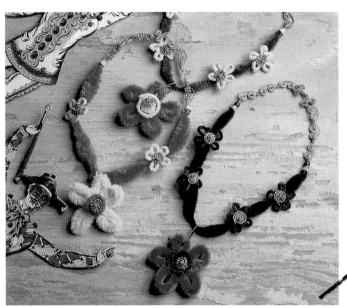

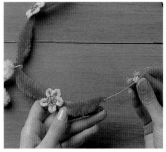

4 Form a loop at each end of the pipe cleaner and attach twisty wire tape to each loop. Form two paper clips into cones, then slide them on to the ends. Bend the ends of straightened paper clips into coils. Join them together to make two chains. Attach the chains to the ends of the pipe cleaner. Make a "hook-and-eye" from paper clips.

Adorn your pockets with these highly original and decorative clips. Galvanized wire has been used here; this can be sprayed with metallic car paint to change its colour.

Pocket Clips

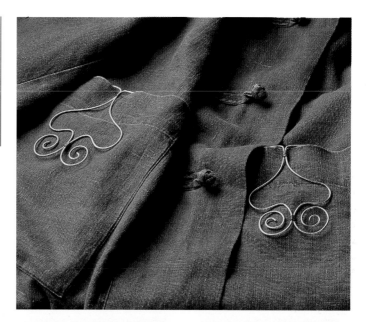

you will need

wire cutters

galvanized wire, 1mm/¹/₂₅in and 0.6mm/¹/₄₁in thick

ruler or tape measure

round-nosed (snug-nosed) pliers

half-round pliers

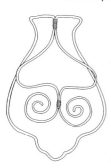

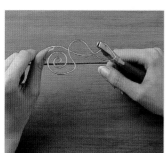

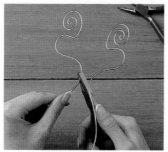

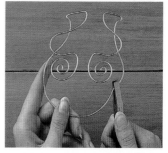

1 Cut a 1m/40in length of 1mm/¹/₂₅in galvanized wire. Make a coil at one end with the round-nosed (snug-nosed) pliers. Bend the wire to make an S-shape, referring to the diagram above. Square off the loop below the coil with half-round pliers.

2 Using half-round pliers, nip in the wire to form one side of the neck, then make a large loop in the wire. From top to bottom the large loop measures 11.5cm/4½in. Make a mirror-image loop and coil on the other side of the large loop, cutting off any excess wire.

3 Fold the structure in half and bend the top of the large loop at both sides to make shoulders. Nip in the bottom of the large loop to make a scallop. Using the 0.6mm/¹/₄₁in wire, bind the coils together. Bind the neck for 12mm/½in.

A homemade card makes a personal gift that will be cherished. The instructions here show you how to make the cherub Valentine card, but templates are provided for the other ideas.

Greetings Cards

you will need

33 x 21.5cm/13 x 8½in red cardboard

21 x 14.5cm/8¼ x 5¾in pink cardboard

paper and felt-tipped pen

scissors

ruler

gold spray paint

round-nosed (snug-nosed) pliers

galvanized wire, 0.6mm/¼1 in and 1mm/¼5in thick

wire cutters

straight pin

needle and thin nylon thread

masking tape

red cotton thread

paper glue

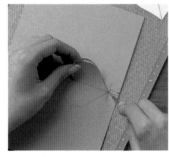

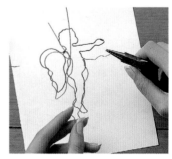

1 Fold the red cardboard in half. Make the heart templates. Centre the small heart on the red cardboard, 2.5cm/1in from the bottom. Centre the large heart on the pink cardboard, 1.5cm/⅗in from the bottom. Cut out the hearts, reserving the pink. Spray the pink cardboard bottom gold.

2 Use the round-nosed (snug-nosed) pliers to bend the thinner wire all around the template of the cherub. Make two. Bind the top of the wings. Form two hearts from the thicker wire. Using a pin, mark the position of the cherubs and one heart, with pairs of holes on the pink cardboard.

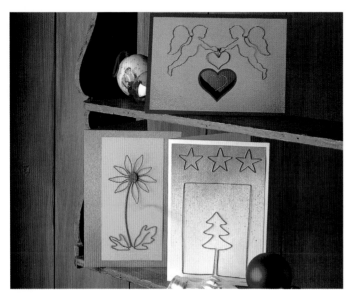

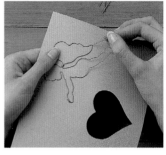

3 Attach the cherubs and heart to the pink cardboard by stitching through the holes with the nylon thread. Secure the ends with masking tape. Hang the second wire heart from the first with cotton thread. Centre the pink cardboard on the red and glue in place. Glue the pink heart inside.

Once you have become dextrous at sculpting in wire, try making this elegant Christmas angel that is sure to take pride of place hanging on the Christmas tree. The soft silver-plated copper wire is easy to bend.

Angel Decoration

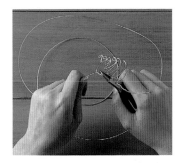

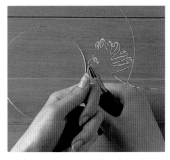

you will need
silver-plated wire,1mm/¹⁄₂₅in thick
round-nosed (snug-nosed) pliers
parallel (channel-type) pliers
wire cutters
narrow ribbon
star-shaped bead or crystal droplet

1 Photocopy the template at the back of the book, enlarging it to the size you require. Leaving 5cm/2in at the end, bend the wire around the angel template, using round-nosed (snug-nosed) pliers and your fingers.

2 Make the hair and the forehead up to the eye. Make the lower lid of the eye, then the upper lid. Halfway along the upper lid, make a loop to form the pupil. Squeeze the corner of the eye with parallel (channel-type) pliers.

3 Shape the nose and make a larger loop around the end of the round-nosed pliers for the nostril. Shape the mouth, closing the lips with parallel pliers, then shape the chin. Refer to the template as you work.

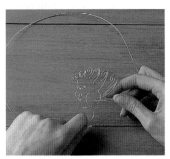

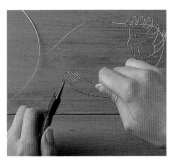

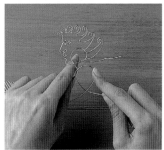

4 Loop the wire around the bottom of the hair to make the cheek. This loop will help to keep the structure flat and more manageable.

5 Follow the template along the arm. Make loops with round-nosed pliers for the fingers, and shape the bottom line of the arm.

6 Make the outline of the shoulder by carefully looping the wire around the point where the top of the arm joins the neck. ▶

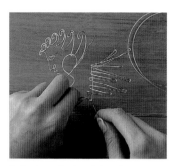

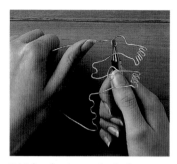

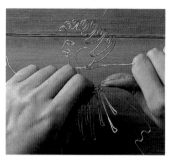

7 At the waist, bend the wire across to form the waistband. Make a series of long horizontal loops with slightly curled ends back along the waistband to represent floaty fabric. When you have made seven loops, secure with a tight twist at the bend.

8 Make a large curve for the lower part of the skirt. Shape a wavy hem around the thickest part of the round-nosed pliers. The legs interrupt the hemline. Make the toes in the same way as the fingers, but make them shorter and rounder. Shape the heels and make a loop at each ankle.

9 Continue bending the wire to complete the wavy hemline and make another, shorter curve to form the back of the skirt. Secure the lower section of the angel by twisting the wire around the waistband as tightly and neatly as possible.

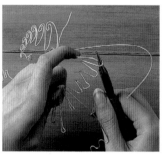

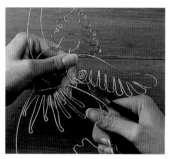

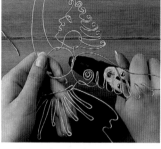

10 Make overlapping loops along the bottom of the wing. Form the curved top of the wing.

11 Loop the wire around the back of the shoulder and also under the bottom of the wing. Finish off with a coil and cut off the wire.

12 Using the 5cm/2in of wire left at the start, bind the shoulder and wing together. Cut off the end. Thread the ribbon through the waistband loops and then hang a star-shaped bead or crystal droplet from the angel's hand.

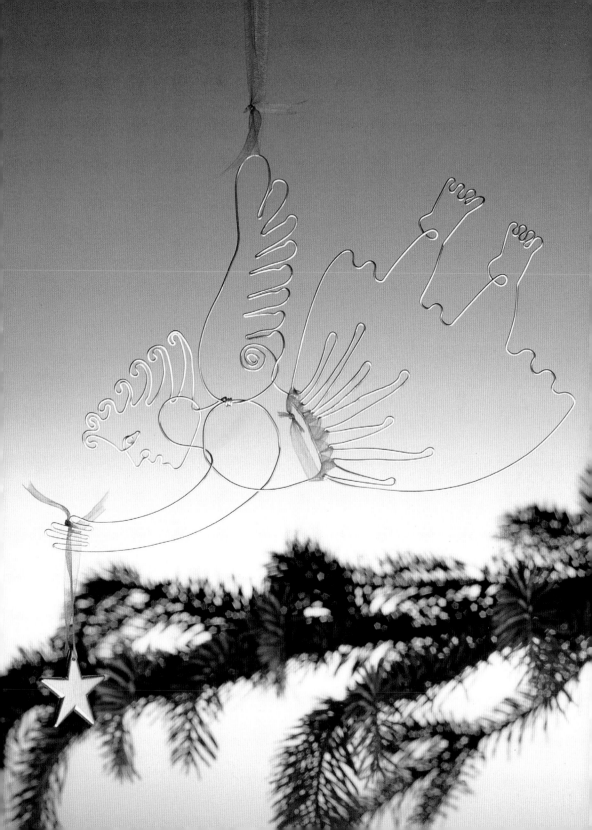

This pretty floral decoration will make a sparkling centrepiece on your Christmas table, but it would also create a magical effect as temporary garden lighting for a party on a summer evening.

Festive Light Bush

you will need

wire cutters

dark green plastic-coated garden wire, 2mm/^{1}/13in and 1mm/^{1}/25 in

ruler or tape measure

flower-shaped fairy (decorative) lights, 12v

pliers

broom handle

large pebble

artificial leaves with wire stems

flower pot

sand

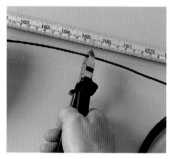

1 Cut a length of the thicker garden wire to the same length as the fairy (decorative) light flex (electric cord) and then turn a neat loop in one end with pliers.

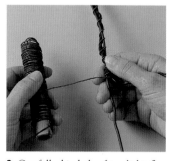

2 Carefully bind the fairy light flex to the thicker garden wire using the finer garden wire. End the binding at a point 20cm/8in beyond the last fairy light.

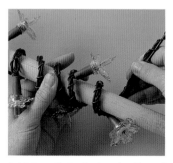

3 Make coils in the length of bound wire by winding it around a broom handle, as shown.

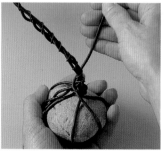

4 At the end of the bound section, wrap the free end of the thick wire around a large pebble.

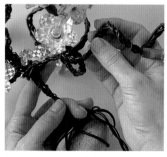

5 Arrange the coiled wire in a bush shape. Support the coils by wiring them together, if necessary.

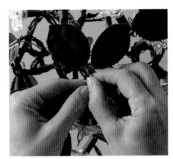

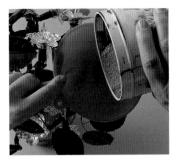

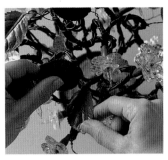

6 Attach the artificial leaves to the coiled wire at regular intervals by winding their stems around it.

7 Half-fill a flower pot with dry sand. Put in the pebble, then support the plant stem with more sand.

8 Adjust the fairy lights so that they are completely clear of the wires and the leaves.

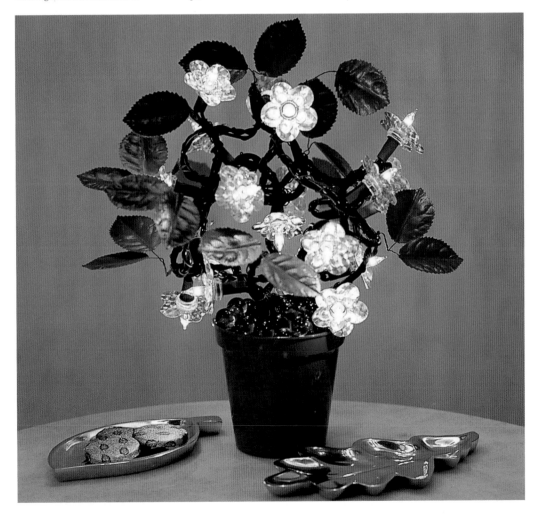

Organize your desk with this smart wire stationery set. The pen pot and note holder are modern wire sculptures, and the notebook has a matching motif. Complete the set with designer paper clips.

Desk Accessories

you will need

paper

pencil

galvanized wire, 2mm/¹/₁₃in, 3mm/¹/₈in and 1mm/¹/₂₅in thick

wire cutters

long-nosed pliers

ruler or tape measure

soldering iron, solder and flux

florist's wire

scissors

thick cardboard

hardback notebook

craft knife

cutting mat

bradawl (awl)

coloured paper

PVA (white) glue

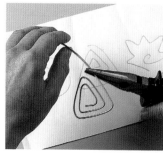

1 Enlarge the spiral, triangle and flower templates from the back of the book to the required size. Cut lengths of the 2mm/¹/₁₃in galvanized wire with wire cutters and then use long-nosed pliers to bend the lengths of wire so that they match the spiral, triangle and flower designs. Set the wire shapes aside.

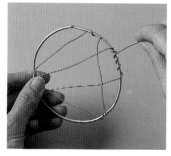

2 To make the pen pot, cut three 30cm/12in lengths of the 3mm/¹/₈in galvanized wire and bend them into circles. Use a soldering iron to join the ends. Stretch some lengths of florist's wire across the centre of one of the rings to form the foundations for the base of the pen pot. Wrap the ends of the florist's wire around the ring to secure.

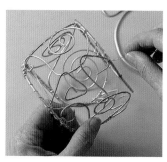

3 Using 1mm/¹/₂₅in wire, bind several shapes to the base and to each other to form the sides. Bind on another ring and repeat. Add the third ring to make the top and cut out and insert a circle of thick cardboard in the bottom.

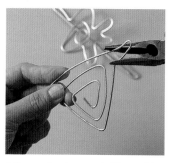

4 Repeat for the note holder, making two squares for the top and base. To make a paper clip, cut a 35cm/14in length of 3mm/¹/₈in wire and bend one end to match one of the template shapes.

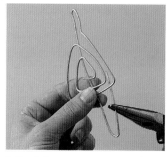

5 Bend the remaining wire so that it runs down behind the centre of the shape and extends below it, as shown. Take the end and bend it back on itself to form a large paper clip (fastener).

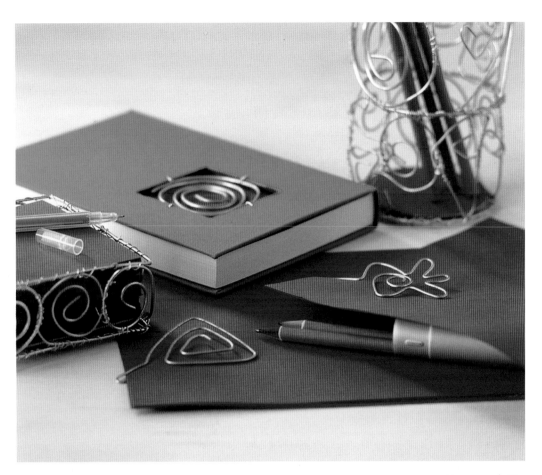

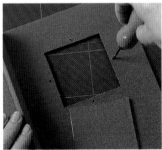

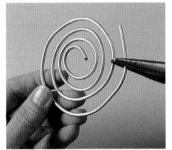

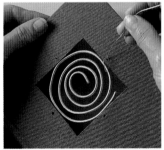

6 For the notebook, use a craft knife to cut a square from the front cover of a hardback notebook. Pierce a small hole halfway along each side of the window using a bradawl (awl).

7 Bend a length of 3mm/⅛in wire into a spiral shape to fit the window in the book cover.

8 Stick a sheet of coloured paper to the inside of the cover. Place the spiral inside the window then bind it to the book using florist's wire.

Simple copper coils with a random sprinkling of brightly coloured glass beads make attractive napkin rings. If you are designing a buffet table setting, scale up the design to make a paper napkin holder.

Spiral Napkin Holders

you will need

wire cutters

ruler or tape measure

copper wire, 0.8mm/¹⁄₃₁in and 1.5mm/¹⁄₁₉in thick

pen or wooden spoon

assorted glass beads

long flat-nosed pliers

cardboard tube from a roll of foil or clear film (plastic wrap)

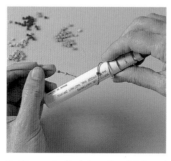

1 Cut a 1m/1yd length of 0.8mm/¹⁄₃₁in copper wire and wind it on to a pen or the handle of a wooden spoon. As you form each loop, add a few small glass beads in assorted colours.

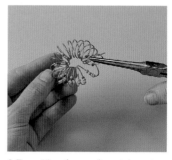

2 Form 18 coils to make a tight spring, then slide it off the pen or wooden spoon. Twist the two ends of the wire tightly together using long flat-nosed pliers.

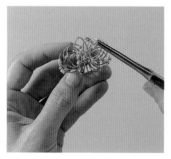

3 Add a small bead and pull the ends of the wire around it to secure.

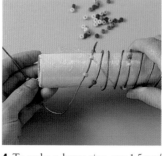

4 To make a larger ring, use 1.5mm/¹⁄₁₉in copper wire and larger beads. Form the coils around a cardboard tube, such as the inside of a roll of foil or clear film (plastic wrap).

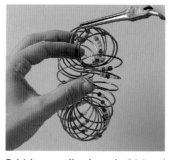

5 Make a small tight coil of 0.8mm/¹⁄₃₁in copper wire using long flat-nosed pliers and slide it over both ends of the ring. Pull the small coil tight. Add a bead to each end of the large ring and loop the ends of the wire over the bead to secure it.

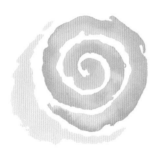

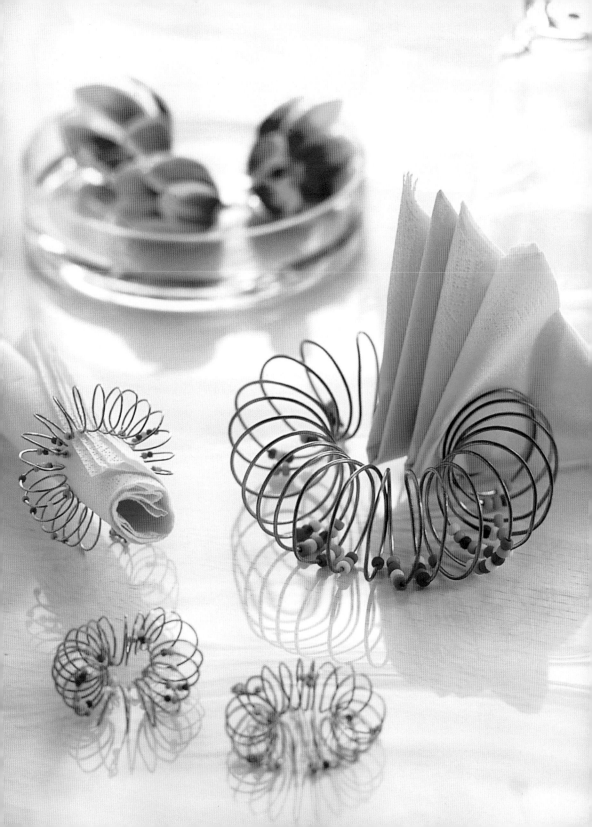

Although it looks intricate, there is nothing more to this colourful tablemat than plain knitting and a simple double crochet stitch. Crystal seed beads add to the glittering effect.

Mesh Place Mat

you will need

50g/2oz each of enamelled copper wire in burgundy and pink, 0.4mm/¹⁄₆₃in thick

pair of knitting needles, 2.75mm/ size 12/US 2

ruler or tape measure

crochet hook, 2mm/size 14/B-1

wire cutters

crystal seed beads

sewing needle

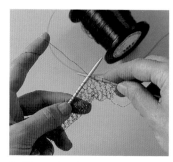

1 Using the burgundy enamelled copper wire and knitting needles, loosely cast on 52 stitches. Knit every row with an even tension until the work measures 22cm/8½ in. Use another combination of colours for the wire if you prefer.

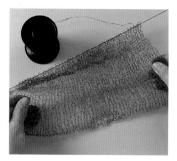

2 When you reach this length, pull the work from the sides and from the top and bottom to stretch the mat out to the final measurement of 23 × 29cm/9 × 11½ in. If necessary, add a few more rows to correct the length, then cast off loosely.

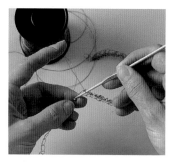

3 Using pink wire and a crochet hook, loosely chain crochet 165 stitches. Turn the work, miss one chain, then double crochet/single crochet into every chain. At the end of this length cut the copper wire, leaving a 2.5cm/ 1in tail.

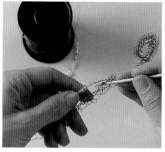

4 Thread 82 crystal seed beads on to a length of pink wire. Holding several seed beads in your left hand, work along the edging strip again in double crochet, adding in one seed bead to every other double crochet stitch.

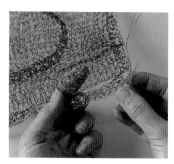

5 Work another two rows in double crochet and cast off. Measure the finished edging around the mat and stretch evenly if necessary to make it fit. Thread a sewing needle with pink wire. Starting in a corner of the mat, stitch on the pink edging.

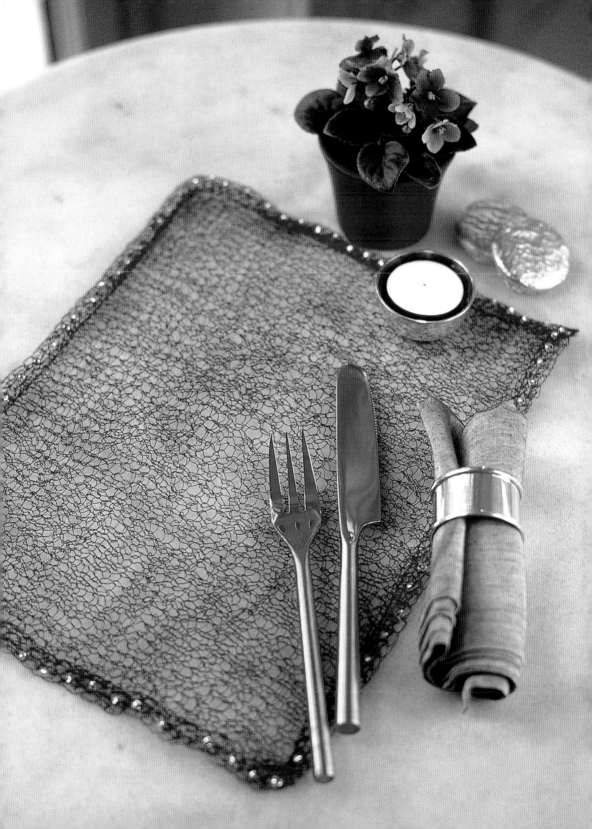

Turn the plainest plate into something special, using flattened wire coils. Bind two layers of coils together with a simple overcast wrap of lilac enamelled wire, which adds a subtle touch of colour.

Pretty Plate Edging

you will need
aluminium wire, 2mm/$\frac{1}{13}$in thick
ruler or tape measure
wire cutters
30cm/12in length of dowel or stiff
cardboard tube, 1cm/$\frac{1}{2}$in thick
white dinner plate, 26cm/10$\frac{1}{4}$in
in diameter
masking tape
flat-nosed pliers
pencil
terry towel or cloth
rolling pin
25g/1oz reel of lilac enamelled
aluminium wire, 0.6mm/$\frac{1}{41}$in thick

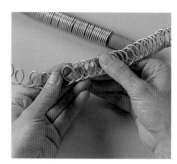

1 Measure and cut a 3m/10ft length of aluminium wire, and wrap it around a piece of 1cm/$\frac{1}{2}$in dowel. Spread the coil so the loops are approximately 5mm/$\frac{1}{4}$in apart, and then flatten it. Working from one end, prise open the flattened rings, leaving a small gap between each.

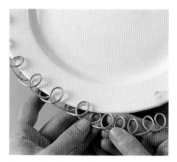

2 Bend the flattened coil into a circle, with the rings facing inwards towards the plate. Place it around the edge of the plate and press it firmly into position by pushing one ring under the rim and the next over the top. Use masking tape to hold the end in place as you work.

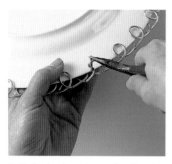

3 Push the last ring under the rim, then turn the plate over. Remove the tape and adjust the spacing of the first and last rings to match the rest. Open out the ends of the wire and twist them together using pliers. Press them towards the base of the plate.

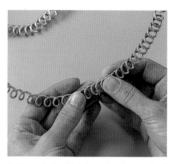

4 Cut a 3.6m/12ft length of wire. Coil it around a pencil and spread the rings out so that there is a 3mm/$\frac{1}{8}$in gap between them. Place the coil on a terry towel or cloth and use a rolling pin to flatten it. Pull the coil apart so a gap shows between the rings.

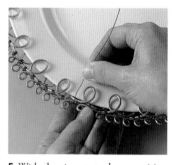

5 With the rings turned out, position the small coil around the outside edge of the large coil. Bind using the enamelled aluminium wire. Wrap the fine wire three times around each loop of the small coil and then fasten off securely.

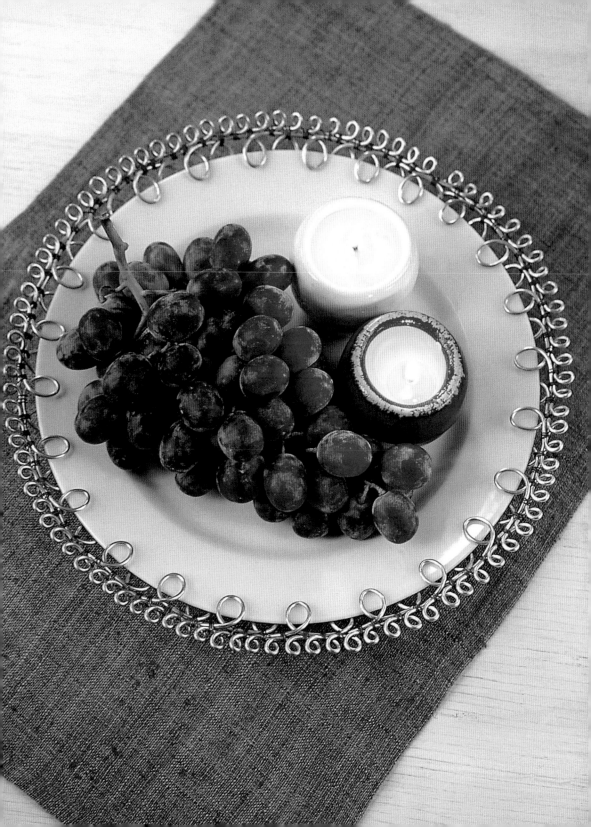

Toasting English muffins over an open fire in winter is always a pleasant activity. This toasting fork is made from four coat hangers and is both light and strong.

Toasting Fork

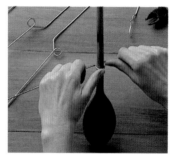

1 To make an inner strut, measure 10cm/4in from the end of one of the straightened coat hangers and wind it around a wooden spoon at this point to create a loop. Measure 2cm/¾in before bending the remaining length of wire straight.

2 Make a second strut a mirror image of the first by winding the wire the other way around the wooden spoon.

3 Make the two outer struts in the same way. This time allow 12.5cm/5in for the prongs and bend a right angle 2cm/¾in beyond the prong loop.

4 Bind the struts together temporarily with tacking wire, loosely enough to allow movement.

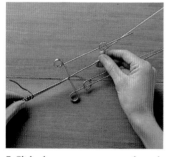

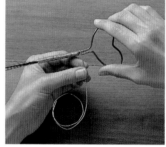

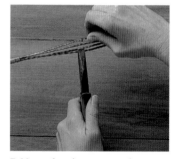

5 Slide the two outer prongs through the loops of the inner prongs. Measure up from the prongs and mark the handle at 4, 18, 4, 20, 4 and 2cm, or 1½, 7, 1½, 8, 1½ and ¾in intervals. Using galvanized wire, bind the 4cm/1½in sections. Do not trim the excess binding wire from the top section.

6 Cut off three of the remaining strut wires at the last mark. Form the fourth strut wire end into a heart shape, using pliers and bending it around a piece of copper piping to create the curves. Leave 2cm/¾in at the end. Bind it in with the other three wires, still using the binding wire.

7 Using the pliers, grip each wire in turn halfway along the 20cm/8in section. Pull the wire so that it bows out. This will be the fork handle so test it in your hand for comfort and adjust if necessary. Trim the ends of the prongs so that they are even and hammer each tip flat.

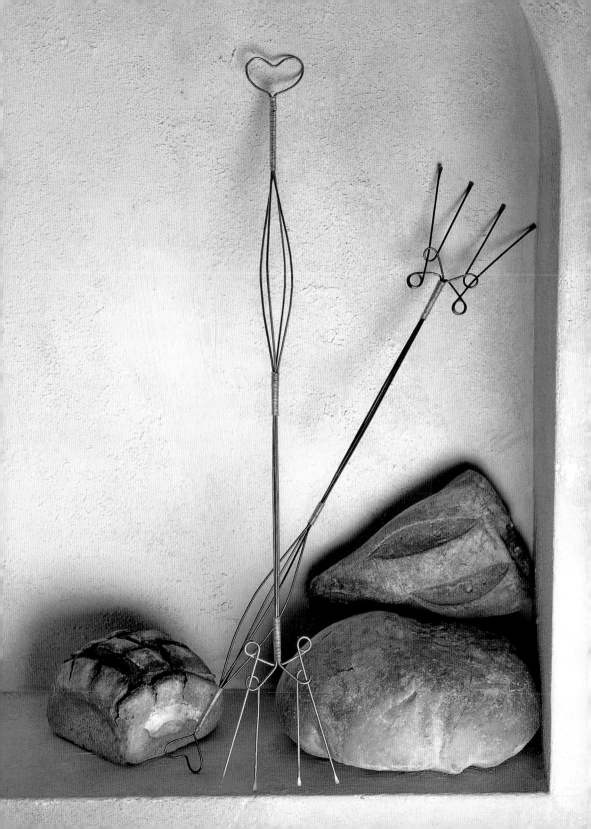

This imposing little picture frame is made from nothing more than cardboard, galvanized wire and metallic paint, yet it looks weighty and solid, and even has its own wire stand.

Picture Frame

you will need
paper and pencil
galvanized wire, 2mm/¹⁄₁₃in,
3mm/¹⁄₈in and 1mm/¹⁄₂₅in thick
wire cutters
ruler or tape measure
long-nosed and flat-nosed pliers
soldering iron, solder and flux
thick white cardboard
craft knife
steel ruler
cutting mat
double-sided adhesive tape
bradawl (awl)
silver metallic paint
paintbrush
epoxy resin adhesive

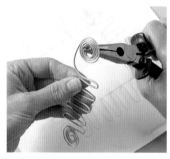

1 Trace the frame template from the back of the book and enlarge it as required. Use the wire cutters to cut four lengths of 2mm/¹⁄₁₃in wire each 70cm/28in long. Using the long-nosed pliers, bend each length of wire so that it matches the spiral and zigzag shapes along the outer edges of the frame.

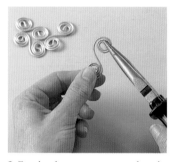

2 For the decoration, cut ten lengths of 2mm/¹⁄₁₃in wire each 30cm/12in and curl each one into a tight S-shape using long-nosed pliers. Cut a 40cm/16in length of 3mm/¹⁄₈in wire and bend into a square to form the centre of the picture frame, arranging the ends in the middle of one side. Solder the ends together.

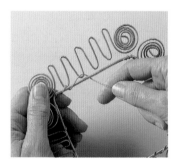

3 Using 1mm/¹⁄₂₅in wire, neatly bind the four decorative side sections to the central frame.

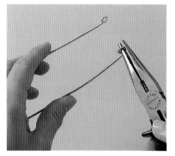

4 For the stand, bend a 30cm/12in length of 2mm/¹⁄₁₃in wire into a U-shape. Curl each end into a tight loop using flat-nosed pliers. Centre it on the back of frame at the top and bind in place with 1mm/¹⁄₂₅in wire.

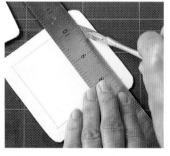

5 Cut two pieces of cardboard to fit the frame. Cut a window from the front and a slightly larger window from the back. Reserve the cut-out window from the back. Stick the frames together using double-sided tape.

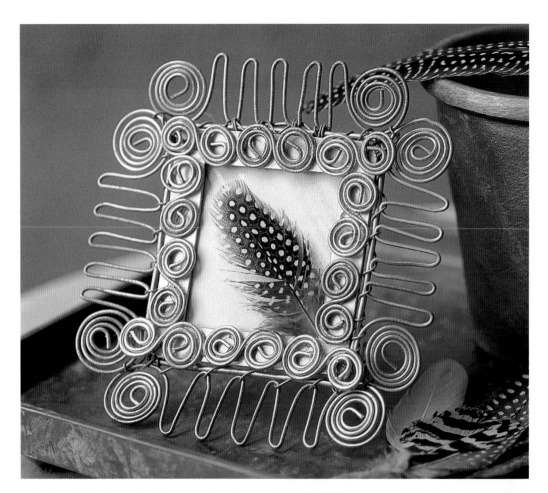

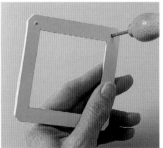

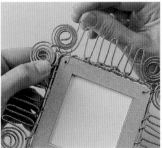

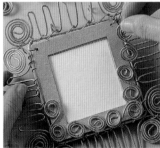

6 Using a bradawl (awl), pierce a small hole in each corner of the cardboard picture holder. Paint the front and edges silver.

7 Bind the picture holder to the frame at each corner using short lengths of 1mm/¹⁄₂₅in wire.

8 Use epoxy resin adhesive to glue the S-shapes to the front of the frame. Insert the picture and replace the reserved square to hold it in place.

Despite its ornateness, this medieval-looking candle sconce is quite easy to make. By making the base of the basket wider and weaving the sides deeper you can adapt the shape to fit a larger candle.

Decorative Candle Sconce

ɣɣɣ

you will need
copper wire, 1.5mm/¹⁄₁₉in and
0.8mm/¹⁄₃₁in thick
ruler or tape measure
wire cutters
general-purpose pliers
masking tape
round-nosed (snug-nosed) pliers
parallel (channel-type) pliers

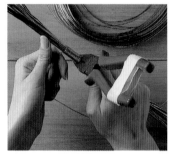

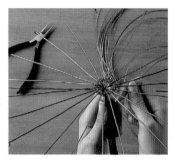

1 Cut 21 lengths of 1.5mm/¹⁄₁₉in wire, each 38cm/15in long. Bundle together so that they are even at the top and bottom, and grip them with the general-purpose pliers 16cm/6¼in from one end. Hold the pliers closed with masking tape so they act as a vice. Using the 0.8mm/¹⁄₃₁in wire, bind the bundle of wires for 2cm/¾in from the pliers. Do not cut off the wire. Release the pliers.

2 Using round-nosed (snug-nosed) pliers, bend a downward-curving loop at the end of each wire. Bend down the wires at right angles at the top of the bound section so they spread out in a circle. Using the 0.8mm/ ¹⁄₃₁in wire that is still attached to the bundle, weave around the wires to make a base with a diameter that measures 7cm/2¾in. This will form the base of the basket.

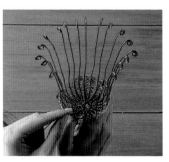

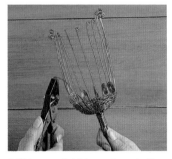

3 Bend up the wires at the edge of the circle and weave the side of the candle basket to a depth of about 2.5cm/1in.

4 Using parallel (channel-type) pliers, coil down the wires to the edge of the candle basket.

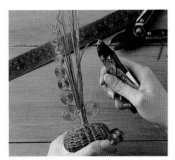

5 Using parallel pliers, make two columns of coils with the wires left under the candle basket. Make nine coils in each column, ensuring that the second column is a mirror image of the first. Trim the end of each wire, increasing the amount you cut off by 12mm/½ in each time, so that the coils decrease in size. Using round-nosed pliers, form waves in the remaining wires. Trim the ends of the outer wires, so that the central one is the longest.

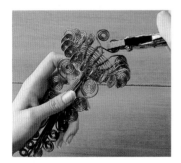

6 Decide which is the back of the sconce. Using the parallel pliers, unwind the two coils at the back a little, cross them over each other and twist flat. Attach the sconce to the wall through the holes in these two coils. Bend back the wavy wires so that they support the sconce at the bottom, holding it away from the wall. Check the distance between the candle flame and the wall.

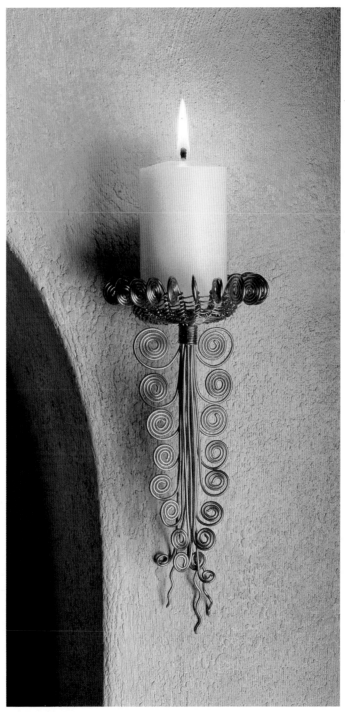

Here's an unusual way of recycling those beautiful bottles that are too nice to throw away. This technique requires patience, but it is not difficult to master.

Woven Bottle

you will need
bottle
enamelled copper wire in two colours,
1.5mm/¹⁄₁₉in and 0.6mm/¹⁄₄₁in thick
ruler or tape measure
wire cutters
masking tape
round-nosed (snug-nosed) pliers

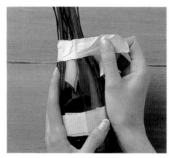

1 Cut four pieces of 1.5mm/¹⁄₁₉in wire 25cm/10in longer than twice the height of the bottle. Cross the wires on the base of the bottle and bend them so that eight struts run up the sides of the bottle. Tuck the wire ends inside the neck and wrap tape around the body and neck of the bottle.

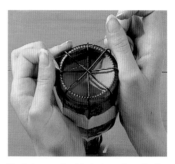

2 Join a doubled length of the 0.6mm/¹⁄₄₁in wire to the point where the wires cross and start weaving. For this project, pass the wire over each strut and then loop it around the strut before continuing to the next one. The rib will be covered by the weave at this stage.

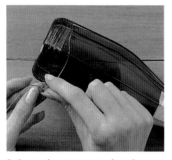

3 Loop the wire around each strut, creating a smooth and closely woven surface. Change wire every so often to achieve a striped pattern. Continue around the sides of the bottle, twisting the wires where you join them.

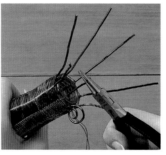

4 When you have woven to the top of the bottle, pull out the ends of the wire struts from inside the bottle. Using the round-nosed (snug-nosed) pliers, make downward-curving coils.

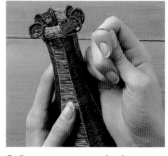

5 Continue to weave the fine enamelled copper wire around the coils. You will now see the reverse pattern of the weave. Secure the last end of wire by wrapping it several times around a strut before cutting it off.

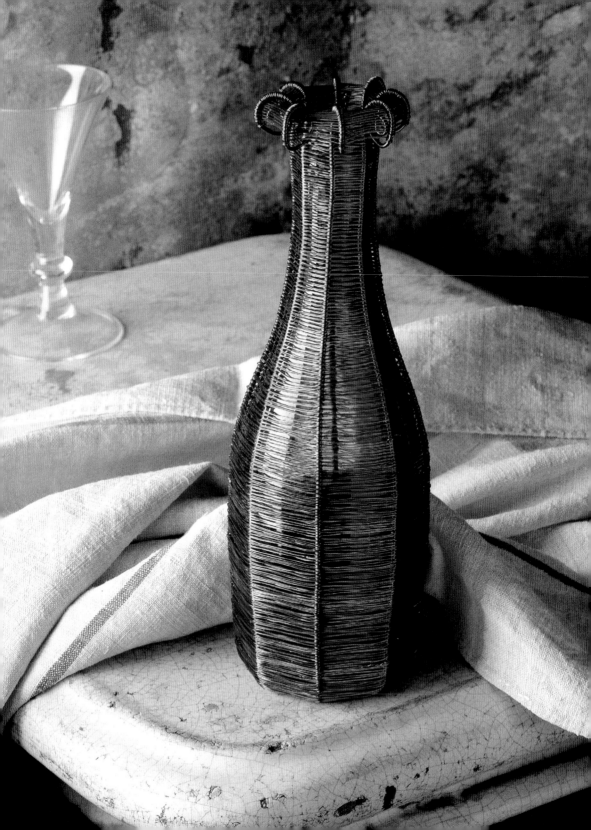

Twisted silver wire, sparingly threaded with beads, has a delicate yet sculptural quality. An assortment of decorative glass beads, following a colour theme, look wonderful entwining a pair of glass candlesticks.

Beaded Wire Candlesticks

ΨΨΨ

you will need

ruler or tape measure

wire cutters

medium silver wire

round-nosed (snug-nosed) pliers

medium decorative glass beads in

yellow, green, silver and clear

pencil

small glass rocaille beads and square

beads in complementary shades

pair of glass candlesticks

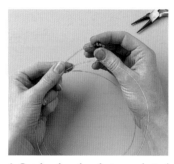

1 Cut four lengths of wire, each 1m/ 40in long for every candlestick. Bend a loop at the end of the first length with round-nosed (snug-nosed) pliers and thread on a decorative bead.

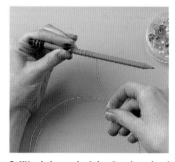

2 Wind the end of the first length of wire around a pencil six times to form a spiral. Make sure you leave some space between the coils, for threading more beads.

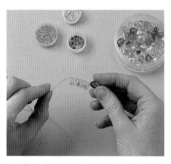

3 Thread on eight small beads and divide them along the spiral. Thread on a medium-sized bead and repeat, forming spirals and threading beads until you reach the end of the wire. At the end, twist the wire with pliers.

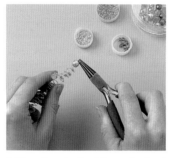

4 Thread on the final decorative bead and finish with a loop at the end of the wire. Make up the other three spirals in the same way, distributing the beads evenly along the spiral.

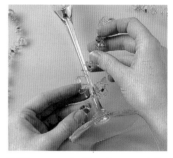

5 Wrap two spiral lengths around the stem of each candlestick to form an interesting shape. Secure the spirals in place by binding them gently to the candlestick stem with more of the silver wire.

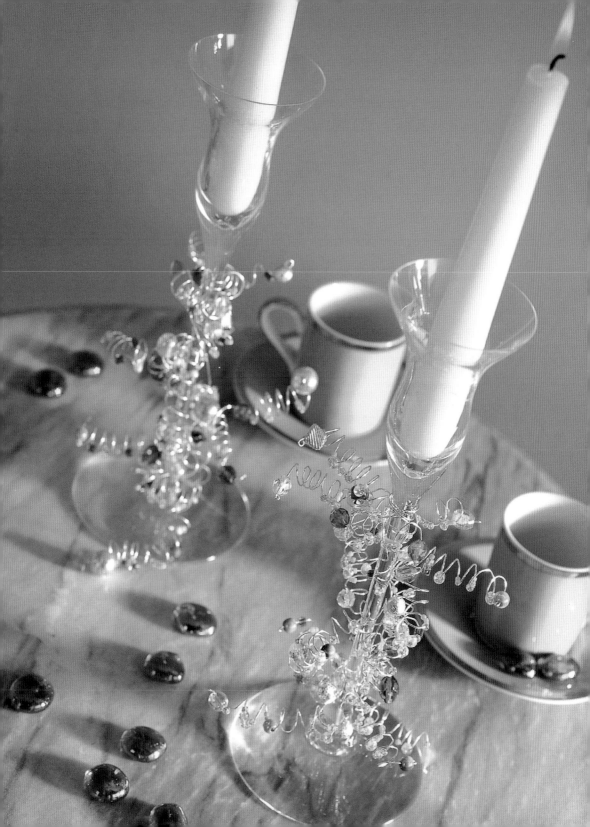

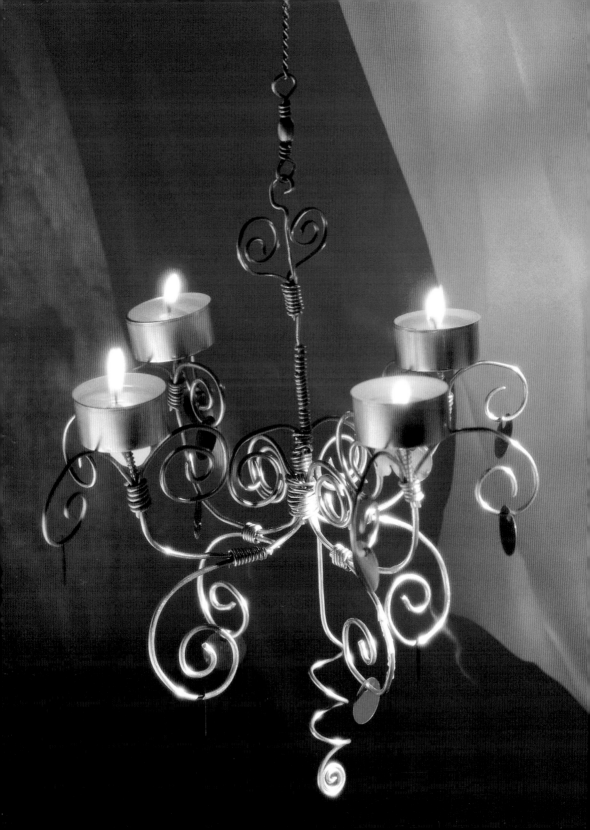

Magically crafted from a roll of wire, this delicate little chandelier was twisted and curled with long-nosed pliers. Hang the chandelier from a chain and hook so that it can twist in passing air currents.

Bent Wire Chandelier

you will need
roll of silver bonsai-training wire
wire cutters
ruler or tape measure
long-nosed pliers
roll of gardening wire
4 self-tapping screws and screwdriver
glue gun with all-purpose glue sticks
4 drawing pins (thumb tacks)
4 night-lights
large sequins

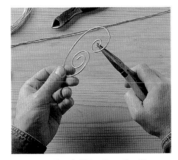

1 Cut a 35cm/13¾in length of bonsai wire to make the first kidney-shaped curl. Hold the wire with your free hand and, gripping the end with the long-nosed pliers, shape it into a curl. Then, holding the first curl in your hand, curl the other end.

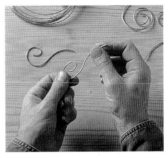

2 Make a single curl from a smaller piece of wire. Make two more single curls. Each branch is made of three single curls and one kidney-shaped curl. There are four branches on the chandelier in total.

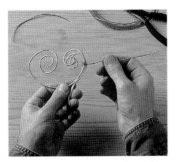

3 With wire cutters cut a 12cm/4¾in length of gardening wire and use it to bind the kidney-shaped curl and two of the single curls together at the point, as shown. Wind the wire round like a spring to make a neat binding.

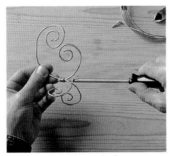

4 Screw a self-tapping screw into the centre of the binding, leaving at least 12mm/½in protruding at the top.

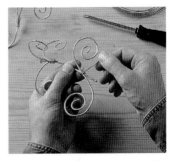

5 Bind the third single curl on to the back of the kidney shape, winding a length of gardening wire into a neat binding as before. ▶

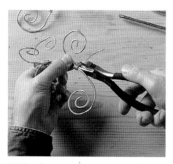

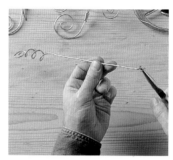

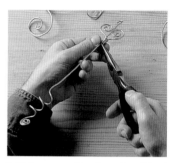

6 Use the wire cutters to neatly snip off the end of the gardening wire at an angle, close to the binding. Repeat the above steps to make the remaining three branches of the chandelier.

7 Cut a 50cm/20in length of bonsai wire for the central column. Twist one end into a decorative spiral and the other into a small hook, as shown. The hook is used for hanging the chandelier from the ceiling.

8 Make two small, tight curls and bind them into the top end of the column, facing inwards. Bind the four branches on to the central column, with the open side of the kidney-shaped curls facing upwards.

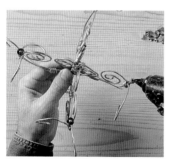

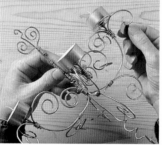

9 Heat the glue gun, apply a dot of glue to one of the screwheads and immediately sit a drawing pin on it, point upwards. Repeat with the three remaining screwheads.

10 Press a night-light down on to each of the points of the drawing pins. Thread the large sequins on to the curls. Take care not to overdo this, as too many could detract from the elegance of the wire twists.

Create this splendid chandelier to hang over your dining table. The length of aluminium wire needed for this project is difficult to work with in the early stages.

Filigree Chandelier

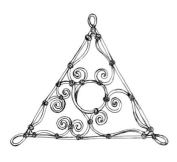

1 Using a permanent marker pen and a ruler and wearing gloves, mark the 3mm/¹⁄₈in aluminium wire at 54.5cm/21½in and 5cm/2in. Repeat another four times, then mark a final point 5cm/2in further on. Using round-nosed (snug-nosed) pliers, bend each 5cm/2in section of wire into a loop, leaving the last 5cm/2in straight for joining. Weave the longer sections over and under each other to form a star shape.

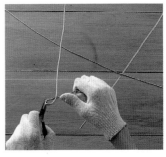

2 Bind the last 5cm/2in to the start of the wire, using the finer wire. Bind each loop closed.

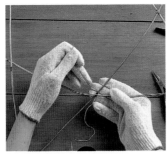

3 To even up the star shape, divide each 54.5cm/21½in length of wire into three equal sections of just over 18cm/7in, and mark the points. Match up the marks where the wires cross and bind them together at these points using 1mm/¹⁄₂₅in wire.

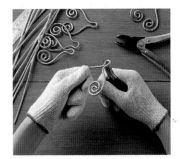

4 Enlarge the templates provided at the back of the book. Cut 30 lengths of the thicker wire, 33cm/13in long. Using the round-nosed pliers, bend 15 of these around the nosed double-coil template. ▶

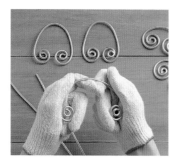

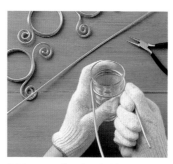

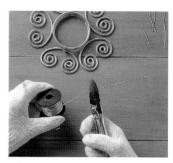

5 Enlarge the templates at the back of the book. Using round-nosed pliers, bend the remaining 15 lengths of wire around the templates to make five double coils, five arched double coils and five single-looped coils.

6 To create the glass holders, cut five lengths of the thicker wire each 50cm/20in. Wrap each wire around a jar twice and overlap the ends. Use the template to coil the wire at each end. To make the central glass holder, cut a 60cm/24in length of wire and wrap it three times around the larger glass or jar to make a plain coil.

7 Using five short lengths of the fine aluminium wire, bind the five double coils on to the central holder. Arrange the coils so that they are evenly placed and sit flat against the bottom of the plain coil. Trim any untidy wire ends carefully, using the wire cutters.

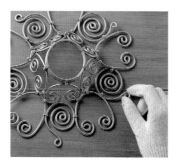

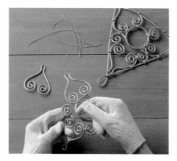

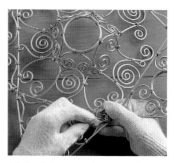

8 Bind the double coils together where the sides touch to make the raised central piece. Then bind the arched double coils and the single-looped coils around the edge of the double coils, alternating the two shapes. Bind the alternating shapes to each other, as well as to the double coils.

9 To each small glass holder, bind one nosed double coil to the coils on the glass holder and two to the ring. Place each structure inside the points of the frame so that the noses of the nosed double coils fit into the corners and the coils of the holder face towards the tip. Bind in place.

10 Bind the central piece to the star frame at all the points of contact. Attach a bath-plug chain to each of the five points where the frame wires cross. Attach the hooks at the ends of the chains to the metal ring and close up. Attach the sixth chain to the top of the metal ring for hanging. Place the glasses or jars in the holders.

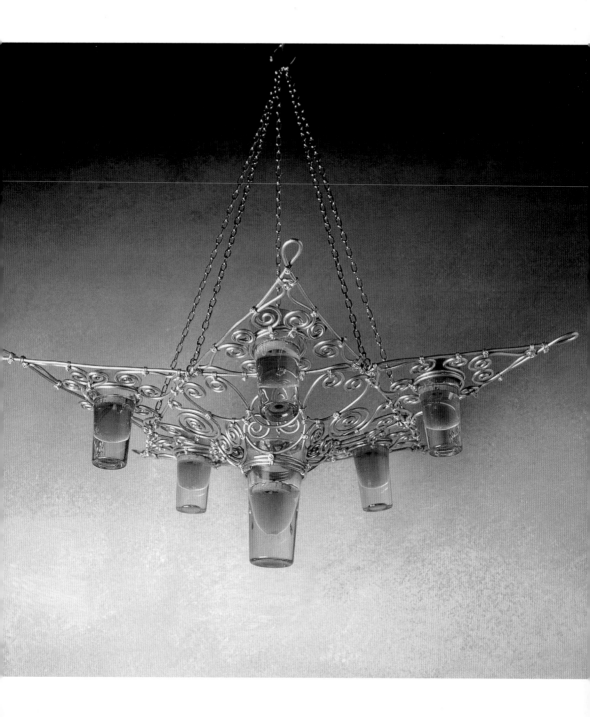

Wire frameworks are essential to many flower arrangements and are usually intended to be unobtrusive, but this one is not only functional but decorative.

Flower Holder

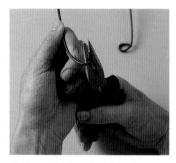

1 Cut eight lengths of garden wire each 90cm/35½ in long to hold eight flower stems. Using flat-nosed pliers, turn a loop in each end of each length to hide the raw end of the wire.

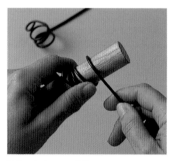

2 Just below each loop, wrap one wire three times around a broom handle to form the stem supports. Repeat this process with the remaining seven lengths of wire.

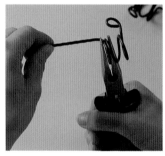

3 Using the pliers, turn the stem through 90 degrees under each coil, and open out the coils a little. Create the final shape of the stem wire by wrapping it around a spray can. Vary the heights of the flower supports.

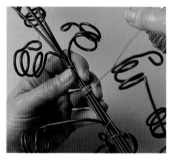

4 Gather all eight stems together and use fine galvanized wire to bind together the lower 8cm/3¼in of the straight sections. Adjust the curved sections so that they are regularly and pleasingly spaced.

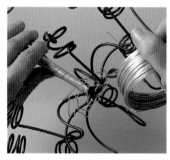

5 Weave the fine wire around the base curves and up the lower part of the flower supports to create a basket. Place the basket in a suitable bowl and weight it with a ring of pebbles. Add flowers of your choice.

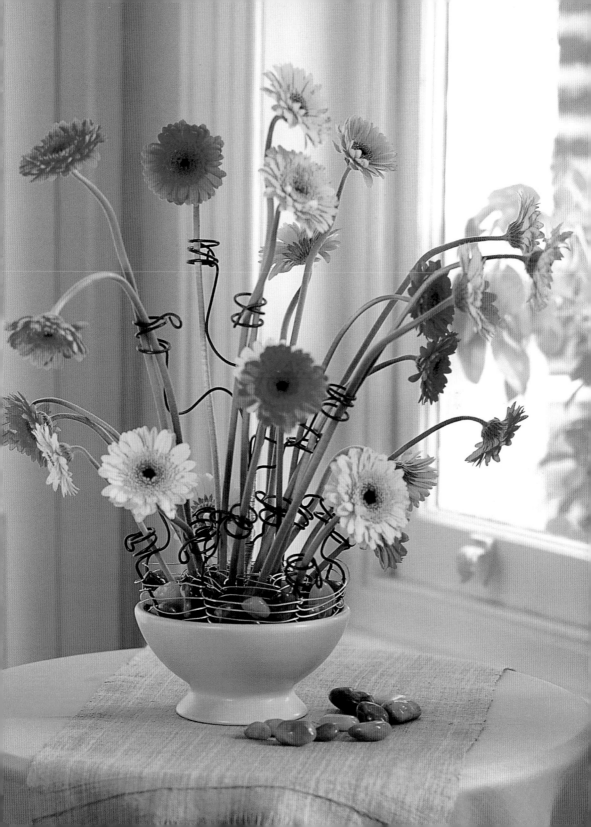

This charming little shade is decorative rather than functional: so use a low wattage bulb, or hang a few together for maximum effect. The choice of paper defines the whole nature of the lampshade.

Flower Lampshade

you will need

copper wire, 1mm/¹⁄₂₅in and
0.5mm/¹⁄₅₀in thick
ruler or tape measure
wire cutters
handmade paper
PVA (white) glue
flame-retardant spray
pencil
scissors
towel
embroidery needle
flat-nosed pliers

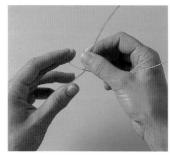

1 Cut a 40cm/16in length of 1mm/ ¹⁄₂₅in copper wire. Twist the two ends of the wire together for 12mm/½in, then pull the loop into a petal shape to match the template at the back of the book. (For a larger flower, work with a 50cm/20in length of copper wire.)

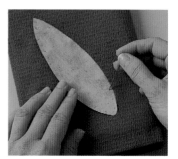

2 Stiffen the paper with diluted PVA (white) glue. Allow to dry completely, then spray the paper with flame-retardant spray. When dry, place the wire petal shape on the paper and draw around it. Cut out the petal, then place it on a towel and use an embroidery needle to punch fine holes around the edge.

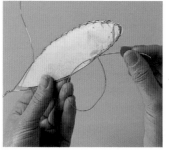

3 Cut a 50cm/20in length of 0.5mm/ ¹⁄₅₀in copper wire and mark the centre. Starting at the petal tip, thread the wire through the first hole and pull it through as far as the centre mark. Sew the petal to the frame. Twist the ends together and trim. Make six petals.

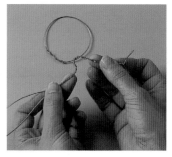

4 Cut a 25cm/10in length of the thicker wire and form a 6cm/2½in diameter circle. Cut two 20cm/ 8in lengths and twist them together for 10cm/4in in the centre. Form a half-loop in the middle, following the template as a guide.

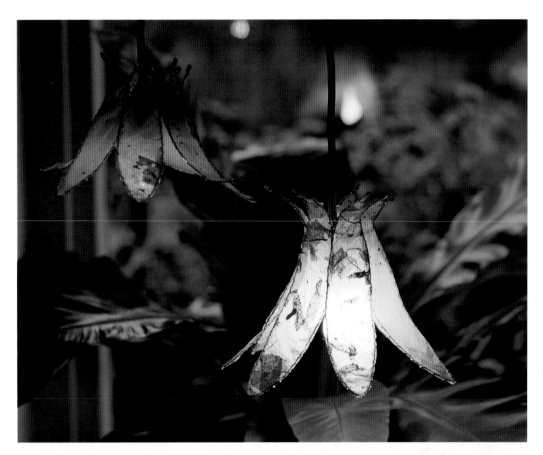

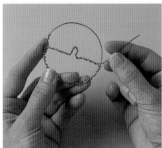

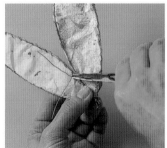

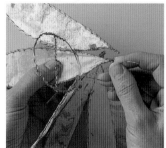

5 Attach the looped rod by winding the untwisted ends of the wire around the circle, to form a frame for the petals, and to enable you to hang the lampshade securely from the electric cable.

6 Join the petals in a row by threading the finer wire through a punched hole on each side of each petal 4cm/1½ in from the top, then twisting and trimming the ends.

7 Attach the petals to the circle in the same way, passing the fine wire through the same hole. Once all of the petals are joined, bend the tops and splay the bottoms of the petals to shape the flower.

Fashion a bunch of fabulous flowers, woven from richly coloured fuse wire. This wire comes in many colours, so you can add the leaves and tendrils by spiralling and coiling the thicker and darker wires.

Fused Flowers

ꙮꙮꙮ

you will need
enamelled copper wire in two colours,
1mm/¹⁄₂₅in and 0.8mm/¹⁄₃₁in thick
ruler or tape measure
wire cutters
hand drill
round-nosed (snug-nosed) pliers

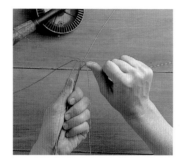

1 Cut six 50cm/20in lengths of the thicker enamelled copper wire. Twist them together along half the length using a hand drill to form the stem. Bend back the wires loosely.

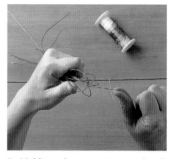

2 Holding the wires in one hand, attach a length of the finer wire to the centre. Start weaving over and under the six wires.

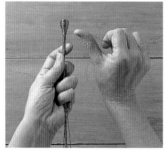

3 Weave a bulb-shaped stamen, 2.5cm/1in high and 1.5cm/⅗in wide. Bend each of the wires back up around the woven stamen between your finger and thumb.

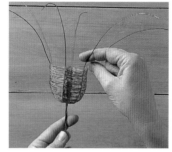

4 Using a different-coloured wire, weave a flower shape 6cm/2½in high.

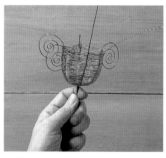

5 Using round-nosed (snug-nosed) pliers, bend each remaining length of wire to form a loose coil. Finally, bind the stem with several lengths of fine enamelled copper wire.

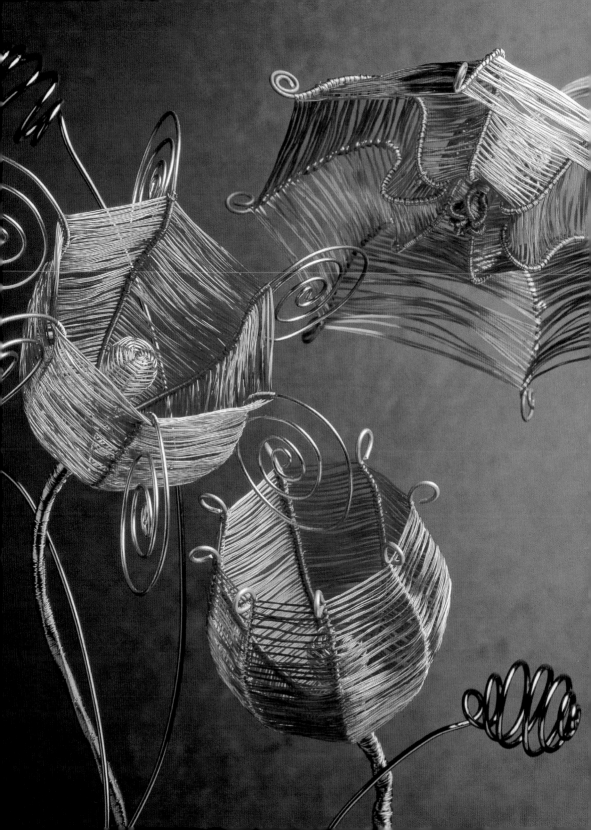

This is an effective way to create a magical container for a night-light. When the candle is lit it looks like a treasure pile and gives a warm, sparkling light as a room decoration or on the table.

Jewel Night-light

you will need
silver-plated wire, 1.5mm/¹⁄₁₉in and
0.8mm/¹⁄₃₁in thick
ruler or tape measure
wire cutters
large rolling pin
75 round glass beads, 14mm/⅝in
75 silver-plated bead cages, 14mm/⅝in
flat-nosed pliers
wooden spoon

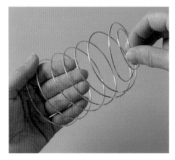

1 Cut a 165cm/65in length of the thicker silver-plated wire and coil it around a large rolling pin to make the frame. Slide the coil off the rolling pin and ease it apart a little. At one end, shape the frame into a cone by making the loops slightly smaller. Pull up the last few loops so that they sit upright.

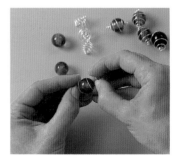

2 To put the glass beads inside the wire cages, pull each cage slightly apart and slip in a bead. The colours of the beads used can obviously be varied to suit your colour scheme, but simple combinations of two complementary shades, as used here, work well.

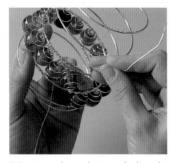

3 Leaving a loop of wire at the base for stability, begin binding the caged beads between the second and third loops, using the fine wire. Pull the wire tight as you work, using pliers. Work around the loops until you reach the point where the coils are twisted upright. There are four rows of beads.

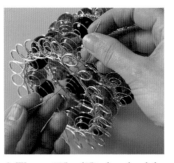

4 Wrap a 115cm/45in length of the thicker wire around the handle of a wooden spoon. Slide the coil off the handle, then flatten it. Join the ends with fine wire to form the circular base. Bind the base to the bottom of the frame with fine wire at three separate points.

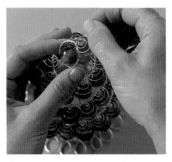

5 Finally, thread a length of fine wire through the middle of a bead and attach it to the top of the frame, where the coils are twisted upright. Wrap the wire around the coils several times to secure the bead to the top of the structure.

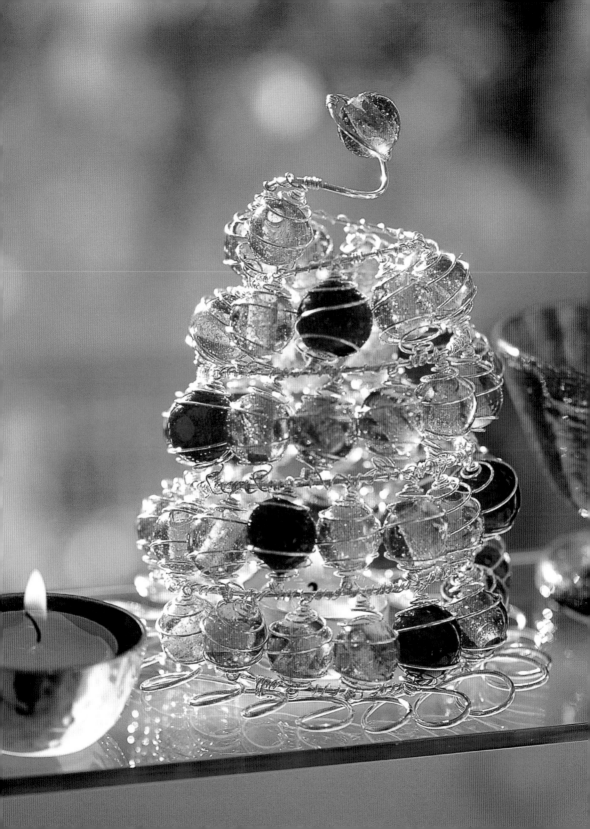

This jazzy coloured, beaded bottle makes the perfect container for salad dressings or olive oil. Its unique cover is made from the fine wires found inside a telephone cable.

Fiesta Oil Bottle

you will need
3m/10ft length of 6-pair
telephone cable
empty thread reels
double-sided adhesive tape
scissors
quarter-size wine bottle
ruler or tape measure
small glass beads in two
contrasting colours
a few larger glass beads
wire cutters
all-purpose instant glue

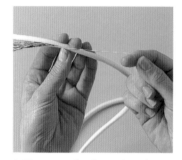

1 To extract the thin coloured wires from the cable, pull the white cotton strand to strip back the coating. Remove the wires, untwist them and roll each colour on to an empty reel. Choose six colours.

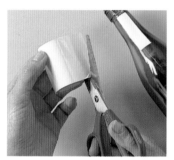

2 Cut thin strips of double-sided tape and stick them down firmly in two lines on opposite sides of the quarter-size wine bottle. Make sure the top strip starts directly under the screw top.

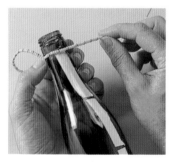

3 Thread on 6cm/2½ in of small glass beads, using alternate colours. Form a loop. Attach the loop to the bottle by twisting the wire back on itself. Thread on more beads to make a circle around the neck of the bottle.

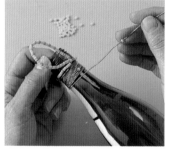

4 Wind the remaining length of coloured wire around the bottle, threading on the odd small bead as you go. The adhesive tape will hold the wire in place.

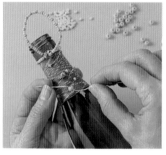

5 To attach each new colour of wire, use a larger bead. Thread both wire ends through the bead and then pull them downwards.

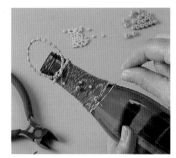

6 Press the wire ends flat against the bottle and trim the ends neatly. Wind the new colour around the bottle as before, covering the loose ends.

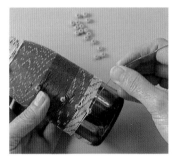

7 Continue to wind the coloured wires down the length of the bottle, attaching new colours as you go. Attach a few larger beads when you reach the main body of the bottle.

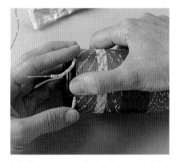

8 When you reach the bottom of the bottle, thread another row of beads on to the last length of wire and glue this all round the bottle using all-purpose instant glue.

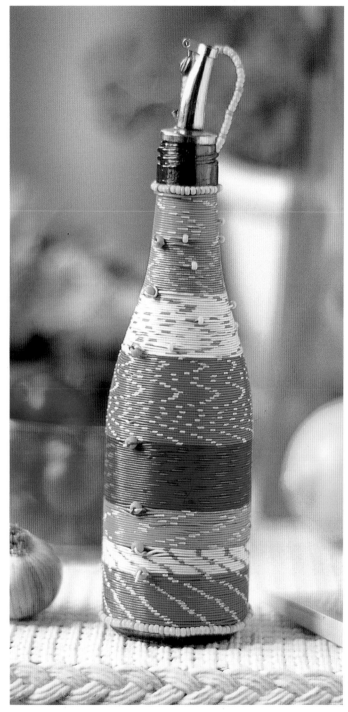

Aluminium wire is light and easy to bend, but a group of these twisted candlesticks makes a substantial centrepiece. The skill in making them lies in plaiting (braiding) the aluminium wire evenly.

Classic Candlesticks

you will need

aluminium wire, 3mm/⅛in and 1.5mm/¹⁄₁₉in thick

ruler or tape measure

wire cutters

coloured copper wire, 0.8mm/¹⁄₃₁in thick

round-nosed (snug-nosed) pliers

glass beads

candle

2 pencils

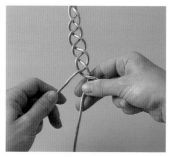

1 Cut three equal lengths of 3mm/⅛in aluminium wire. These should be 45cm/18in for the small, 50cm/20in for the medium and 55cm/22in for the tall candlestick. Bind the three pieces together 10cm/4in from the top using coloured copper wire, then plait (braid) them together.

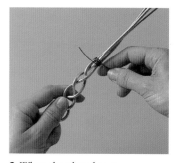

2 When the plaited section measures 10cm/4in, 15cm/6in or 18cm/7in, depending on the size of candlestick you have chosen to make, bind the three wire pieces together with the coloured copper wire, as at the top. The binding should be directly under the plaited section.

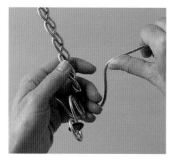

3 Separate the three wires beneath the binding and shape into legs, bending each wire up and then down to make a double curve. Use round-nosed (snug-nosed) pliers to curl each end into a loop, which must be equal in height, and add a bead.

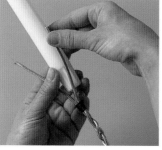

4 Open out the wires at the top of the candlestick, then position a candle between the wires and mould them around it.

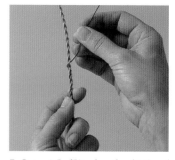

5 Cut a 1.5m/59in length of 1.5mm/¹⁄₁₉in aluminium wire and fold it in half. Loop a pencil into each end of the doubled wire and twist, using the pencils as handles. Cut a 75cm/30in length of coloured wire and wind it over the twisted aluminium.

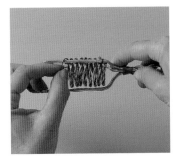

6 Coil a 50cm/20in length of the twisted wire gently around the candle base, then bind this coil inside the shaped spikes with a few turns of coloured wire at the top and bottom of each spike.

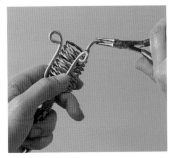

7 To complete the candlestick, use round-nosed pliers to curl the spikes down into three loops.

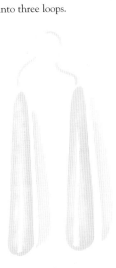

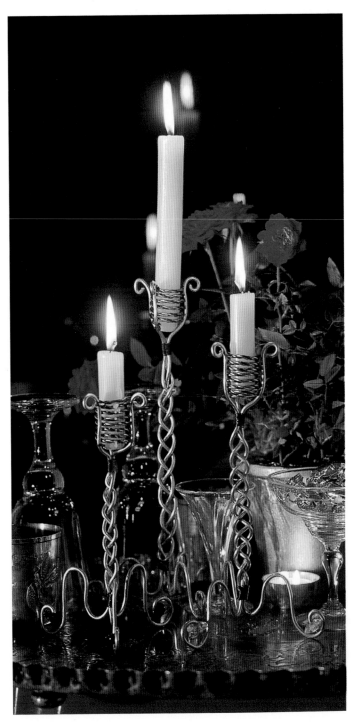

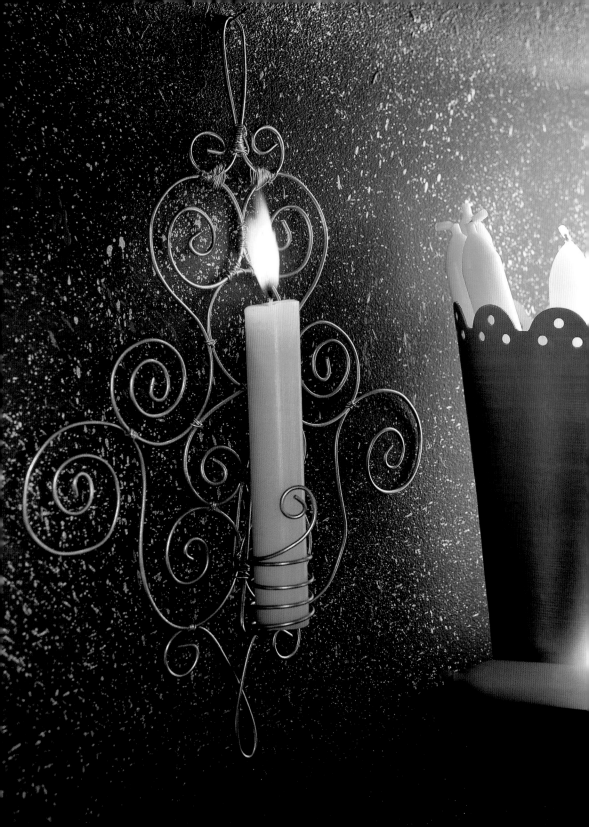

Delicate coils of pale galvanized wire make an ornate candle holder to hang on the wall. Enlarge the template to the size required, then place the wire coils over it as you bend them to check that they match.

Swirled Candle Sconce

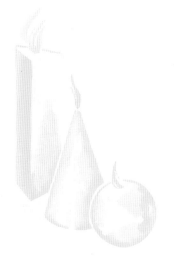

you will need

paper

pencil

wire cutters

galvanized wire, 2mm/¹/₁₃in thick

ruler or tape measure

long-nosed pliers

fine galvanized wire

clear adhesive tape

candle

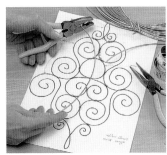

1 Enlarge the template at the back of the book to the finished size and draw it on a piece of paper. Cut the 2mm/ ¹/₁₃in wire into two lengths of 30cm/ 12in for the top hanger and lower coil; one of 50cm/20in for the centre piece; four of 55cm/21½in for the side pieces; and one of 80cm/32in for the candle holder.

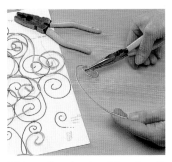

2 Using pliers, bend each length to fit the relevant coiled shape on the sconce design. It may help to have a second photocopy of the design, so that you can position each length as soon as you have shaped it.

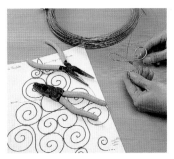

3 Take the top hanger piece and wind the fine wire around the crossover point, trim the wire and take the ends to the back of the sconce.

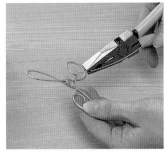

4 Turn the shape over and twist the ends of the fine wire together securely, then clip off any excess. Use this method for all the seams described.

▶

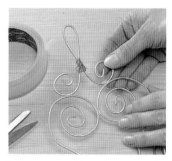

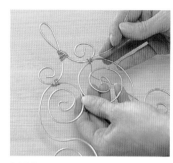

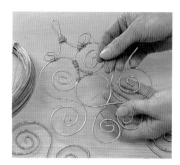

5 Secure two of the side pieces under the hanger with tabs of adhesive tape at the points indicated. This tape will hold the coils steady while you make the wire seams.

6 Make strong wire seams at the taped points using fine wire.

7 Tape the centre piece into position between the two side pieces, then wind the fine wire around the small round shape in the centre, securing it to the side pieces.

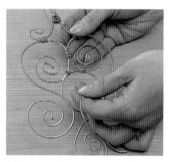

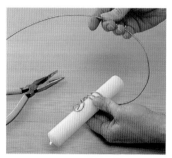

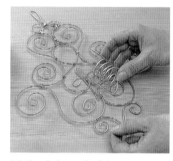

8 Tape the other pieces into place and make small wire seams to secure them, winding a short piece of fine wire around three times. Secure the ends of the fine wire by twisting them together at the back.

9 Make the candle holder with the remaining length of 2mm/¹⁄₁₃in wire. Begin with a small spiral, then wind the wire around the candle about five times, as shown.

10 Bend the end of the wire under the coil across the base (the base of the candle will rest on this), and then into an elongated hook shape at the back. Hook the holder on to the sconce and wire securely in place.

An African toy was the inspiration for this project. Handmade from wire and scrap materials, it was ingeniously designed so that a little figure pedals a bicycle when the toy is pushed along.

Bicycle Toy

you will need

galvanized wire, 1.5mm/¹/₁₉in thick
ruler or tape measure
wire cutters
permanent marker pens
bottle
parallel (channel-type) pliers
twisty wire tape in two colours
cotton reel
coloured pipe cleaners
small cardboard tube
paper clips (fasteners)
selection of large and small wooden beads
strong glue
ribbon
doll's straw hat
fabric in two colours
scissors
needle and thread
double-sided adhesive tape
freezer-bag ties
doll's basket
silk flowers
green bamboo cane

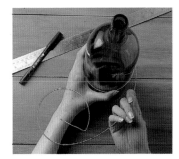

1 To make the bicycle, cut a 1m/40in length of galvanized wire. Mark the wire at intervals of 5cm/2in, 31cm/12¼in, 5cm/2in, 3cm/1¼in, 2cm/¾in, 2cm/¾in, 4cm/1½in, 2cm/¾in, 2cm/¾in, 3cm/1¼in, 5cm/2in, 31cm/12¼in and 5cm/2in. Wrap both 31cm/12¼in sections around a bottle with a diameter of approximately 10cm/4in to form the wheels. Using pliers, bend in the 5cm/2in at each end of the wire to form a radius.

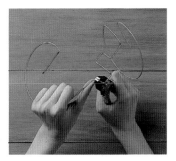

2 Bend in the other two 5cm/2in sections into the centre of the wheel. Make the bicycle pedals by bending right angles in the wire at the marked points. Bend each wheel so that it is at a right angle to the pedals.

3 Transfer the twisty wire tape to a cotton reel to make it easier to handle. Bind tape around the wheel, along the radius, across the pedals and around the second wheel.

▶

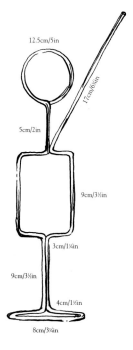

12.5cm/5in

17cm/6¾in

5cm/2in

9cm/3½in

3cm/1¼in

9cm/3½in

4cm/1½in

8cm/3¼in

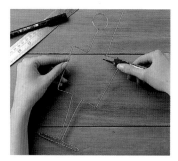

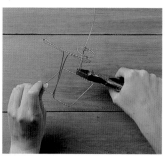

4 To make the bicycle body, cut a 1m/40in length of galvanized wire and mark it at intervals of 12.5cm/5in, 5cm/2in, 3cm/1¼in, 9cm/3½in, 3cm/1¼in, 9cm/3½in, 4cm/1½in, 8cm/3¼in, 4cm/1½in, 9cm/3½in, 3cm/1¼in, 9cm/3½in, 3cm/1¼in, 17cm/6¾in. Cut off any excess and follow the diagram to shape the bicycle. Bend the 12.5cm/5in section into a circle to form the seat.

5 Bend up the handlebars, seat and stick at right angles. Bind wire tape in another colour all around the handlebars, leaving a tiny gap near each end for the doll's hands. Bind the handlebar neck and the frame. Halfway along, bind to the wheel. Bind the seat, leaving the stick bare. Continue binding the frame, binding on the other wheel. The wheels should rotate.

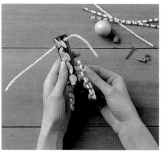

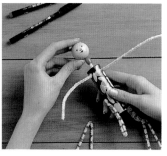

8 Bend two pipe cleaners in half to make the lower legs and thread through the upper legs. Wrap a brown pipe cleaner around the bottom of each leg and bend up to make the doll's shoes. Glue three brown pipe cleaners on to the top of the head and plait (braid) on each side to make the hair. Tie a ribbon on to the end of each plait. Glue on a doll's hat.

6 To make the doll's body, twist together the ends of two pipe cleaners. Make a hole at either side of the top and bottom of the cardboard tube. Thread the pipe cleaners through the top holes for the arms. For the upper legs, bend two more pipe cleaners in half and twist the ends together. Loosely attach to the bottom holes with a paper clip (fastener).

7 Using a permanent marker pen draw a face on a large, plain bead. Make a hole in the tube end. Thread a pipe cleaner through the hole. Thread on a small bead for the neck and then the large bead. Bend the pipe cleaner over the top of the head and over the bottom edge of the tube so that the head is held on securely.

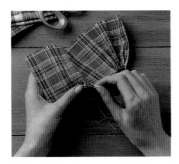

9 Cut a 10cm/4in square of fabric and fray. Cut a slit from one corner to the centre to make the shawl. Cut a 10 × 33cm/4 × 13in rectangle from another fabric. Sew a line of running stitch along the top edge and then gather to make the skirt. Wrap a piece of strong double-sided tape around the doll's body. Dress the doll and tie a length of ribbon around the waist.

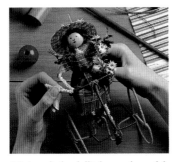

10 Attach the doll's feet to the pedals with freezer-bag ties. Wrap each arm around the handlebars, twisting the excess length around the arm. Place a little basket over one arm first and fill it with silk flowers.

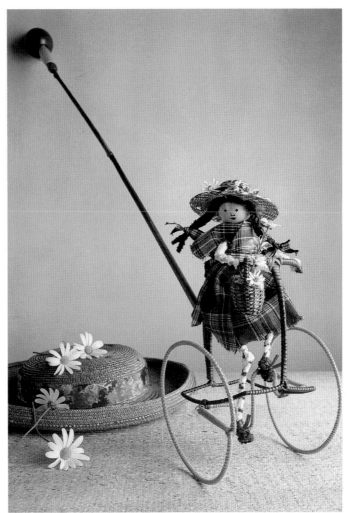

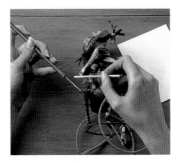

◀ **11** Apply strong glue to the piece of wire projecting from the bicycle seat and insert into the hollow centre of a green bamboo cane. Allow the glue to dry. Apply glue to the top end of the cane and slide on two or three beads to make a handle. Toddlers' beads are best for this as they have large holes.

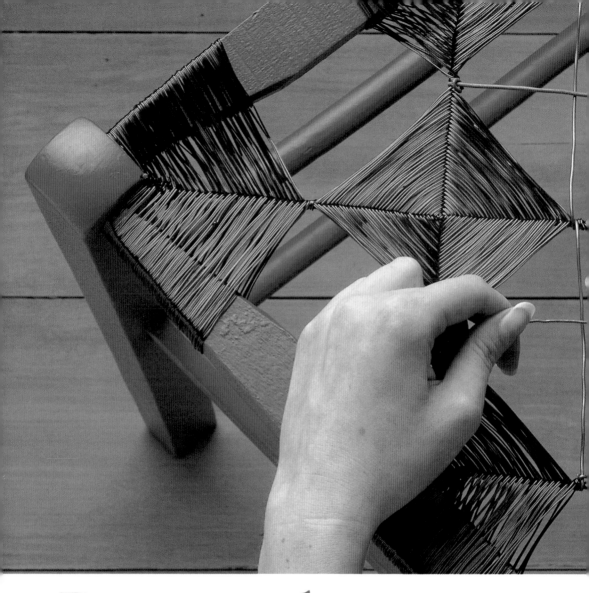

Practical
Wire Objects

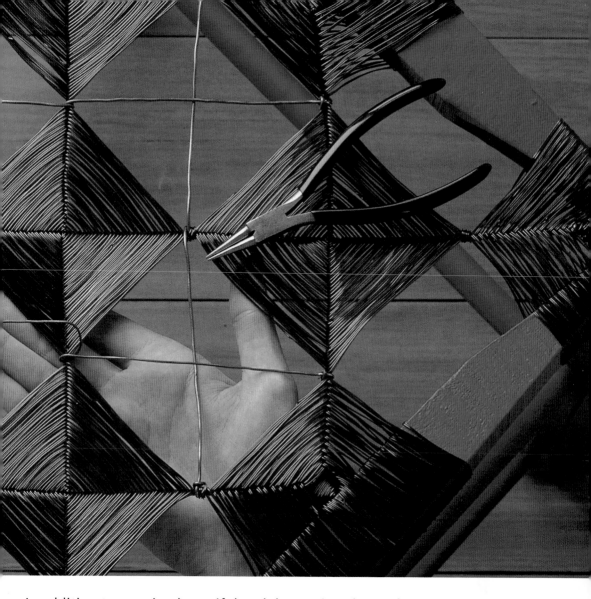

In addition to creating beautiful and decorative objects for around the home, you can use wire to create all manner of useful, practical items. You can twist and sculpt wire to make an enormous variety of holders and dishes for the bathroom and kitchen, as well as creating attractive containers for bottles and glasses, and building strong racks and shelves for storing all those essential items needed in every home.

Coil and Weave

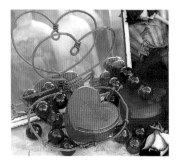

Wire is one of the most useful materials to have in the home as it has a wide variety of functional uses. Where would we be without wire coat hangers or metal hooks? In this chapter, wire is used to make a selection of practical but decorative objects for the home, ranging from toothbrush holders and soap dishes for the bathroom, toast racks and shelves for the kitchen, to a wire bird feeder for the garden.

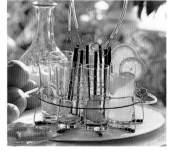

Wire is extremely practical. It is easy to use. Thicker gauges, once woven together, are strong and capable of supporting a heavy weight, and are usually rustproof, making wire ideal for use in bathrooms and kitchens. What's more, it is easy to clean, and hard to break.

Galvanized wire is used in this chapter to sculpt items, and to provide a

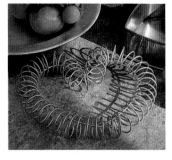

framework over which a flimsier material can be wrapped. Wire coat hangers can be recycled for small-scale projects that still require strength. Gardening wire is ideal to use outdoors; its plastic coating means that it does not tarnish. Another

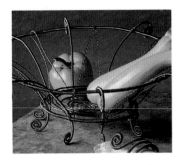

wire worth using is tinned copper wire; this has a lovely colour and, again, does not tarnish. Chicken wire has a range of practical uses, both indoor and outdoor, and even food and drinks cans may be given an imaginative new function.

Wire is an attractive material in its own right and needs little adornment. Its clean and functional appearance complements a stainless steel kitchen. A wire trivet, toast rack and utility rack would look ideal in a more modern kitchen with minimal decor

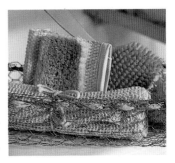

and clean unfussy surfaces. For functional items, simplicity is the important factor. Decorative motifs and curlicues are unnecessary and detract from the

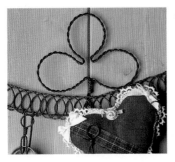

finished piece. Keep edges straight and neat for the best effect.

Many of the wire items featured in this chapter can also be made as gifts for friends and family. Handmade items are always treasured. If you make a project as a gift, try to personalize it somehow, perhaps by incorporating a monogram in the design.

These monogrammed clothes hangers make lovely gifts, or a charming gesture in a guest's bedroom. The instructions show how to make the hanger as well as the decoration.

Monogrammed Clothes Hanger

you will need
galvanized wire, 2mm/¹/₁₃in,
1mm/¹/₂₅in and 0.3mm/¹/₈₃in thick
ruler or tape measure
wire cutters
large pliers
beads
round-nosed (snug-nosed) pliers

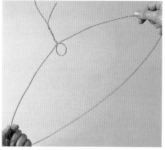

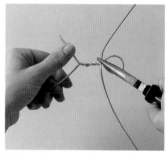

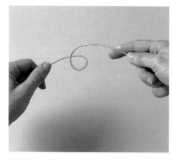

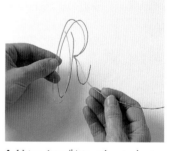

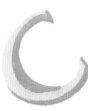

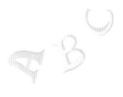

1 Cut a 140cm/55in length of the 2mm/¹/₁₃in galvanized wire. Bend it to form a loop 25cm/10in from one end, as shown.

2 Cross the two ends over at the loop and, holding them at the crossing-point with pliers, twist the two ends together for 5cm/2in.

3 Above the twist, trim off the short end and shape the longer end to form the hook. Holding the circle of wire with the hook at the top, pull out the sides to form the hanger shape.

4 Using 1mm/¹/₂₅in galvanized wire, shape the initial letter for the centre of the hanger following the relevant template from the alphabet at the back of the book.

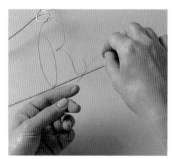

5 Bind the letter to the hanger at the top and bottom using the 0.3mm/⅛₃in galvanized wire.

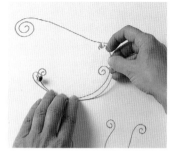

6 With 1mm/⅑₅in wire, make the decorative shapes using the templates at the back of the book as a guide. Thread beads on to the ends of the wires, then twist into shape using round-nosed (snug-nosed) pliers.

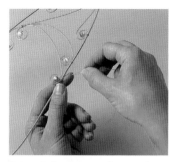

7 Attach the shapes to the main frame in the order of the numbers shown on the template. Bind each one to the top and bottom of the hanger, using fine wire as before.

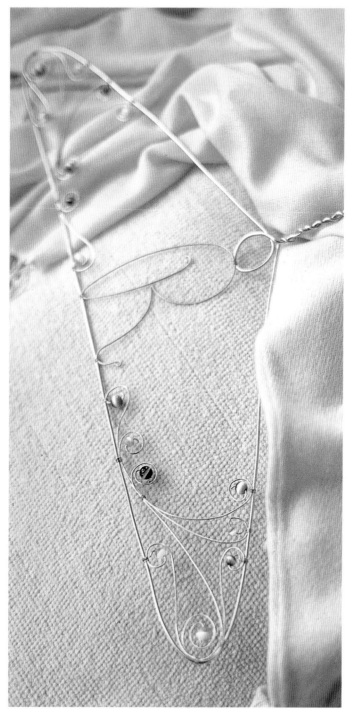

A quirky design using coloured, plastic-coated wire makes a holder for a glass and four toothbrushes that will get you smiling in the morning. Glass beads add colourful decoration.

Toothbrush Holder

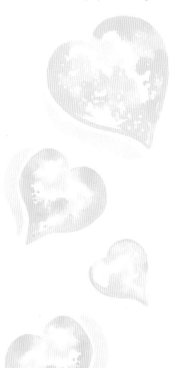

you will need

glass

plastic-coated steel wire, 1mm/¹⁄₂sin thick

ruler or tape measure

wire cutters

glass beads, 5mm/¹⁄₆in

pen

all-purpose instant glue

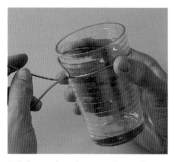

1 Select a glass that is wider at the top than the bottom. Cut a 1m/40in length of wire and circle the glass with it, twisting the ends to secure.

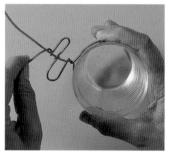

2 Twist one end of the wire firmly around the other, forming two loops on opposite sides to each other as you do so.

3 Thread eight glass beads on to the straight wire and twist the second wire between them to hold them in place and create a solid spine.

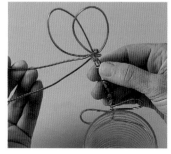

4 Form two loops with the ends of the wires to make a heart. Twist the ends together at the base of the heart and trim off any excess wire.

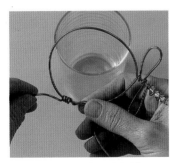

5 To make the toothbrush holders, cut two 30cm/12in lengths of wire and then coil the central part of each one tightly around the circle.

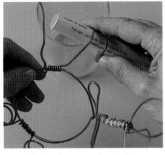

6 Coil the loose ends of the wires around a large pen to make four circles large enough to hold your toothbrush.

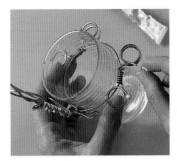

7 Glue beads to the wire ends as a finishing touch.

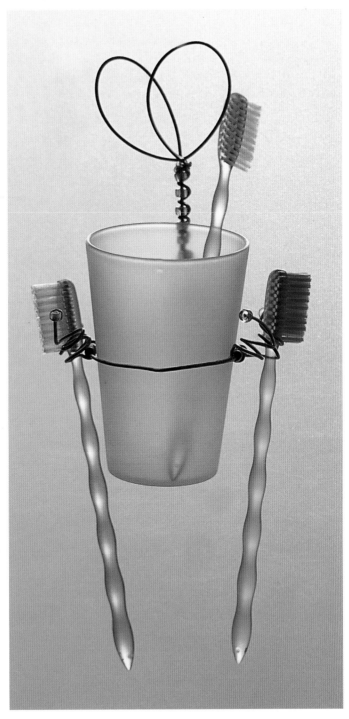

This unusual fly swatter is simple to make and extremely effective. It is designed to resemble a giant flower, and is an attractive addition to the kitchen or conservatory.

Flower Fly Swatter

you will need
straightened wire coat hanger
wire cutters
pliers
broom handle
ruler or tape measure
wooden ball, 2.5cm/1in diameter
paper
pencil
plastic mesh
scissors
cotton knitting yarn
needle

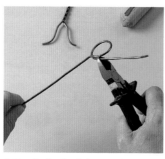

1 Cut the hook off the coat hanger. To form the flower centre, using pliers, bend one end of the wire and form a loop using a broom handle to bend the wire around. Trim.

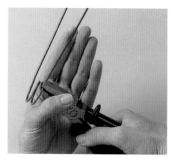

2 To form the handle of the fly swatter, measure down 45cm/18in from the top of the loop and bend a 90° angle. Turn this end around the broom handle twice, then bend at 90° again and cut off, leaving a 4cm/1½in length parallel with the stem. Twist the end of the wire around the stem. Open the double loop and insert the wooden ball.

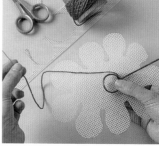

3 Enlarge the flower template at the back of the book to the required size. Trace it on to the plastic mesh, and cut out neatly. Centre the top loop of the wire stem on the flower shape and oversew firmly in place with cotton yarn.

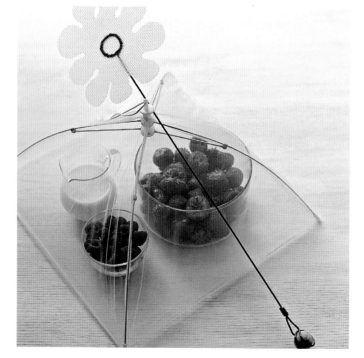

Made from galvanized wire, this practical yet decorative accessory for the kitchen will co-ordinate with any style of kitchen decor. You could make a set of trivets in different shapes and sizes.

Heart-shaped Trivet

you will need
galvanized wire, 2mm/¹⁄₃in thick
wire cutters
ruler or tape measure
broom handle
pliers

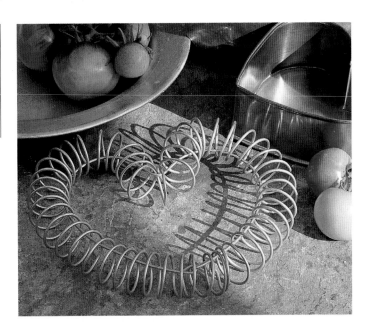

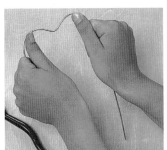

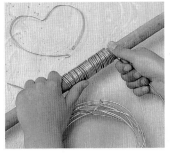

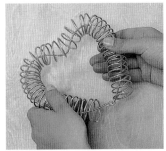

1 Cut a 50cm/20in length of wire, and form it into a heart shape by bending the wire in the centre to form the dip in the top of the heart. At the ends, make hooks to join the two ends of the wire together.

2 Make a coil by tightly and evenly wrapping more wire round a broom handle 50 times. Make hooks in the ends in the same way as before.

3 Thread the coil over the heart. Connect the ends of the heart by crimping the hooked ends together with pliers. Manipulate the coil, to make it sit evenly around the heart, before joining and crimping the ends together with pliers.

A novel idea to brighten up your bathroom – a soap dish made from gardening wire. It is easy to make and can be attached to the wall by inserting a screw through the hoop.

Sweetheart Soap Dish

you will need
thick plastic-coated gardening wire
wire cutters
ruler or tape measure
pencil
pliers

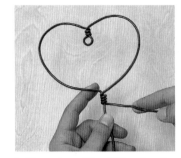

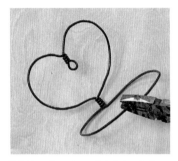

1 Cut an 88cm/35in length of wire and wrap it, at the halfway point, round the pencil. Make a coil, by twisting the pencil a couple of times.

2 Using about 17cm/6¾in of garden wire on each side of the coil, make a symmetrical heart shape and then finish off at the point, by twisting the wire into a coil again.

3 Using the wire ends left, hook them together and join the ends together by crimping them with pliers. Make this loop into an even oval, which will form the rim of the soap dish.

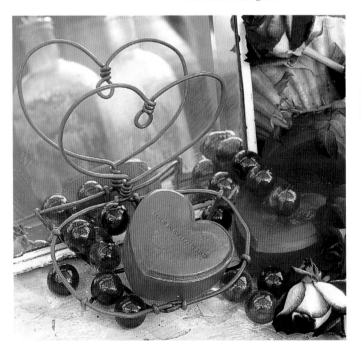

4 Cut four 14cm/5½in lengths of wire. Hook over the outside of the oval, making two crosses. Attach a shorter length across the centre.

This wire tidy is ideal for storing all those bathroom brushes and sponges that need to dry out between use. It is made from galvanized chicken wire and raffia.

Wire Bath Tidy

you will need
wire cutters
galvanized chicken wire, small gauge
natural raffia
large-eyed needle

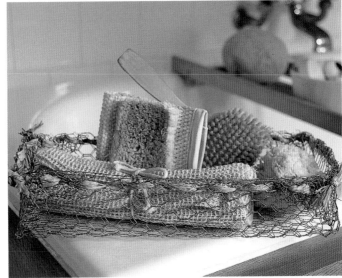

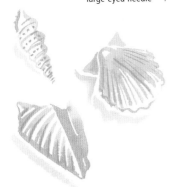

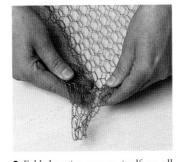

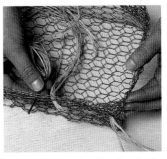

1 Use the wire cutters to cut a 50cm/20in length of chicken wire. Fold it in half lengthways, so that the smooth edges meet. Fold over the cut ends at each end to make them smooth as well.

2 Fold the wire over on itself, on all four sides. The folds should be 7.5cm/3in deep. To form the corners of the tidy, first press the folds firmly to ensure sharp creases and then unfold and open out the corners. Fold the opened-out wire corners flat against the long sides of the tidy.

3 Thread two or three lengths of raffia on to the needle and use it to make running stitches around the edge of the tidy, from corner to corner. Where it meets at the corners, tie a reef knot and trim the ends.

Transform a wire coat hanger into this charming toilet-tissue holder. Hearts are a traditional motif in folk-art designs, and transform the most functional of objects into personal works of art.

Toilet-tissue Holder

you will need

wire coat hanger

wire cutters

parallel (channel-type) pliers

piece of wood

drill

screw and screwdriver

ruler or tape measure

permanent marker pen

general-purpose pliers

galvanized wire, 0.8mm/¹⁄₃₁in thick

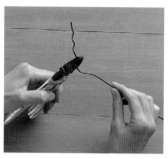

1 Open out the coat hanger hook and cut off the hook and the twisted wire with wire cutters. Straighten the wire using parallel (channel-type) pliers.

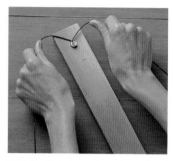

2 Drill a hole in a piece of wood and insert a screw. Wrap the wire around the screw halfway along its length. The screw will hold the wire firmly. Mould the wire into a heart shape.

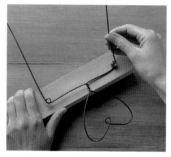

3 Allow 6.5cm/2½in between the eye and the bottom of the heart. Twist the wires together twice at the bottom of the heart. Bend out the remaining wires at right angles. Unscrew the wire heart and replace the screw in the piece of wood. Measure 6.5cm/2½in from the bottom of the heart along each wire, then wrap each wire once around the screw at this point and bend up the end at a right angle.

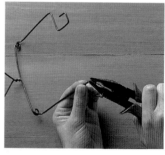

4 Using a marker pen, mark each remaining length of wire at intervals of 7.5cm/3in, 3cm/1¼in, 3cm/1¼in, 2cm/⅘in and 2cm/⅘in. Bend the wire into right angles at the marked points using general-purpose pliers, so the ends that will hold the toilet tissue point inwards. To decorate, loosely wrap a length of 0.8mm/¹⁄₃₁in galvanized wire around the whole of the structure.

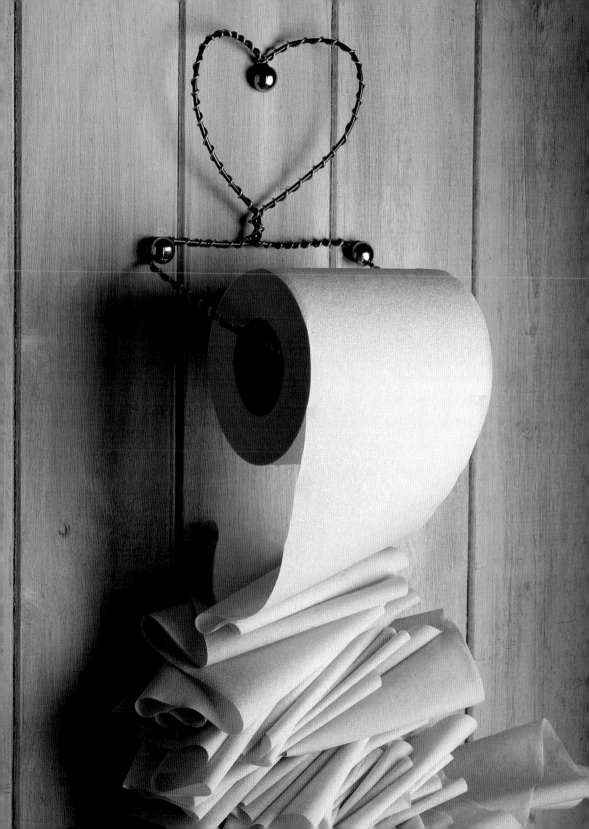

Extremely useful, bottle carriers can be quite hard to find. This version is made from thick galvanized wire formed into a clover leaf shape and holds three bottles.

Bottle Carrier

you will need

galvanized gardening wire, 2mm/¹/₁₃in and 0.8mm/¹/₃₁in thick

ruler or tape measure

wire cutters

bottle

general-purpose pliers

permanent marker pen

nail, 5mm/¹/₅in long

large wooden bead

strong glue

hammer

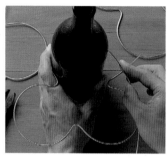

1 Cut three 80cm/32in lengths of the thicker wire. Leave 10cm/4in at one end of each wire and wrap the next section around a bottle. At the point of overlap, bend back the wire to form a second, then a third curve. Make a loop at each end of the wire and close together. Cut off any excess wire. Make two more clover shapes.

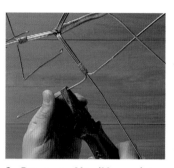

2 Cut seven 80cm/32in and two 91.5cm/36in lengths of thicker wire. Bundle them together so that the longest are in the centre and stick out at one end. This end forms the handle. Starting where the longer wires stick out, bind the bundle with thin wire for 42cm/16½in. To form the base of the bottle carrier, divide the wires into groups of three. Bend each group away from the central shaft at right angles. Arrange the wires in each group side by side. Measure 3cm/1¼in from the handle and bind together for 2cm/⁴/₅in. Bend out the outer two wires at right angles. Measure 5cm/2in from the bound section and mark each wire. Bend each wire up at a right angle so that it stands parallel to the handle. Make a hook at the end of each wire.

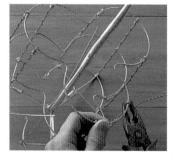

3 Slot the three clover shapes into the structure, and then close up the hooks around the top clover shape. Bind the bottom clover in place. Bind up each strut, securing the middle clover shape halfway up. Bind over the wire ends at the top of the structure.

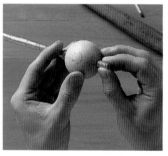

4 Wrap a length of 2mm/¹/₁₃in wire around the nail to make a coil. Thread the bead on to the wires at the top of the central shaft. Apply strong glue to the coil and hammer on the bead.

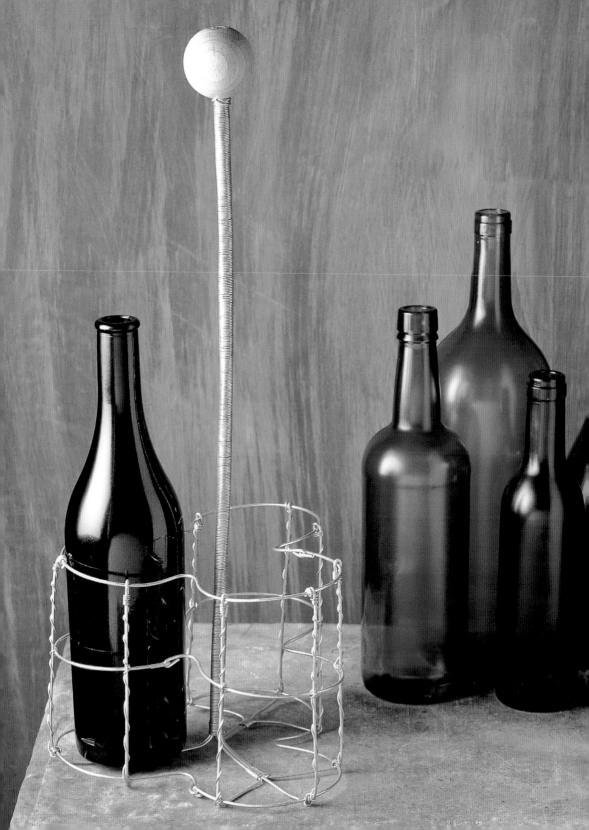

This clever little device made of two recycled coat hangers will give your rolling pin its own place on the kitchen wall, looking decorative as well as being out of the way.

Rolling Pin Holder

you will need

galvanized wire, 2mm/¹⁄₁₃in thick

wire cutters

ruler or tape measure

screwdriver

pliers

fine brass picture-hanging wire

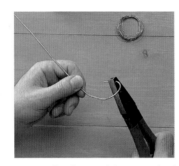

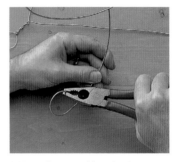

1 Cut two 75cm/30in lengths of the galvanized wire. Find the middle of one length and then bend it around a screwdriver handle to make a loop. Twist the two halves six times.

2 Using the pliers, curl the two ends of the wire forwards. The curls form the handle that holds the rolling pin, so check the fit as you work.

3 Twist the second length of wire into a heart shape – bend it sharply in the middle, then bring the ends down in opposite directions so that they cross over. Curl the ends.

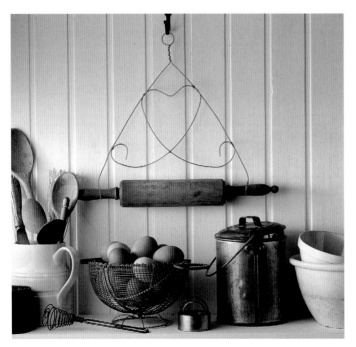

4 Using short lengths of brass picture-hanging wire, bind the two lengths together at the points shown. Place your rolling pin between the curled hooks to judge the width needed.

The design for this whimsical egg tree derives from eastern European folk art. The basket at the bottom is traditionally used for bread. Tinned copper wire has been used – it is malleable but does not tarnish.

Decorative Egg Tree

you will need
ruler or tape measure
tinned copper wire, 2mm/¹/₁₃in and
1mm/¹/₂₅in thick
rolling pin
wire cutters
permanent marker pen
pencil
tacking wire
general-purpose pliers
strong tape

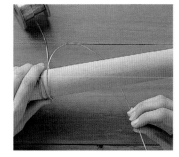

1 Measure 60cm/24in of 2mm/¹/₁₃in wire but do not cut off. Beginning at this point, wrap this section of wire three times around a rolling pin. Remove from the rolling pin and grip the middle of the final loop between your thumb and forefinger.

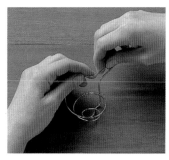

2 Wrap the loop around your thumb and then pull it down. The second loop will reduce in diameter. The loops form the egg holder. Bend the remaining end of wire up the outside of the egg holder to meet the wire still attached to the spool.

4 Make ten more egg holders. The bound section of the six lower holders measures 7.5cm/3in, and the section for the five upper holders measures 4cm/1½in.

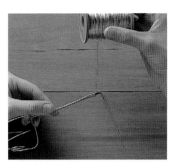

3 Bend both wires away from the egg holder to make the branch. Bind the two branch wires together for 7.5cm/3in using the thinner wire. Trim the thinner wire, leaving 2cm/⁴/₅in free. Bend the branch wires down at a right angle. Measure 60cm/24in of the branch wire from the spool and trim.

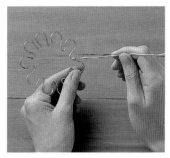

5 Measure 6.5cm/2½in of 2mm/¹/₁₃in wire and mark the point. Wrap the next section ten times around a pencil to form petals. Bend these round to form a flower. Use the first 6.5cm/2½in of wire to join the flower and cut off. Bend down the remaining wire at a right angle. Cut at 76cm/30in. ▶

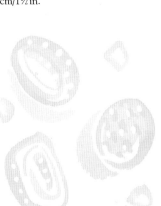

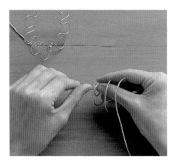

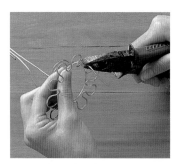

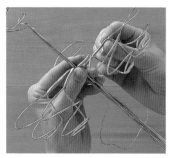

6 Form the top egg holder by measuring another 60cm/24in piece of 2mm/¹⁄₁₃in wire, without cutting off. As before, begin at this point and wrap the section three times around the rolling pin. Remove from the rolling pin and wrap the first loop around your thumb and pull down. Measure 70cm/27½in and cut off the wire from the spool.

7 Bind the end of the top egg holder on to the flower, opposite the joint. To hold the wires in place while you are working, bind them together with tacking wire. Bend the long wire extending from the flower to curve down the outside of the spiral. Using 1mm/¹⁄₂₅in wire, start binding the two stem wires tightly together. Bind for 7cm/2¾in.

8 Bunch the stem wires of the upper five egg holders around the two stem wires to form the trunk. Wrap with a piece of strong tape to keep them in place. Using 1mm/¹⁄₂₅in wire, start binding the trunk from just below the point at which the egg holders join the stem. Bind the trunk for 7cm/2¾in. Then bind on the six lower egg holders. Bind the trunk for 25cm/10in below this second tier.

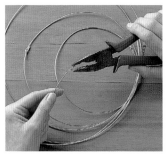

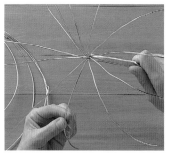

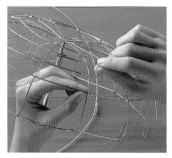

9 To make the basket, cut six lengths of 2mm/¹⁄₁₃in wire measuring 91cm/36in, 90cm/35½in, 89cm/35in, 76cm/30in, 66cm/26in and 46cm/18in. Using pliers, bend hooks at both ends of each wire. Form each length into a ring and hook the two ends together. Squeeze the hooks together using pliers to close.

10 Splay out the wires from the base of the egg tree and curve upwards to form the side struts of the basket. Check that the diameter at the top is the same as that of the largest ring.

11 Tack the rings on to the struts. Start with the smallest at the bottom and work up to the largest at the top. Allow 2.5cm/1in between each ring. Attach the largest ring by wrapping the ends of the strut wires around it. The basket should be about 9cm/3½in in height. Finally, bind the rings on to the struts.

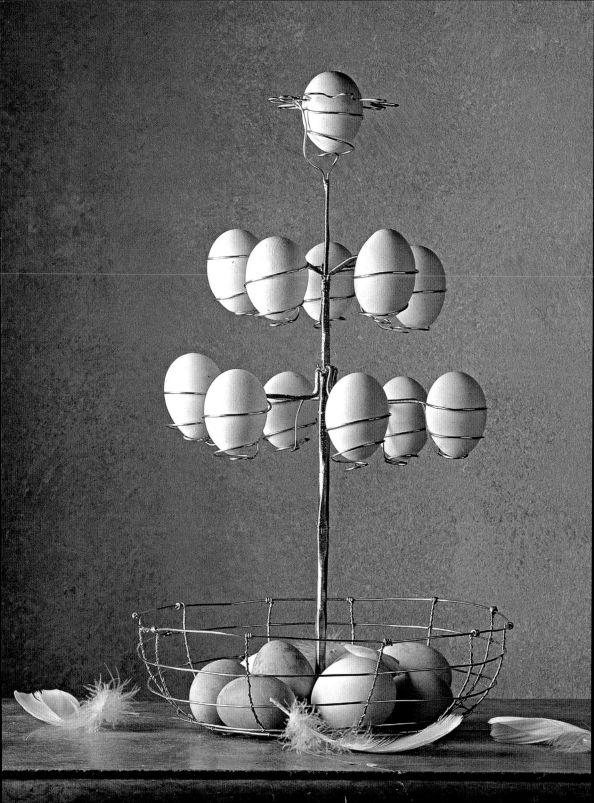

This intriguing little basket is made using a simple wrapping technique. The tightly woven pipe cleaners give a softness that is irresistible to touch. Use this basket to hold jewellery.

Woven Pipe Cleaner Basket

you will need
galvanized wire, 1.5mm/¹⁄₁₉in and
0.5mm/¹⁄₅₀in thick
ruler or tape measure
wire cutters
50 lilac and 24 grey pipe cleaners,
30cm/12in long
flat-nosed pliers
round-nosed (snug-nosed) pliers

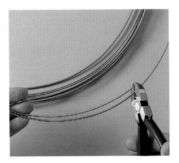

1 For the struts of the basket, measure and cut eight lengths of 1.5mm/¹⁄₁₉in galvanized wire, each 36cm/14in. Retain the curve of the wire as you cut the lengths from the coil. Cut one 30cm/12in length of the 0.5mm/¹⁄₅₀in galvanized wire.

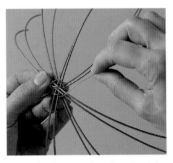

2 Use the fine wire length to bind the struts together at the centre. Bind two pairs together at right angles, then place the remaining pairs diagonally. Wind the fine wire around all the individual struts to hold them in position, evenly spaced.

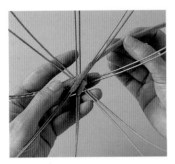

3 Weave a lilac pipe cleaner over the centre of the basket so that all the fine wire is covered.

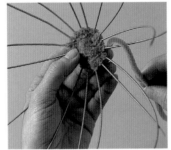

4 Take the pipe cleaner under each wire, back around it and then on to the next, pushing the pipe cleaners in towards the centre to keep the weave tight. Adjust the wires as necessary to keep the shape and spacing even. Work in lilac until the woven piece measures 7.5cm/3in.

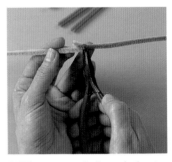

5 When you reach the end of a pipe cleaner or want to use a different colour, join the lengths by bending a small hook in the end of each. Hook them together and flatten the hooks with flat-nosed pliers.

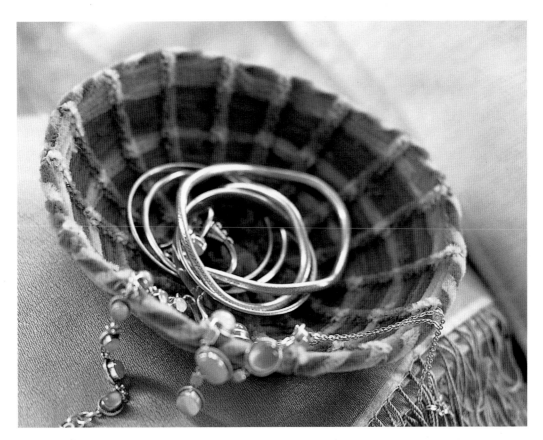

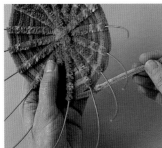

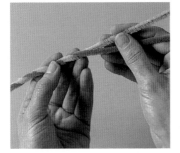

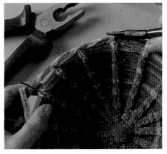

6 Work two rows of weaving in the grey pipe cleaners, then three lilac, two grey, four lilac, two grey, five lilac, and four grey, to bring you to the top edge of the basket.

7 Take two lilac pipe cleaners and hook them together, and do the same with two grey pipe cleaners. Hold the two colours together at one end and twist them firmly together. Join the twisted length to the last grey length on the basket and arrange it around the top edge, outside the struts.

8 Trim the tops of the struts to 5mm/ ⅕in and use round-nosed (snug-nosed) pliers to bend them over the edging. Weave the ends of the twisted edge into its beginning.

These ingenious containers look like fat little pots, but are actually made of brightly coloured fabric stretched over wire frames. Use them as containers for cotton wool.

Fabric-covered Baskets

you will need
galvanized wire, 3mm/⅛in,
2mm/¹⁄₁₃in and 1mm/½₅in thick
ruler or tape measure
wire cutters
long-nosed pliers
masking tape
two-way stretch fabric
scissors
sewing machine
sewing thread
needle

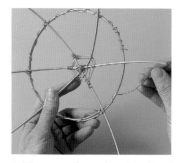

1 Measure and cut three lengths of 3mm/⅛in galvanized wire 45cm/18in long. Cross the wires at the centres and bind together using 1mm/½₅in wire so that the six prongs splay out evenly in a star shape. Using 2mm/¹⁄₁₃in wire, make a double ring 13cm/5in in diameter and bind it centrally to the framework to form a base.

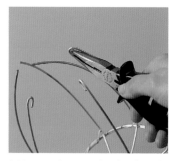

2 Use your fingers to bend each of the six prongs of the framework upwards where it joins the ring that forms the base. These prongs will form the structure for the sides of the container. Bend the end of each of the prongs into a tight loop using long-nosed pliers, as shown.

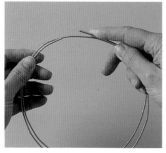

3 Make a second double ring of 2mm/¹⁄₁₃in wire to match the base, and then hold the two ends together temporarily using masking tape.

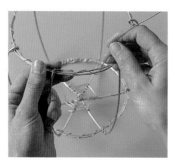

4 Slip the wire ring into the loops at the top of the framework, then bind in place using 1mm/½₅in wire.

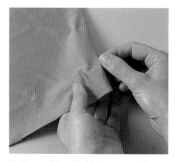

5 Cut a 35cm/13¾in square of two-way stretch fabric. Fold in half and stitch down the long side to make a tube, using a machine stretch stitch.

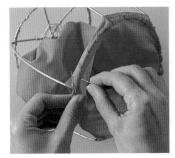

6 Place the fabric tube inside the wire framework. Hand stitch the raw edge to the top ring.

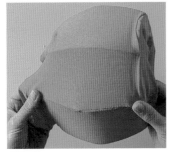

7 Pull the fabric up from inside the framework and carefully stretch it down around the outside of the tube. The fabric should be right side out.

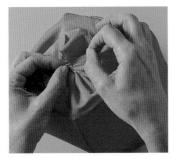

8 Gather the raw edge under the base and stitch to the centre of the framework. Ease any remaining fabric up towards the top of the container, and secure it with curly clips made from galvanized wire.

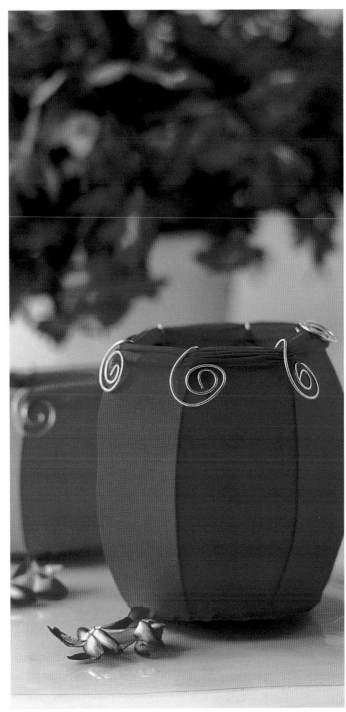

An elegant wire cage will ensure that a ball of string is always there when you need it and that it never gets into a tangle. Easy to refill and attractive, this dispenser is a useful accessory for the potting shed.

Hanging String Dispenser

you will need

galvanized wire, 2mm/¹⁄₁₃in and
1mm/¹⁄₂₅in thick
ruler or tape measure
wire cutters
broom handle
ball of string
pliers
length of garden cane
pencil

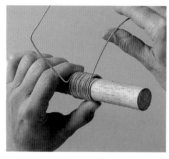

1 Cut a piece of 2mm/¹⁄₁₃in galvanized wire 1.7m/67in long. Bend a right angle about 30cm/12in from one end, then make 11 coils by turning the wire around a broom handle.

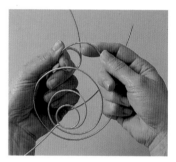

2 Loosen and spread the coils to form a shape that resembles a cone or half sphere. The shape needs to be large enough to fit loosely around the ball of string.

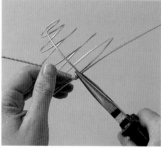

3 Bend the end of the wire down around the cone and use it to bind the last circle closed with pliers, leaving enough wire to create the feed loop for the string.

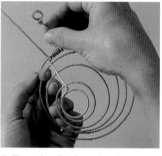

4 To make the loop for the string, wind a double coil around a garden cane about 2.5cm/1in along the remaining wire. Twist the end tightly around the stem and trim.

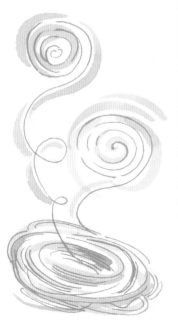

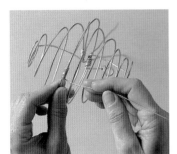

5 Make a second, matching cone, omitting the string loop. Using 1mm/¹⁄₂₅in wire, bind the two halves on the side opposite the loop.

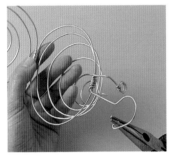

6 On each half, bend the free end of the wire at 90° to the circle and create two matching hanging hooks. Complete each hook with a tight loop at the end.

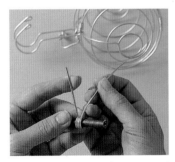

7 Cut a length of 2mm/¹⁄₁₃in wire and coil it several times around a pencil to make a closing ring for the dispenser. Trim and thread the ring over the hooks to keep the two halves shut.

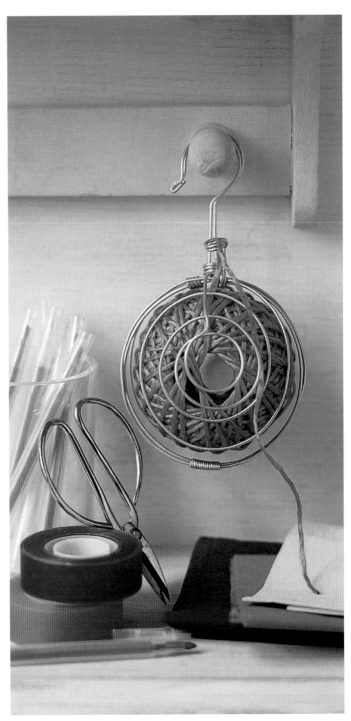

This sturdy basket is particularly suitable for gathering vegetables in from the garden. The mesh allows the soil to fall through and, because the wire is galvanized, the contents can be hosed down outside.

Wire Vegetable Basket

you will need

small-gauge chicken wire

wire cutters

gloves

ruler or tape measure

straining wire

galvanized wire, 1.5mm/^{1}/$_{19}$in and 0.8mm/^{1}/$_{31}$in thick

round-nosed (snug-nosed) pliers

permanent marker pen

tacking wire

broom handle

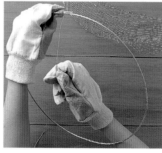

1 To make the cylinder, cut a piece of chicken wire 28 × 89cm/11 × 35in. Form it into an oval and join the short edges together. Cut a 94cm/37in length of straining wire and form it into an oval that will fit snugly inside the chicken-wire cylinder. Bind the ends together with the 0.8mm/^{1}/$_{31}$in galvanized wire.

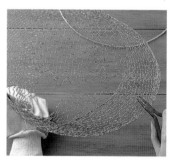

2 To shape the basket, count up ten holes from the bottom of the cylinder. This section will be the base. Use the round-nosed (snug-nosed) pliers to bend all the holes into heart shapes. To make the base support, cut a 70cm/28in length of straining wire and bind it into an oval.

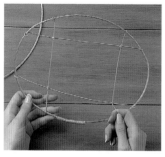

3 Cut two 18cm/7in lengths and two 23cm/9in lengths of the 1.5mm/^{1}/$_{19}$in galvanized wire. Use round-nosed pliers to attach the wires to the oval to form a grid, binding where the wires cross.

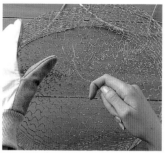

4 Push the bottom edges of the basket together and bind with 0.8mm/^{1}/$_{31}$in galvanized wire to close up the base section neatly.

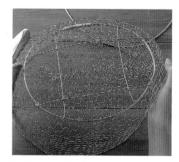

5 Position the base support on the bottom of the basket and bind it on to the chicken wire all the way around.

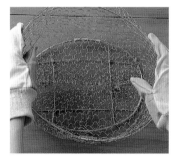

6 Place the large oval of straining wire inside the basket, 5cm/2in from the top. Fold the chicken wire over it, as shown. This will reinforce the top rim of the basket.

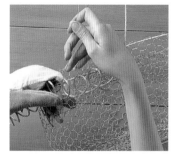

7 Mark a 54.5cm/21½in length of straining wire but do not cut it. Tack the end to one side of the basket and bend to form the handle. Secure the wire to the other side of the basket at the marked point. Wrap the next section of the straining wire around a broom handle to form ten loops. Bind these loops around the basket to the other side of the handle.

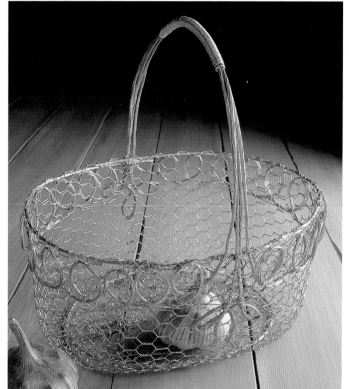

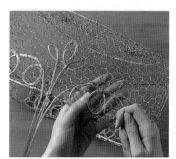

8 Bend the wire over the basket to double the handle. Bend the wire into a three-petalled decoration, as shown, and bind it to the basket. Loop the handle across again and make another three-petalled decoration on the other side.

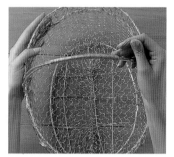

9 Bend the wire back over the basket to form a fourth handle loop. Using the broom handle, make ten more loops in the wire and bind around the basket. Using 0.8mm/¹⁄₃₁in galvanized wire, bind the handle wires together, tucking the ends inside.

These semi-circular copper shelves have a Spanish style and will look good anywhere. The flattened coil edging adds strength to the framework as well as creating a shallow lip to stop anything from slipping off.

Decorative Shelves

you will need

paper

felt-tipped pen

ruler or tape measure

copper wire, 2mm/¹⁄₁₃in, 1.5mm/¹⁄₁₉in
and 0.5mm/¹⁄₅₀in thick

wire cutters

flat-nosed pliers

round-nosed (snug-nosed) pliers

masking tape

30cm/12in length of wooden dowel,
1cm/²⁄₅in thick

2 picture hooks and nails

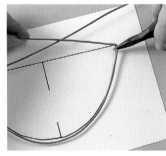

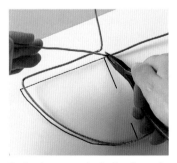

1 Enlarge the template at the back of the book to a width of 18cm/7in. Cut an 80cm/32in length of 2mm/¹⁄₁₃in copper wire and use the template as a guide to form the shelf frame. Use flat-nosed pliers to bend the wire, and start with the centre of the wire length at the centre front of the frame.

2 At the centre back, bend a right angle in the two ends of the wire so that they are vertical and parallel with each other. These will form the struts under the shelf. Using a pair of round-nosed (snug-nosed) pliers, turn each end of the wire to form a 5mm/¼in outward-facing hook.

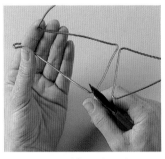

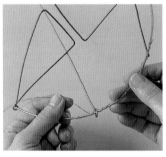

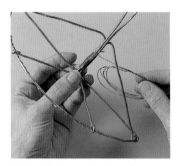

3 Measure 6cm/2½in along the struts from the base and bend them out to the sides, so that the hooks meet the back corners of the base. Attach and firmly close the hooks.

4 Cut two 23cm/9in lengths of 2mm/¹⁄₁₃in wire and form a hook in one end of each. Attach these to the outer curved frame one-third of the way in from each side and close the hooks firmly. To hold them in place, wrap 0.5mm/¹⁄₅₀in wire along the front edge and around both hooks.

5 Bring both wires back to the centre back. Bend them up at right angles so that they run parallel to the central support wires. Cut a 150cm/59in length of 0.5mm/¹⁄₅₀in wire and bind the four wires together. Trim, leaving a 2.5cm/1in tail. Use pliers to tuck the end under the coils to secure it.

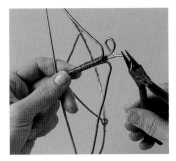

6 Trim the two ends at the bottom to 4cm/1½in and use round-nosed pliers to bend them into outward-facing loops which will lie flush with the wall.

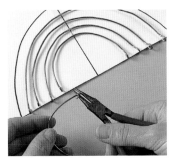

7 Make the wire hoops using 1.5mm/ ¹⁄₁₉in wire. Turn a hook in one end then bend the wire in a semi-circle 1cm/⅖in in from the template edge and finish with a hook at the other end. Tape this piece in place and then repeat, working inwards in 1cm/⅖in steps until you have a total of six semi-circles, as shown.

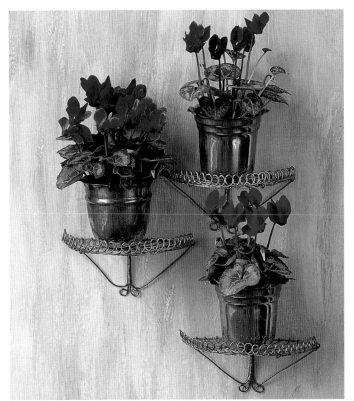

8 Wrap a 60cm/24in length of 0.5mm/ ¹⁄₅₀in wire once around the centre back struts. Hook the smallest semi-circle of wire into position on the back edge and firmly close the hooks.

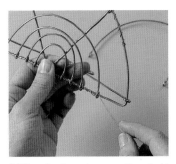

9 Wrap the fine wire around it to hold it in place, then repeat to attach the other semi-circles. Fasten off the fine wire tightly at the corners. Using the fine wire, attach the semi-circles to the shelf supports in the same way, first working in along one support and then working back out along the other.

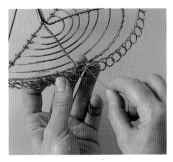

10 Cut a 1.2m/47in length of 1.5mm/ ¹⁄₁₉in wire, and wrap it around a length of 1cm/⅖in dowel to make a flattened coil. Pull out the coil so that it stretches evenly around the curved outside edge of the shelf, and bind it in place with a 60cm/24in length of 0.5mm/¹⁄₅₀in wire. Hang the shelf using a picture hook in each corner.

The elegance of this fresh green rack will add style to your kitchen and ensure that your kitchen implements, such as brushes and spoons, are always close at hand.

Spoon Rack

you will need
thick gardening wire
ruler or tape measure
wire cutters
rolling pin
round-nosed (snug-nosed) pliers
piece of copper piping
permanent marker pen
screwdriver and 4 screws

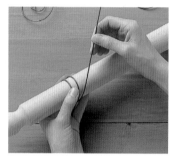

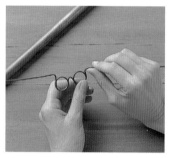

1 Cut three 1m/40in lengths of thick gardening wire. Wrap one end of each wire three times around a rolling pin. Using the round-nosed (snug-nosed) pliers, make a small loop in the coiled end of each wire large enough to take a screw. Shape the coils into a spiral in each wire. Bend back the wire from one of the lengths at a right angle to make the central stem.

2 To make the spoon holders, cut three 58cm/23in lengths of wire. Bend each wire at a right angle 12.5cm/5in from one end. In the next section of wire, make a row of three circles by wrapping the wire one and a half times around a piece of copper piping (or similar tube) for each of the circles.

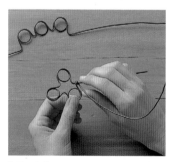

3 Bend the remaining wire away from the third circle at a right angle. Bend the three circles around to form a clover shape and bind the long end of wire around the 12.5cm/5in end for 7cm/2¾in. Do not cut off the ends.

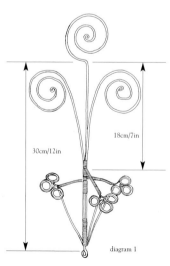

30cm/12in

18cm/7in

diagram 1

◀ **4** Arrange the three spiralled wires together with the right-angled one in the centre. Measure 30cm/12in down from the right angle on the central stem and then mark this point. Cut a 36cm/14in length of wire and make a small loop in one end. Leave 2cm/⅘in next to the loop, then bind the wire tightly around the spiralled wires, upwards from the marked point (see diagram 1).

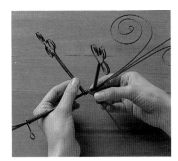

5 Measure 18cm/7in from the right angle of the central stem (see diagram 1), and, using the excess wire on one of the clover shapes, bind it on to the stem at this point. Bind upwards for 2cm/⅘in and cut off the wire. Bind on the second clover shape 2cm/⅘in below the first in the same way. Attach the third shape below the second, binding downwards for 4cm/1½in. Make a bend halfway along the stems of the second and third clover shapes to angle them inwards slightly.

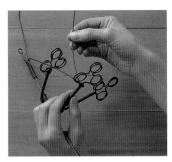

6 Bend up the three stem wires at the bottom and bind each to the neck of one of the clover shapes. Cut off the ends. Screw the spoon holder on to the wall through the loop in each spiral and at the bottom of the stem.

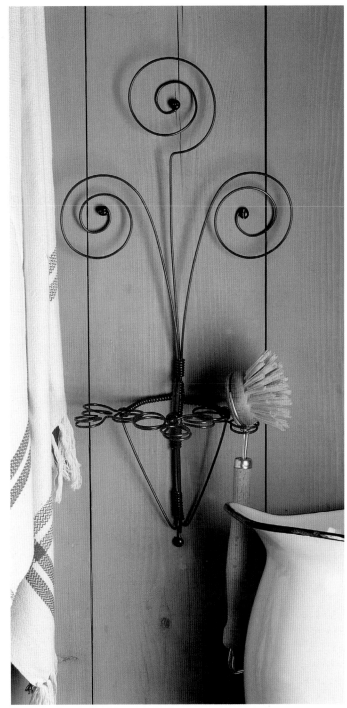

Small aluminium drink (soda) cans and aluminium mesh form the basis of this bird feeder. It can be filled with various types of nuts, scraps and larger seeds.

Wire Bird Feeder

you will need
small aluminium drink (soda) cans
old scissors
permanent marker pen
aluminium mesh
wire cutters
small pliers
bradawl (awl)
galvanized wire

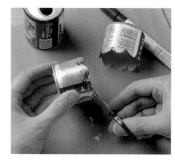

1 Cut a small aluminium drink (soda) can in half, then draw a decorative scalloped border around each half with a permanent marker pen and cut out. Trim off any jagged edges with a pair of old scissors.

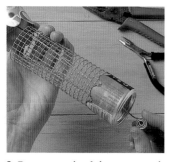

2 Cut a rectangle of aluminium mesh to fit, rolled up, inside the can. Join the edges by hooking the cut ends through the mesh and bending them over, using pliers. Pierce a hole in the bottom of the can. Fit the mesh cylinder into the two halves of the can, then thread on to galvanized wire. Coil the lower end of the wire so that the feeder cannot slide off.

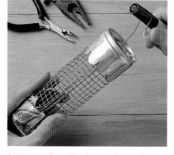

3 Leave a length of wire above the top of the can long enough for the top to slide up off the mesh, for refilling, then allow an extra 7.5cm/3in. Cut the wire. Twist the end into a flat coil, then make a hook by bending the wire over a marker pen. Repeat with the remaining cans.

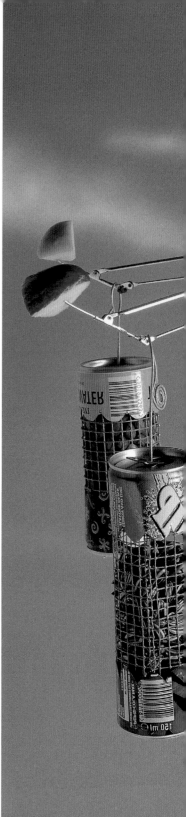

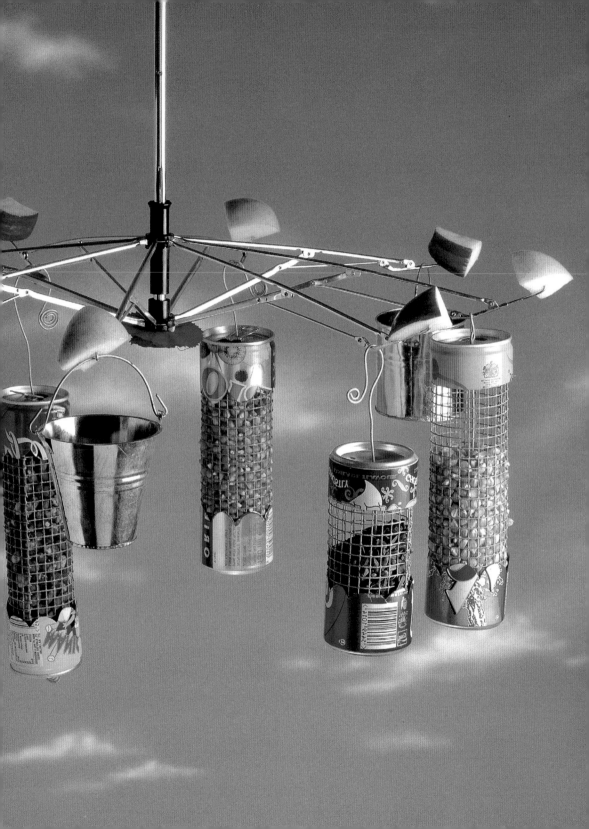

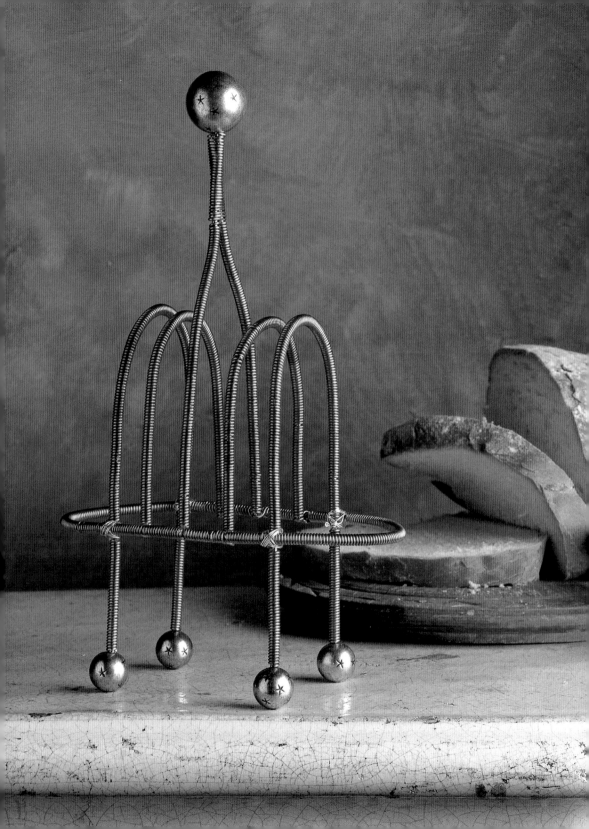

Grace your breakfast table with this sculptural toast rack. The tight wire wrapping and the star patterns on the handle and feet beads give the piece an original space-age quality.

Toast Rack

you will need

copper wire, 2.5mm/¹⁄₁₀in and 1mm/¹⁄₂₅in thick

ruler or tape measure

wire cutters

round-nosed (snug-nosed) pliers

tacking wire

bottle

file (optional)

permanent marker pen

strong glue

silver-plated copper wire, 0.8mm/¹⁄₃₁in thick

4 medium-sized beads

large bead

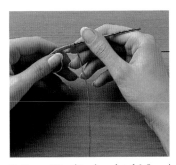

1 Cut a 10cm/4in length of 2.5mm/¹⁄₁₀in copper wire, and use round-nosed (snug-nosed) pliers to bend a loop in one end to make a "key". Attach the 1mm/¹⁄₂₅in copper wire next to the loop and wrap for 2cm/⁴⁄₅in. Do not cut off the wire.

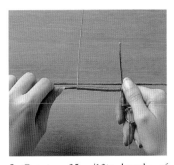

2 Cut two 25cm/10in lengths of 2.5mm/¹⁄₁₀in copper wire for the main shafts. Place the key at a right angle to one of the 25cm/10in lengths of wire, 1cm/½in from the end. Wrap the shaft with the same length of 1mm/¹⁄₂₅in wire for 23cm/9in by turning the key.

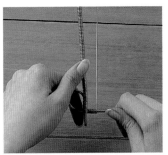

3 Remove the key from the initial 2cm/⁴⁄₅in of wrapping and place at a right angle to the other end of the 25cm/10in piece of wire. Wrap the key for another 2cm/⁴⁄₅in, making sure that this coil sticks out from the shaft wire at the same side as the first. Cut off the wrapping wire and remove the key from the coil.

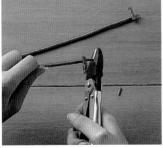

4 Trim the shaft wire close to the coil at each end. Wrap the second shaft wire in exactly the same way. Cut two 35cm/13¾in lengths of 2.5mm/¹⁄₁₀in wire. Wrap these wires in the same way again, leaving 7cm/2¾in unwrapped at each end. Do not trim the unwrapped sections – these form the legs.

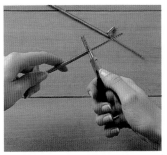

5 Using pliers, adjust all the 2cm/⁴⁄₅in coils so that they stick out from the wrapped wires at right angles and point in the same direction. To make the handles, cut two 21cm/8¼in lengths of 2.5mm/¹⁄₁₀in wire. Make a 2cm/⁴⁄₅in coil as before, then begin wrapping one of the wires 1cm/½in from the end. Wrap for 14cm/5½in.

▶

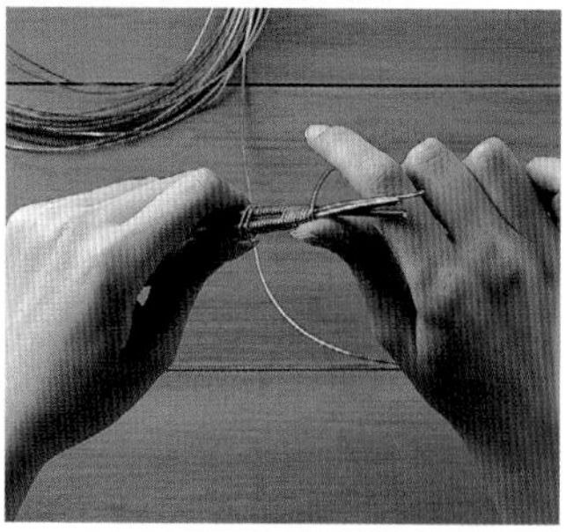

6 Trim the wrapping wire, leaving a long end. Wrap the second handle strut, but do not cut off the wrapping wire. Tack the two handle struts together using tacking wire, checking that the coils are facing in the same direction. Wrap them together, continuing up from the 14cm/5½in wrapped sections. Leave 2cm/⅘in at the top unwrapped.

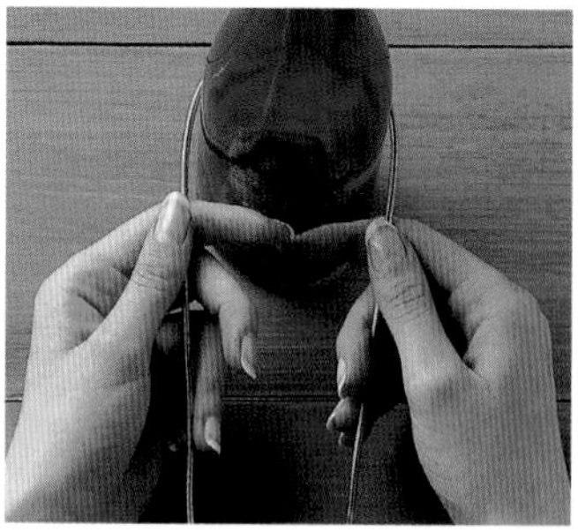

7 To make the base, cut a 50cm/20in length of 2.5mm/⅒in wire. Leave 15cm/6in at one end and bend the next section around a bottle 6cm/2½in in diameter. Wrap another length of 2.5mm/⅒in wire for 12.5cm/5in. Trim the wrapping wire. Remove the length of wire and thread the 12.5cm/5in coil on to the bent wire. Move it along until it sits in the bend.

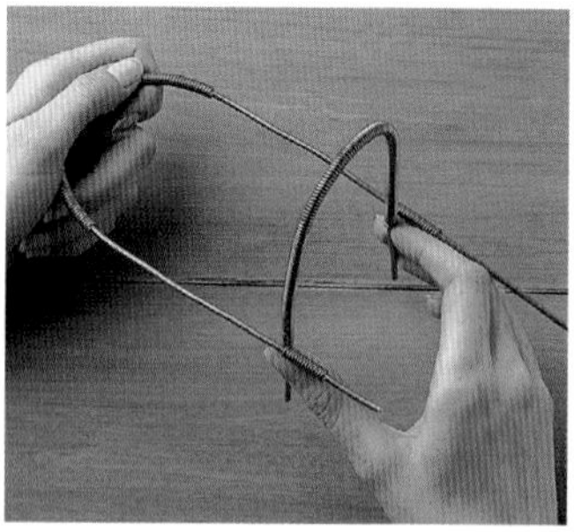

8 Bend each of the four wrapped pieces to make a curve in the centre. Thread the first wrapped section on the base. It should be one of the pieces with 7cm/2¾in legs. If you find it hard to push the wires through the coils, file the ends of the base wire. Pull apart the individually wrapped struts of the handle section and bend them to make an arch shape.

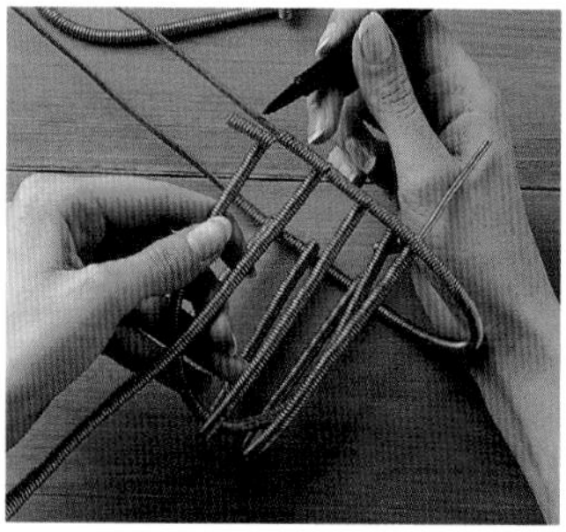

9 Thread on the next piece (with no legs), followed by the handle arch. Before threading on the next piece, mark the base wire halfway along the length of the next coil. You will cut the wire at this point later. Thread on this piece, followed by the second piece with legs. Wrap a length of 2.5mm/⅒in wire for 9cm/3½in and then remove the coil. Thread the 9cm/3½in coil on to the long end of the base wire.

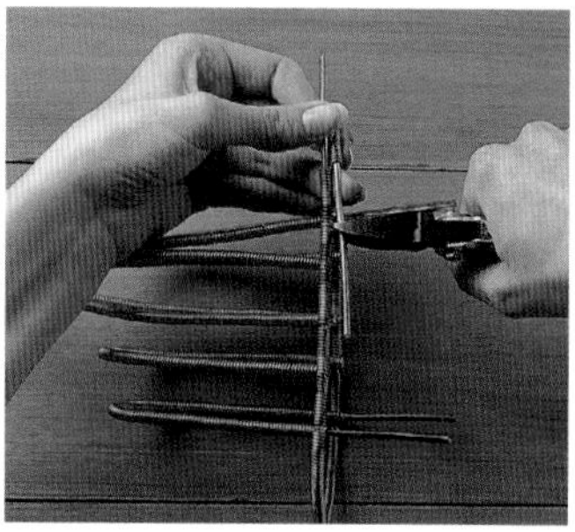

10 Bend the wire to mirror the first curve and until the two wrapped sections meet. Cut off the wire where it meets the marked point. Remove the last two coils from the base wire and cut off at the marked point. Thread the first coil on to the base wire next to the curve. Slot half of the next coil back on to the other end of the base wire. Apply glue to the end of the base wire next to the curve and slot it into the empty section of the next coil. Allow to dry.

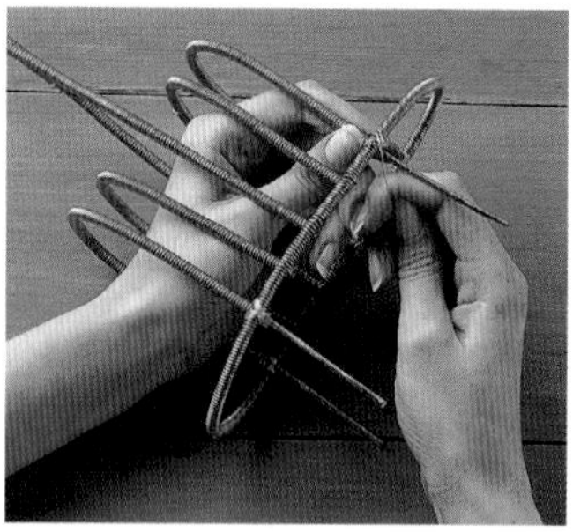

11 Using silver-plated copper wire, bind crosses around the leg joints to add stability. If you find that the rack is too springy, carefully apply a little glue to the joints. Make four 5cm/2in coils of 1mm/1⁄25in wire by wrapping around a length of 2.5mm/⅒in wire and then removing. Thread these coils on to the legs and then glue on bead feet. Glue the large bead on to the top of the handle. If necessary, make the hole in the bead a little larger by drilling carefully.

You don't need DIY skills to create fashionable designer furniture. Wooden chairs with a removable seat are easy to find. Paint the chair in one colour and choose wire of a contrasting colour.

Woven Chair

you will need
wooden chair
8 screw eyes
parallel (channel-type) pliers
enamelled copper wire in two colours,
2.5mm/¹⁄₁₀in and 1mm/¹⁄₂₅in thick
wire cutters
round-nosed (snug-nosed) pliers

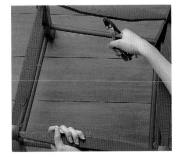

1 Screw the screw eyes into the inside of the chair frame, one in each corner of the seat section and one in the middle of each side piece, as shown. Tighten them securely with parallel (channel-type) pliers and make sure that all of the ring ends lie flat.

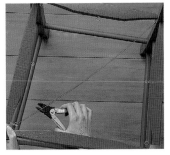

2 Attach the 2.5mm/¹⁄₁₀in wire to one corner by threading it through the eye and twisting the end around the wire, using pliers. Stretch it diagonally across the frame and secure it to the opposite eye. Repeat across the other diagonal. Make a diamond between the four side screws with four more pieces of wire.

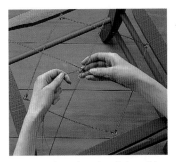

3 Cut a long length of 1mm/¹⁄₂₅in enamelled copper wire and fold it in half. Attach it by passing the loop under the centre of the copper wire cross and threading the end back through to secure.

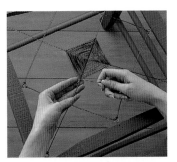

4 Weave a square so that you cover half the distance from the centre to the point where the copper wires cross. Cut off the wire, then wrap it around several times and tuck in the end. Weave four more squares, one at each point where the wires cross.

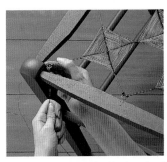

5 Attach another double length of 1mm/¹⁄₂₅in enamelled copper wire to one of the corner screw eyes.

▶

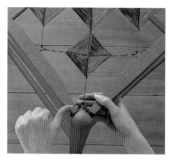

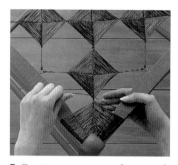

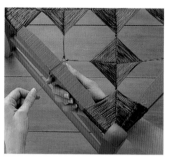

6 Weave first around one side of the chair frame, then work back around the diagonal copper wire and continue around the other side of the chair frame to make a herringbone pattern at the corner.

7 Continue weaving until you reach the square nearest to that corner. Secure the wire and trim, tucking in the end as before. Weave the other three corners of the chair in the same way.

8 Loop a double length of 1mm/¹⁄₂₅in enamelled copper wire around one of the side screw eyes. Weave around the chair frame to one side of the eye, then over the eye, around the other side of the chair frame and back under the eye. Continue in this way until the eye is completely covered.

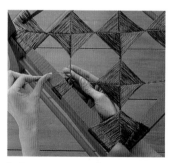

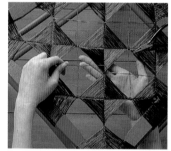

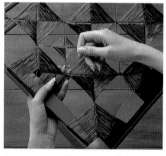

9 Continue weaving by wrapping the wire around the two diagonal copper wires as well as the chair frame. Weave until you reach the two nearest squares. Secure the wire and cut it off. Weave the other three sides.

10 Stretch two lengths of 2.5mm/ ¹⁄₁₀in copper wire across each of the spaces between the five central woven squares. Attach the wire ends to the corners of the squares and secure with round-nosed (snug-nosed) pliers.

11 Use 1mm/¹⁄₂₅in enamelled copper wire in a second colour to weave a square in each space. Weave the four squares so that they are smaller than the first five and there are gaps in the finished pattern.

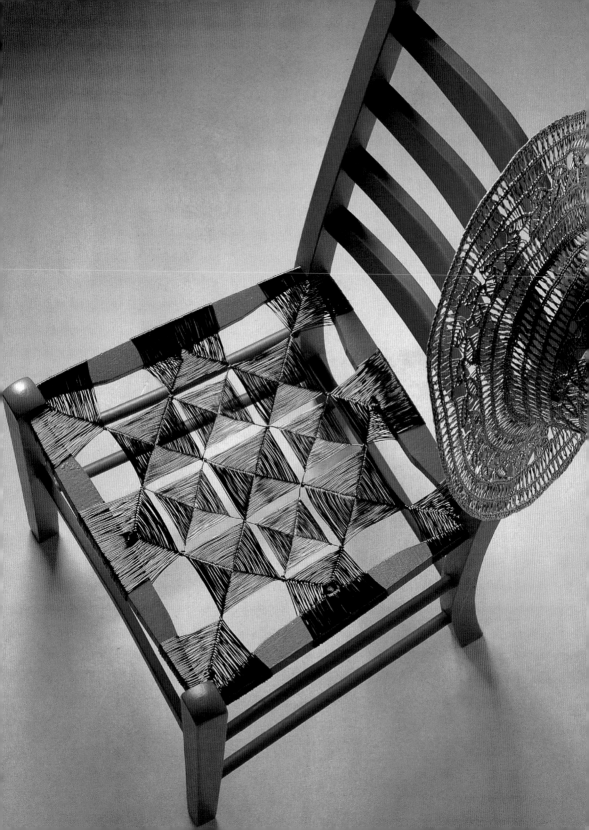

Copper wire is naturally warm in colour, and the wrapping technique used here enhances its rich appearance. The bowl looks particularly soft and sumptuous when displayed by candlelight.

Copper Bowl

ῠῠῠῠ
you will need
copper wire, 2mm/¹⁄₁₃in,
0.8mm/¹⁄₃₁in, 2.5mm/¹⁄₁₀in,
1mm/¹⁄₂₅in and 1.5mm/¹⁄₁₉in thick
ruler or tape measure
wire cutters
parallel (channel-type) pliers
bowls in two sizes
quick-drying glue
permanent marker pen
general-purpose pliers

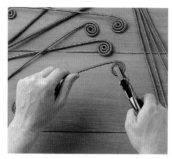

1 Cut eight 42cm/16½in lengths of 2mm/¹⁄₁₃in copper wire. Wrap with 0.8mm/¹⁄₃₁in wire. Make a coil with a diameter of about 4cm/1½in at one end and one of 2.5cm/1in at the other, using parallel (channel-type) pliers.

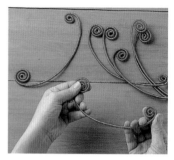

2 Bend each wire to form the curved side struts of the bowl. To make the rims of the bowl, cut two lengths of 2.5mm/¹⁄₁₀in wire, one 80cm/32in and the other 50cm/20in. Wrap the longer length in 1mm/¹⁄₂₅in wire and the shorter in 1.5mm/¹⁄₁₉in wire.

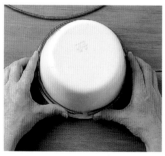

3 Release 2cm/⅝in at each end of the coil. Bend the longer wrapped wire around the larger bowl and the shorter wrapped wire around the smaller bowl to make two wire hoops.

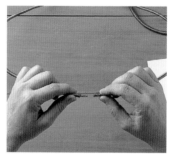

4 Insert a little quick-drying glue into the empty end of each coil and slot in the projecting end of wire. Hold it firmly in place until the glue is dry.

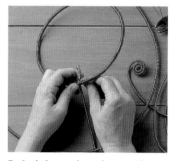

5 Lightly mark eight equidistant points around each of the hoops. Cut 16 lengths of 1mm/¹⁄₂₅in wire, each measuring 12.5cm/5in. Use these to begin binding the side struts to the hoops. Allow the struts to extend above the top rim by 6cm/2½in and below the bottom rim by 4cm/1½in.

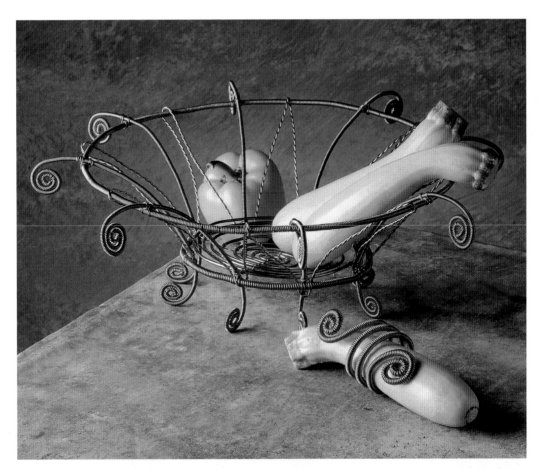

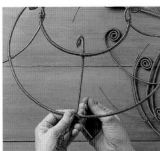

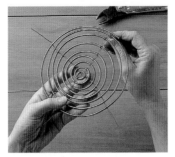

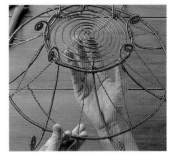

6 Continue to bind the struts to the hoops, wiring alternate ones first. This gives the bowl stability. Bind the last four struts to the hoops, adjusting any that become misshapen in the process.

7 Make an open coil with a diameter of 15cm/6in, from the 2.5mm/¹⁄₁₀in copper wire. Hold the shape of the spiral by binding it with two lengths of 1mm/¹⁄₂₅in copper wire, leaving about 10cm/4in spare wire at each end.

8 To attach the base coil, bind the excess wire around four of the struts. Twist a 2.3m/2½yd double length of 1mm/¹⁄₂₅in wire and wrap it around the bowl. Make a zigzag between the struts and halfway between the top struts.

Chicken wire becomes an exotic material when used to make this lantern, which is perfect for hanging in the garden. Place long-lasting night-lights in the jam jars.

Garden Lantern

ψψψψ

you will need

gloves

small-gauge chicken wire

wire cutters

ruler or tape measure

aluminium wire, 1mm/$^1/_{25}$in thick

galvanized wire, 1.5mm/$^1/_{19}$in thick

round-nosed (snug-nosed) pliers

general-purpose pliers

bottle with cone-shaped lid

jam jar

large beads

bath-plug chain

metal ring

flat-headed jewellery pins

narrow ribbon (optional)

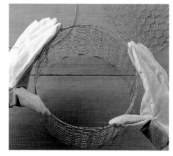

1 Wearing gloves, cut one piece of chicken wire 18 × 61cm/7 × 24in and one piece 22 × 55cm/8½ x 21½in. Form two cylinders with the wire and join the short edges together with the aluminium wire. Cut one length of the galvanized wire 66cm/26in and one length 61cm/24in. Bend to form two hoops with the same diameter. Bind the ends with aluminium wire.

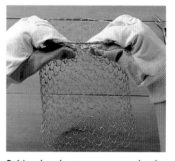

2 Use the aluminium wire to bind a hoop on to the edge of each cylinder. To shape the large cylinder into the lantern, carefully bend each of the holes in the chicken wire into heart shapes (see Basic Techniques). Use round-nosed (snug-nosed) pliers and your hands to mould the cylinder. (If necessary, refer to the step 7 picture for guidance with the shape.)

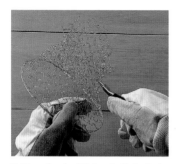

3 To make the lid, bend all the holes in the second cylinder into heart shapes, then mould the wire to form a curved lid shape. You will need to squash the holes together at the top.

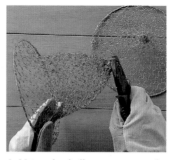

4 Using the hollow section in the mouth of the general-purpose pliers, carefully crimp the chicken wire in the centre of each section to give you a central core.

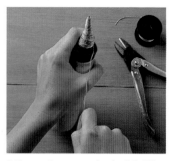

5 Form a long cone for the lid. Wrap the aluminium wire around the tapered top of a paint or glue bottle. The bottom of the cone must fit over the central core of the lid.

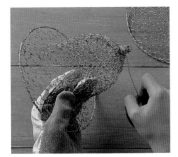

6 Secure a length of thin wire inside the centre of the lid and push it through the core. Thread the coiled cone on to the wire and slip over the core. Leave the length of wire hanging loose from the centre of the cone. Wrap another length of wire around the core of the lantern section to make a smaller coil.

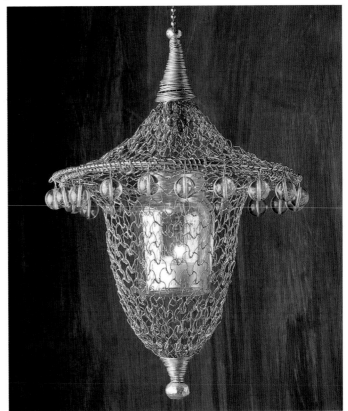

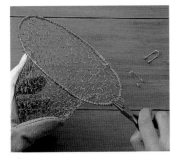

7 Cut four 10cm/4in pieces of the galvanized wire. Using round-nosed pliers, bend each piece into a loop with a hook at each end. Curve up the bend in each loop slightly. Position evenly around the rim of the lantern section and close up the hooks with pliers. Cut two lengths of galvanized wire and twist together around the neck of a jam jar so that the ends stick out on each side. Attach the wires to the lantern rim on each side of two opposite loops. This will hold the jam jar securely in place.

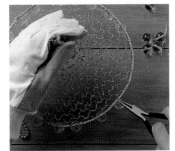

8 Thread a large metallic bead on to the loose wire in the lid. Bind the bath-plug chain on to the wire and trim any excess. Attach a metal ring to the other end for hanging. Thread beads on to flat-headed jewellery pins and hang evenly around the rim. Add a large bead to the lantern core.

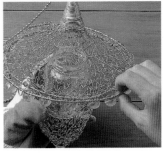

9 Put the lid on the lantern and slot the four loops on the lantern rim through the chicken wire of the lid. Press them down firmly. It is very important for safety that the loops hold the bottom securely in place. Reinforce with extra pieces of wire or tie with narrow ribbon.

Instead of balancing them precariously on a tray, a bottle and glasses can be safely carried into the garden in this stylish and sturdy carrier made from wire and bamboo.

Garden Drinks Carrier

you will need

black bamboo canes

ruler or tape measure

saw

skewer or length of thick wire

broom handle

galvanized wire, 2mm/¹⁄₁₃in and 1mm/¹⁄₂₅in thick

wire cutters

flat-nosed pliers

food can

fine wire

plastic coated garden wire, or length of thick wire 3.5mm/¹⁄₇in thick

length of plastic tubing (aquarium air line)

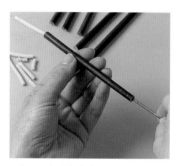

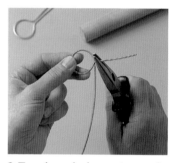

1 From the black bamboo canes, cut eight 15cm/6in lengths for the base of the drinks carrier and eight 17cm/6¾in lengths for the uprights. Use a skewer or length of thick wire to remove the pith from the centre of each cane.

2 To make each glass carrier, use the broom handle to turn a loop in the end of a length of the 2mm/¹⁄₁₃in galvanized wire. Bend the short end to lie against the length and then thread both ends of the wire through the centre of one of the hollowed-out base canes.

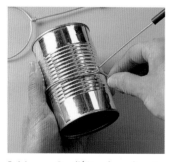

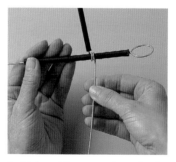

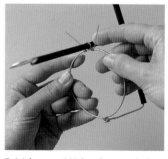

3 Measure 8cm/3¼in along the wire from the end of the cane, and at this point form a circle around a can. Twist the end around the wire to secure, and cut off the excess. Repeat to make eight base cane sections.

4 Make eight more looped wire lengths and thread them through the upright canes. Use the end of the wire to bind each upright cane to a base cane, 8cm/3¼in from the end with the small loop, and trim.

5 Make two 90° bends in each long wire, one at the end of the base cane and the other before the ring, and bind the ring to the upright with a short length of fine wire.

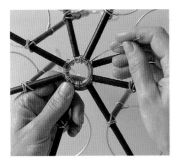

6 When the eight sections are all completed, arrange them in a circle, laying down each pair of opposites together. Using fine wire, bind all the central loops together and bind the rings to each other.

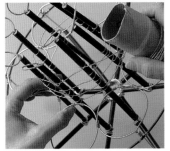

7 Cut a length of the plastic-coated garden wire to fit around the edge of the carrier and twist the ends to make a circle. Use fine wire to bind this in place just under each ring, and to bind the upright canes together. Turn the carrier upside down and loop fine wire around the base canes to make a firm platform for the glasses.

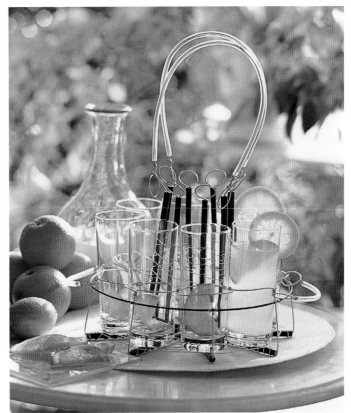

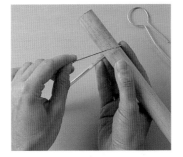

8 To make the carrying handles, use the broom handle to form a loop in one end of two short and two long lengths of wire and thread the wire into two lengths of plastic tubing (aquarium air line). Form another loop at the other end of the wires.

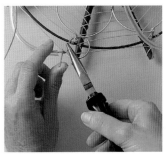

9 Thread the loops of the two long carrying handles through the loops at the top of four uprights, and secure them by twisting the ends of the wires around the handles. Attach the short handles around the garden wire ring in the same way.

Keep your herb and spice jars neat in this heart-rimmed rack, which is designed to hold five standard-sized spice jars. It can be hung on the wall or used free-standing on a shelf or kitchen surface.

Spice Rack

you will need

galvanized wire, 1.5mm/^{1}/$_{19}$in and 0.8mm/^{1}/$_{31}$in thick

ruler or tape measure

wire cutters

permanent marker pen

round-nosed (snug-nosed) pliers

general-purpose pliers

galvanized wire, 1.5mm/^{1}/$_{19}$in thick, doubled and twisted

tacking wire

broom handle

1 Cut five 45cm/18in lengths of the 1.5mm/^{1}/$_{19}$in wire. Mark at intervals of 5cm/2in, 5cm/2in, 25cm/10in, 5cm/2in and 5cm/2in.

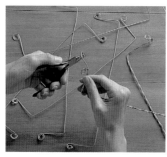

2 Using round-nosed (snug-nosed) pliers, bend the 5cm/2in sections at the ends of each wire into coils. Using general-purpose pliers, bend each at right angles at the next 5cm/2in marks. Cut two 45cm/18in lengths of twisted wire and mark in the same way. Untwist 5cm/2in at each end and make two coils. Bend right angles at the next marks.

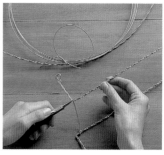

3 Cut two 9cm/3½in lengths of 1.5mm/^{1}/$_{19}$in galvanized wire. Make the box section of the spice rack by joining together the two twisted wire struts. Twist the ends of the 9cm/3½in lengths around the bent corners of the struts, leaving a distance of 6cm/2½in between the two struts.

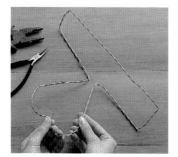

4 Cut a 104cm/41in length of twisted wire and mark it at intervals of 20cm/8in, 12.5cm/5in, 6cm/2½in, 25cm/10in, 6cm/2½in, 12.5cm/5in and 20cm/8in. Bend at the marked points to form a rectangle and heart.

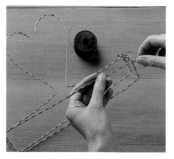

5 Attach the four corners of the heart rim to the top of the box section using tacking wire. Cut four 54.5cm/21½in lengths of twisted wire and mark each at intervals of 5cm/2in, 5cm/2in, 6cm/2½in and 38cm/15in.

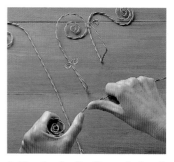

6 Untwist the 5cm/2in end of each wire and make into two coils. Bend right angles at the next two marked points. Bend each 38cm/15in section into a coil. Bend a curve in the wire next to two of the coils.

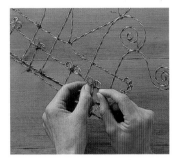

7 Slot the box section inside these four pieces so that the four large coils are at the back beside the heart. Tack into place where the pieces touch.

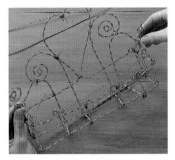

8 Slot the plain wire struts made in step 1 inside the box structure. Space them evenly across the width of the box and tack into place.

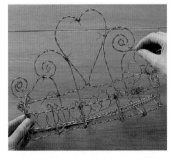

9 Wrap a long length of 1.5mm/¹⁄₁₉in galvanized wire several times around a broom handle to make a loose coil. Flatten the coil and position it inside the front edge of the spice rack.

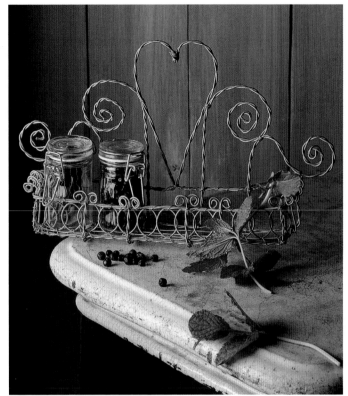

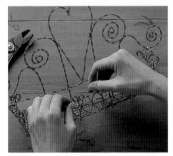

10 Using 0.8mm/¹⁄₃₁in galvanized wire, bind around the top rim of the box, securing each piece in position and removing the tacking wire as you go. Then bind from front to back along the bottom struts. Finish the spice rack by binding the heart closed at the top and bottom. Bind all of the decorative spirals where they touch.

One of the great things about wire is that it gives structure to otherwise flimsy materials. Here the wire used is completely covered with raffia to create a rustic tray.

Garden Tray

1 For the handles, cut two 1m/40in lengths of wire. Using a marker pen, mark each wire at intervals of 25cm/10in, 5cm/2in, 40cm/16in, 5cm/2in and 25cm/10in.

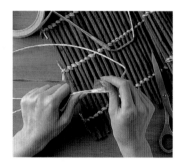

2 Using parallel (channel-type) pliers, bend each wire at the marked points into two handle shapes. The 25cm/10in sections double up to form the tray base. The two 5cm/2in sections make the sides and the long 40cm/16in section curves over the top. Hold each handle together at the base with double-sided adhesive tape.

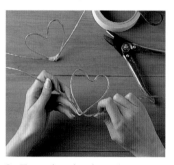

3 To make the hearts, cut two 1m/40in lengths of straining wire and mark at intervals of 38cm/15in, 25cm/10in, and 38cm/15in. Make the middle section into a heart shape and cross the wires over at the marked points. Bend up the wire and then secure it with tape. Wrap the heart wires and the handles with tape, then bind them closely with raffia.

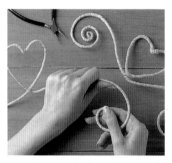

4 Using round-nosed (snug-nosed) pliers, bend the ends of the heart wires into coils, so that they will fit inside the handles.

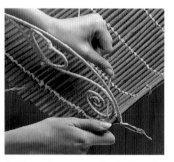

5 Place the mat inside the handle. Bind in place with raffia. Thread the raffia between the mat sticks and also around the sides and base of the handle. Place the heart inside the handle. Bind in place.

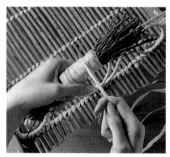

6 Bind the second handle and heart wire to the other end of the mat. Make two bundles of twigs and bind tightly to the top of the handles with double-sided adhesive tape. Wrap with raffia to cover all the tape.

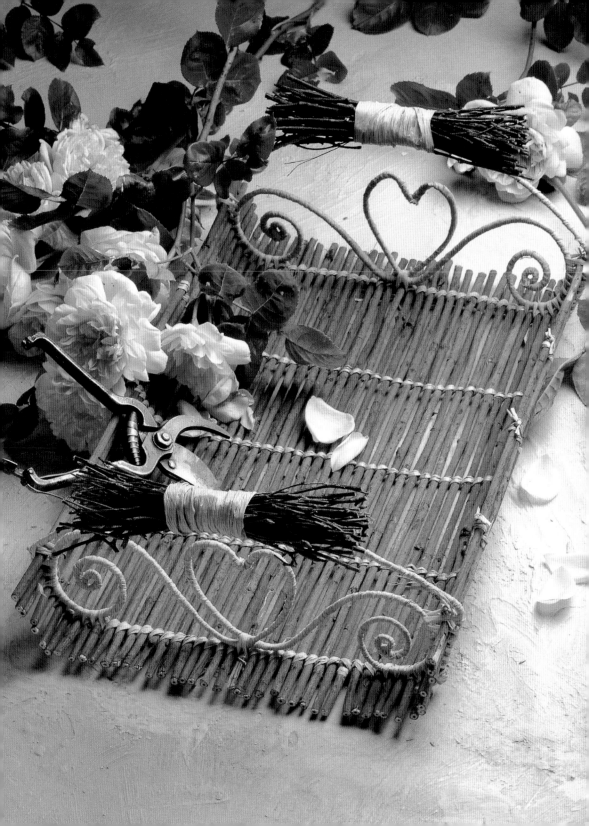

A rack of hooks is always useful, and can be hung in the hall for keys, in the bathroom for towels and in the kitchen for utensils. This project is ideal to make with children, as the plastic-coated wire is safe to use.

Kitchen Hook Rack

you will need
green gardening wire
broom handle
ruler or tape measure
wire cutters
permanent marker pen
pencil
wooden spoon
screwdriver and 3 screws

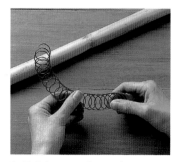

1 Tightly wrap the gardening wire 40 times around a broom handle. Leave 10cm/4in of wire at each end and cut off. Flatten the coil. The coil should be about 30cm/12in long.

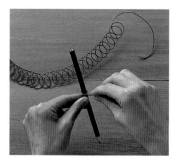

2 Cut a 56cm/22in length of wire. Mark the centre and the point 15cm/6in from each end. Form a loop at each of the points by wrapping the wire around a pencil. Thread the wire through the flattened coil, and then thread the circle at each end of the coil through the end loops on the wire.

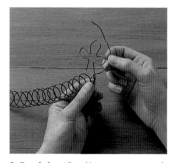

3 Bend the 15cm/6in section at each end of the gardening wire around the handle of a wooden spoon to create a three-leaf clover shape, as shown. There should be about 2cm/¾in left at the end to bend back down the stem. Use the 10cm/4in of wire left at the ends of the coil to bind the stem.

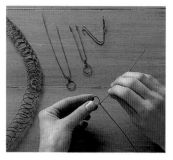

4 Cut four 30cm/12in lengths of wire. Bend each in half and wrap the bend around the handle of a wooden spoon to make a circle. Twist to close. Bend small hooks in the ends of the wires. Bend each wire in half. Loop the hooks around the coil and bottom wire of the frame, and close tightly.

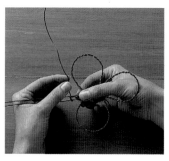

5 Cut a 2m/79in length of wire. Bend in half, wrap the bend around the handle of a wooden spoon to make a circle. Twist closed. Mark 15cm/6in from the circle. Ask a friend to hold this point while you twist the wires, then bend them around the broom to make a clover shape. Bind closed.

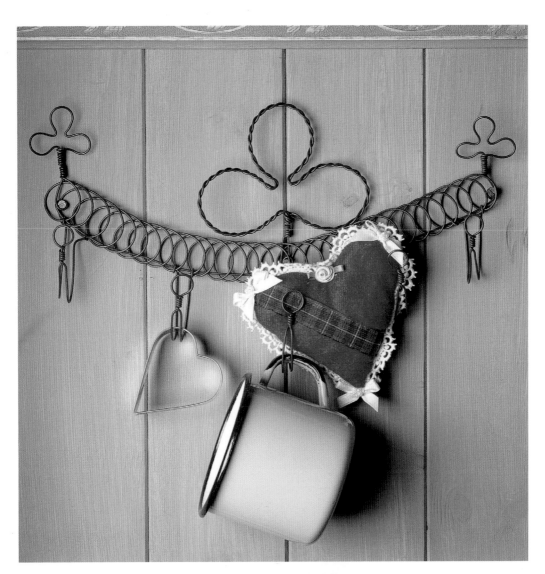

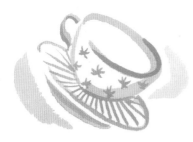

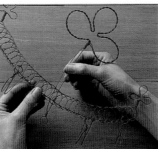

◀ **6** To finish, slot the clover hook through the middle of the coil, so that its shank lies on either side of the central loop in the base wire. Bend up the hook 5cm/2in from the circle end. Screw the rack to the wall through the three loops in the bottom wire. The central screw holds the hook firmly in place.

The shelf at the bottom of this simply designed rack is wide enough to hold four food cans. Stripped of their labels, the cans make useful storage containers that complement the design of the rack.

Utility Rack

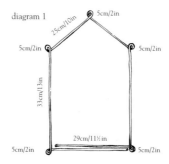

diagram 1

25cm/10in · 5cm/2in

5cm/2in · 5cm/2in

33cm/13in

29cm/11½in

5cm/2in · 5cm/2in

1 To make the frame, cut a 2m/79in length of straining wire. Twist the ends to stop them from unravelling. Mark the wire at intervals of 29cm/11½in, 5cm/2in, 33cm/13in, 5cm/2in, 25cm/10in, 5cm/2in, 25cm/10in, 5cm/2in, 33cm/13in, 5cm/2in, and 29cm/11½in.

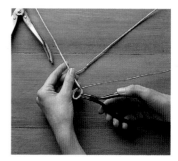

2 Using round-nosed (snug-nosed) pliers, make a loop with each 5cm/2in section, making sure that the pen marks match up and that all the loops face outwards (see diagram 1). Using the 0.8mm/$\frac{1}{31}$in wire, bind the 29cm/11½in sections together to make the bottom of the frame.

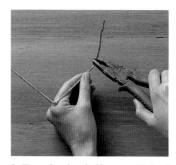

3 To make the shelf, cut a 73.5cm/29in length of straining wire and mark it at intervals of 2.5cm/1in, 9cm/3½in, 10cm/4in, 30cm/12in, 10cm/4in, 9cm/3½in and 2.5cm/1in. Using general-purpose pliers, bend the wire at right angles at the marked points (see diagram 2).

diagram 2

2.5cm/1in

10cm/4in · 9cm/3½in

2.5cm/1in

30cm/12in · 10cm/4in

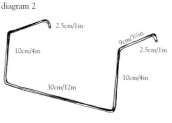

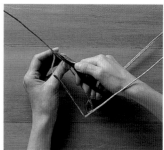

4 Mark each side of the frame 10cm/4in from the bottom. Twist the 2.5cm/1in ends of the shelf wire tightly around the frame at these points.

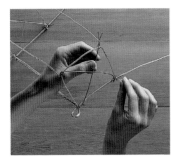

5 For the rim and sides of the shelf, cut a 104cm/41in length of 1.5mm/¹⁄₁₉in galvanized wire and mark it at intervals of 2.5cm/1in, 12.5cm/5in, 9cm/3½in, 12.5cm/5in, 30cm/12in, 12.5cm/5in, 9cm/3½in, 12.5cm/5in and 2.5cm/1in. Using round-nosed pliers, make a loop with the 2.5cm/1in section at each end of the wire. Bend the wire at the 12.5cm/5in and 9cm/3½in points at each end at 45° angles to form the side crosses of the shelf. Bend the 30cm/12in section in the middle at right angles to form the top rim (see diagram 3).

diagram 3

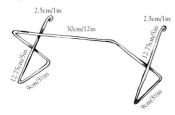

6 Tack the loops at the ends of the rim wire to the 10cm/4in markings on the sides of the main frame. Tack each corner of the side crosses to the frame.

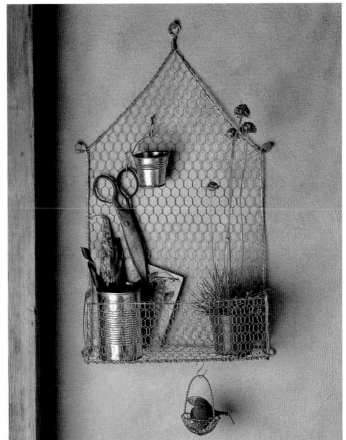

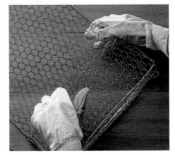

◀ **7** Lay the frame on to a piece of chicken wire and cut around the frame. Allow 30cm/12in at the bottom for wrapping around the shelf, so that there is a double thickness of wire at the front of the shelf where it tucks inside. Using 0.8mm/¹⁄₃₁in galvanized wire, bind the edges of the chicken wire to the frame. Wrap any rough edges at the top around the frame before binding. Bind the shelf firmly to the frame as you bind on the chicken wire, and remove the tacking wire.

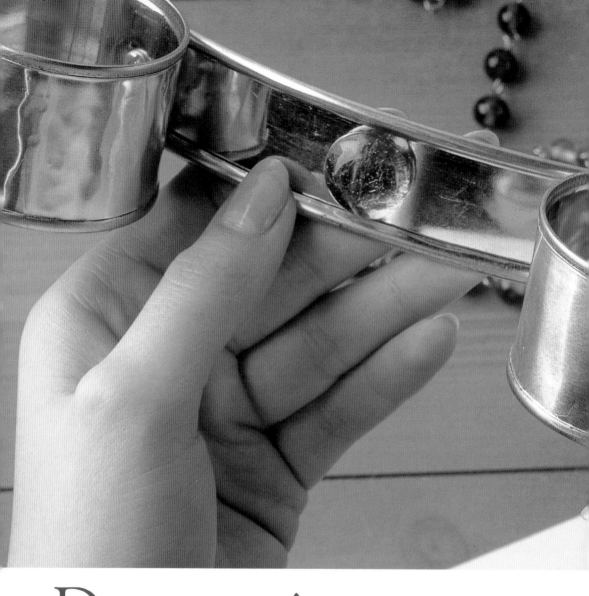

Decorative

Tinwork

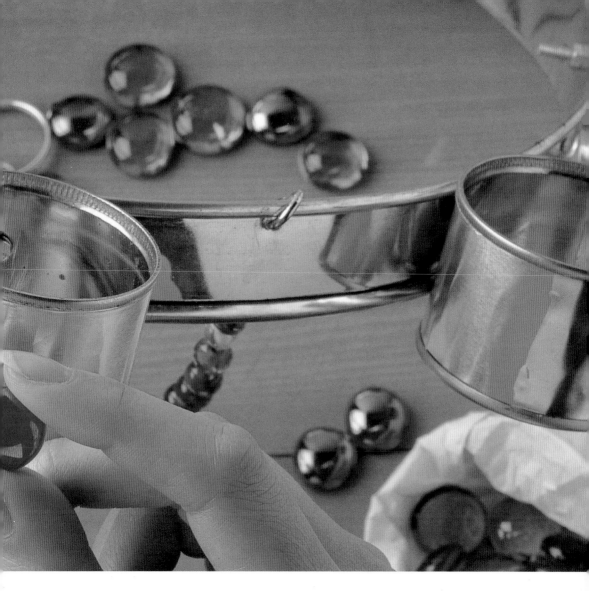

Metal is a marvellous material to use in creating decorative items. With its smooth texture, reflective sheen and stark graphic appeal, metal is the new material for the home. A combination of punching, embossing, soldering and mosaic enables you to create jewellery, decorative candle sconces, ornamental picture frames, a Moorish blind and even a musical scarecrow.

Embossed Trinkets

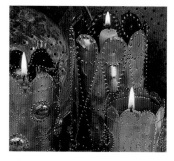

This chapter shows you how to make use of metal in all its guises to create beautiful decorative projects for the home. Starting with easy embossing and simple punching, you can create pretty ornaments and jewellery. Then you can progress on to more complex mosaic and soldering to make chandeliers, incense holders and even a shimmering temple for the garden.

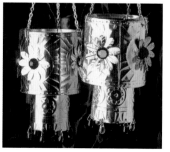

Aluminium and other metal foils are frequently used to create decorative motifs. You can trace or stencil designs on to the metal, then cut out the shapes with scissors. Use foils to make decorations for greetings cards, ornaments for the Christmas tree and cladding for picture frames. Metal foil is easy to emboss with decorative patterns and motifs. Recycle aluminium drinks (soda) cans to create decorative objects using the

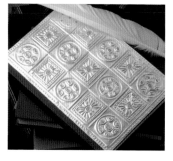

decoration of the can as part of the final pattern. Foil pie dishes and baking tins (pans) make ideal bases for ornaments and have been used in several of the tin projects in this chapter. When making items to hang from the ceiling or a window frame,

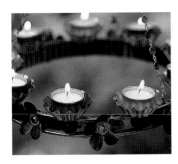

use a material that highlights the sheen of the metal, such as metal link chains or gold thread.

An easy way to decorate a metallic surface is to emboss it using a dry ballpoint pen. This creates a raised surface on one side of the metal, rather like

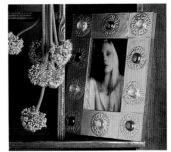

the look of stamped tin, but is easier and quicker to achieve. Traditional punched patterns are made using a centre punch or chisel; you could punch folk art motifs or graphic patterns or create your own designs. Punched tin can be used to decorate picture frames, cupboard doors and even book jackets.

The projects in this chapter are inspired by art from all over the world.

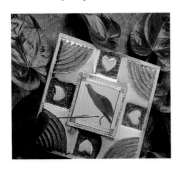

Celtic motifs are used for some of the repeating patterns, while aspects of Islamic art are featured in other items. Vibrant Mexican designs provide the inspiration for some of the bold patterns, while traditional American folk art is used for much of the decoration of the punched tin projects. Your surroundings will provide other inspiration for creating your own designs.

Make this exquisite embossed heart decoration to personalize a special gift. Metal stencils come in a variety of designs and make embossing foil simple, so this is an easy project to start with.

Embossed Heart

you will need
small, pointed scissors
pewter or aluminium foil, 36 gauge, (0.1mm/¹⁄₂₅₀in thick)
metal stencil
double-sided adhesive tape
self-healing cutting mat
double-ended embossing stylus
sewing needle (optional)
pinking shears (deckle-edged scissors) (optional)
album, box or greetings card

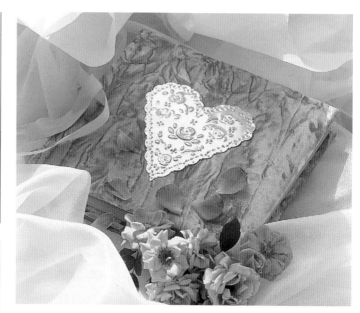

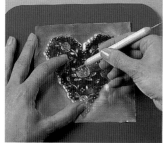

1 Cut a piece of foil large enough to fit the metal stencil plus a small border all around it. Tape the stencil on to the foil, then place on a cutting mat. Use the thin end of the embossing stylus to outline the stencil. Indent the pattern by drawing the outlines, then rubbing over the whole area. Use the thin end of the stylus for small shapes, and the wide end for large areas. For very small shapes, use the blunt end of a needle.

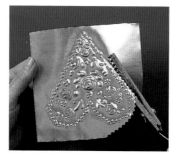

2 Remove the stencil and continue to work on the image to refine it. Cover the indented side of the foil with double-sided adhesive tape, then turn the foil over and cut out the heart shape. For a decorative border, use pinking shears (deckle-edged scissors).

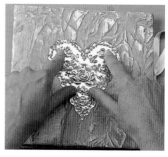

3 Remove the adhesive backing and stick the tin motif on to an album, box or greetings card. To make it even more secure, work the stylus around the edge, pressing in between the raised dots.

Greetings cards decorated with aluminium foil motifs are quick and easy to make. The foil is soft and can be cut with scissors. Designs can be drawn into the back of the foil to make a raised, embossed surface.

Embossed Greetings Cards

you will need
tracing paper
soft pencil
masking tape
aluminium foil, 36 gauge
(0.1mm/¹/250in thick)
thin cardboard
dry ballpoint pen
scissors
thick coloured paper
all-purpose glue

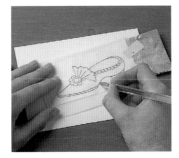

1 Trace the motifs from the templates at the back of the book, then tape the tracing to a piece of aluminium foil and place it on top of a piece of thin cardboard. Carefully draw over the motif with a dry ballpoint pen to transfer it to the foil.

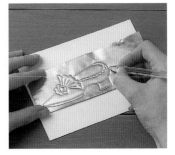

2 Remove the tracing paper from the foil and redraw the lines to make the embossing deeper. Add detail to the design at this stage. Remember any mistakes will show so be sure to follow the markings of your paper template accurately.

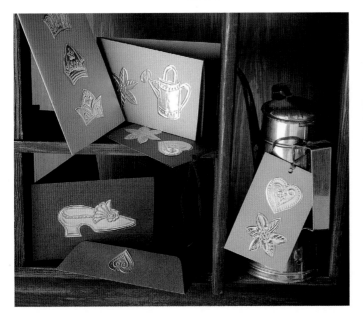

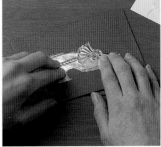

3 Turn the sheet of foil over and cut around the motif, leaving a narrow margin of foil around the outline of the design. Cut a piece of thick coloured paper and fold it in half to make a greetings card. Carefully spread a little glue over the back of the foil motif and stick it to the card, raised side up.

Dainty ladies' gloves make a pretty motif for a traditional glittering tree ornament at Christmas time. Use translucent glass paints to decorate the gloves; they adhere well and let the foil shine through the colour.

Lacy Silver Gloves

you will need
tracing paper
soft pencil
heavy-gauge aluminium foil
masking tape
dry ballpoint pen
scissors
oil-based glass paints
paintbrush
fine gold cord

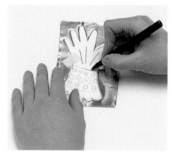

1 Trace the template from the back of the book and attach the tracing to a piece of foil with masking tape. Draw over the design to transfer it to the foil. Remove the tracing and complete the embossing with a ballpoint pen.

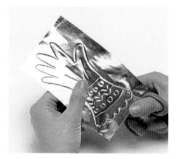

2 Cut out the glove, leaving a narrow border of about 2mm/¹⁄₃in all around the edge; don't cut into the embossed outline. Carefully make a hole in one corner of the glove with the point of the scissors.

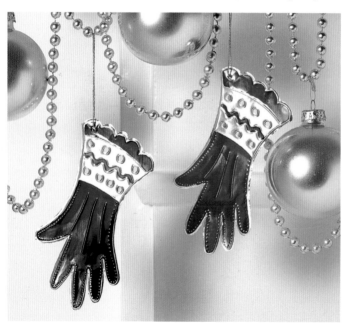

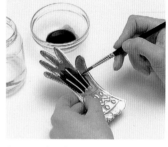

3 Paint the design with glass paints, keeping the colours within the embossed outlines. Allow to dry for at least 24 hours. Thread a loop of fine gold cord through the hole for hanging on the tree.

This delicate foil picture frame demonstrates that repoussé work can be used on objects that are to have a practical, as well as a decorative purpose. Choose foil that is a thicker gauge for such projects.

Repoussé Frame

you will need

tracing paper and pencil
copper foil, 36 gauge
(0.1mm/^{1}/250in thick)
adhesive tape
self-healing cutting mat
dry ballpoint pen
ruler
dressmaker's tracing wheel
small, pointed scissors
foam board
double-sided adhesive tape or
all-purpose glue

1 Trace the template from the back of the book. Stick the tracing paper to the copper foil using adhesive tape. Rest the foil on a cutting mat and transfer the design by drawing lightly over the lines with a dry ballpoint pen. Use a ruler for the straight lines.

2 Remove the tracing paper and then use the ballpoint pen to press firmly over the lightly drawn lines. Use an even pressure throughout the whole piece to make the marks consistent.

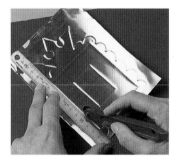

3 Outline the outer and inner edges using a tracing wheel, then add the crown detail.

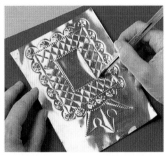

4 Draw the crossed lines. Draw a star in each scallop. Use scissors to cut around the frame. Carefully cut out the centre. Use the template provided to cut out a sheet of foam board. Mount a picture in the centre of the foam board and tape or glue it in place to the board and to the back of the frame. The finished decoration is positioned raised side up.

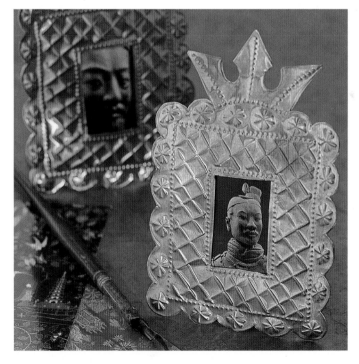

Plant an instant border of flower candleholders. The materials are easy to find, and are soon transformed into shimmering flower heads, with tall green stems.

Garden Candleholders

you will need
permanent markers
deep-sided foil pie dishes
scissors
stained-glass paints
paintbrush
small foil pie dishes
brightly coloured foil sweet (candy)
wrappers (optional)
epoxy adhesive
night-lights
large flat-headed nails, 2.5cm/1in long
medium green garden canes (stakes)
large foil flan tin (pie pan) (optional)
foil strips (optional)
heavy-duty double-sided adhesive
tape (optional)

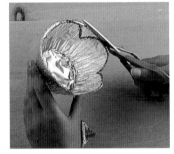

1 Draw the outline of rounded petals on the inside of a foil pie dish with a permanent marker. Cut out the flower shape. Paint the flower, inside and out, with stained-glass paint in a bright, vibrant colour. Leave it to dry thoroughly. Repeat all the above to make more candleholders, painting them in single contrasting colours.

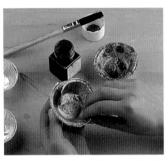

2 Cover a small pie dish with bright sweet (candy) foils if available, smoothing out the foil and wrapping it over the rim to hold it secure. Alternatively, paint with stained-glass paint in a colour that will stand out against the petals already painted.

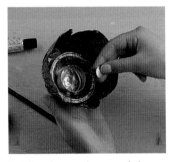

3 Glue the metal surround from a night-light into the pie dish. Then stick the pie dish inside the flower and push a nail through the centre point of all three layers to hold them together firmly.

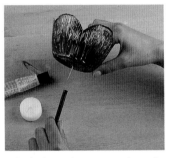

4 Push the nail point into the pithy hollow at one end of a garden cane (stake) to fix the assembled flower to it. Add a blob of glue to the joint so it all holds firmly together. When the glue has dried, put the candle into the centre of the flower.

5 If you want to make leaves, mark a large foil flan tin (pie pan) into eight segments with a green permanent marker. Draw curves between the lines along the rim to make heart shapes. Cut out all the segments – each will become an individual leaf.

6 Attach a thin folded strip of foil to the underside of each leaf with heavy-duty double-sided adhesive tape. Paint the leaves on both sides with stained-glass paint. Stick the leaves to the flower stems with another piece of double-sided tape.

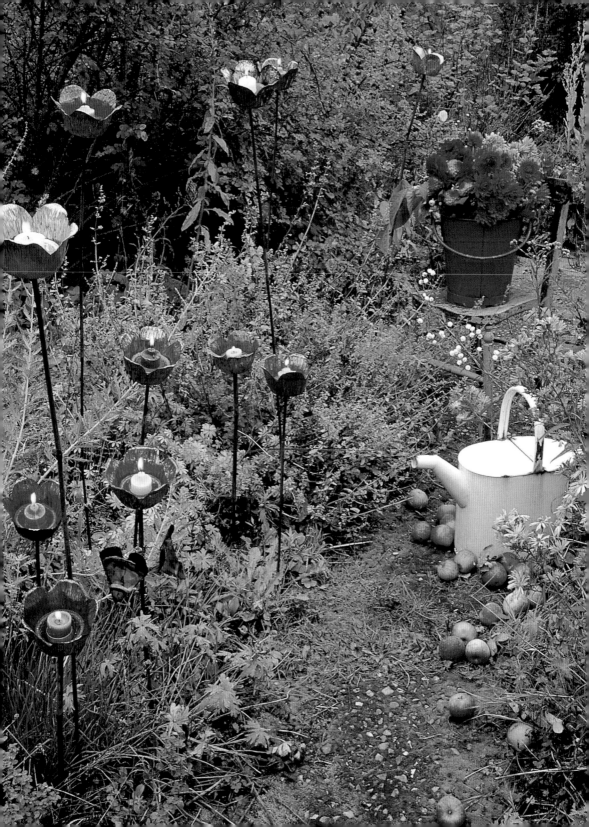

These candle collars are based on flower and leaf forms and are embossed from the back in imitation of veining. The beading, though seemingly intricate, is very simple to attach using thin jeweller's wire.

Candle Collars

you will need
tracing paper
soft pencil
thin cardboard
scissors
masking tape
copper foil, 40 gauge
(0.08mm/^{1}/$_{300}$in thick)
sharp pencil
bradawl (awl)
dry ballpoint pen
wooden block
fine jeweller's wire
glass beads

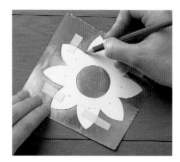

1 Trace the template provided. Enlarge it as required. Transfer it to thin cardboard and cut out. Tape the template to a piece of copper foil. Draw around it using a sharp pencil to transfer the shape to the foil.

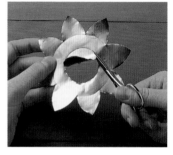

2 Remove the template and cut around the outside of the collar. Pierce the centre of the collar using a bradawl (awl). Insert the scissors through the hole and carefully cut out the centre of the collar.

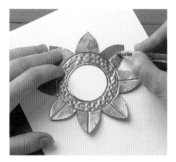

3 Place the collar face down on a sheet of thin cardboard. Redraw over the lines of the outer and inner circles using a dry ballpoint pen. Press a random pattern of dots into the surface of the foil between the two rings. Draw veins on each petal.

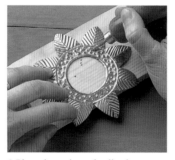

4 Place the embossed collar face up on a block of wood. Carefully pierce a hole directly below the centre of each petal using a bradawl.

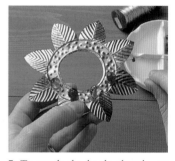

5 To attach the beads, thread wire through a hole in the collar, from the back to the front, leaving a short end. Bend the end. Thread a large bead on, then a small bead. Loop the wire over the small bead, thread back through the large bead and up through the next hole at the back of the collar. Attach the beads, cut the wire leaving an end. Twist the ends together.

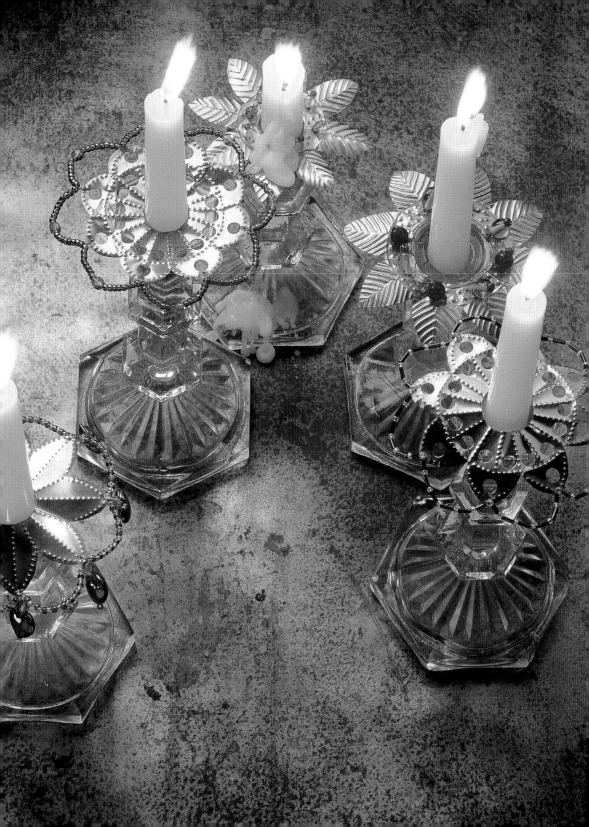

Adapted from the simple paper angels that we all made as children, this embossed pewter design will add a touch of elegance to the top of your Christmas tree or provide a festive ornament on the mantelpiece.

Treetop Angel

you will need

pencil

paper

masking tape

pewter shim

self-healing cutting mat

dressmaker's tracing wheel

dry ballpoint pen

pinking shears (deckle-edged scissors)

craft knife

permanent marker pen

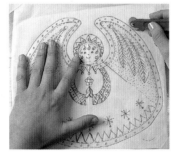

1 Enlarge the template at the back of the book to the required size. Tape to the pewter shim. Place the sheet on a self-healing cutting mat and use a dressmaker's tracing wheel to trace over the double outlines.

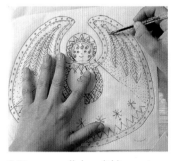

2 Draw over all the solid lines using a dry ballpoint pen. Indent the dots using a pencil.

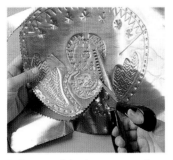

3 Cut around the shape using pinking shears (deckle-edged scissors). Be very careful when cutting around the halo and wing tips. If you bend some of the zigzag edging, smooth back into shape with your fingers.

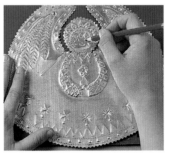

4 Turn the angel over. Following the paper pattern, complete the remaining embossed markings from the reverse side, pressing in dots for the eyes and at the centre point of each star.

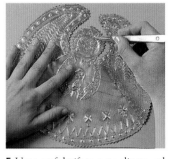

5 Use a craft knife to cut a slit around the head, inside the halo. Be careful not to cut too near the neck so as not to weaken it. Cut the two slits beside the wings where marked.

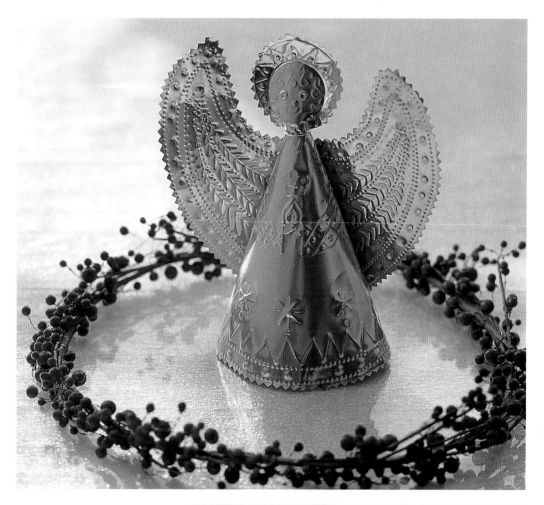

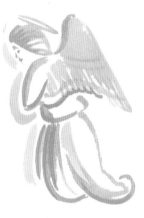

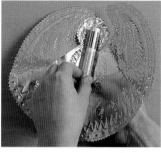

6 Roll the head and neck slightly around a cylindrical object such as a marker pen.

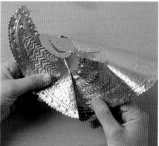

7 Bend the angel's body into a curve and slot together as shown.

Inspired by European folk-art motifs, these foil birds make very pretty ornaments for hanging on the Christmas tree, where their embossed decorations will catch the light as they twirl.

Embossed Birds

you will need
tracing paper
pencil
paper
small, pointed scissors
aluminium foil, 36 gauge
(0.1mm/¹⁄₂₅₀in thick)
adhesive tape
self-healing cutting mat
dry ballpoint pen
dressmaker's tracing wheel
hole punches, 5mm/¹⁄₅in and 3mm/¹⁄₈in

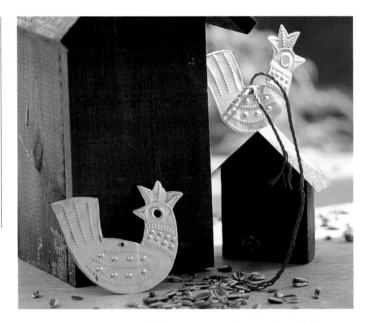

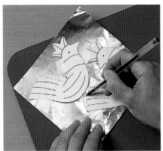

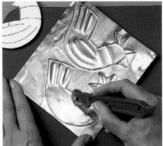

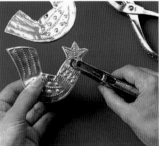

1 Trace and transfer the templates from the back of the book and cut out of paper. Place the templates on the aluminium foil and secure with tape. Place the foil on a cutting mat and draw around the shapes using a dry ballpoint pen.

2 Remove the templates. Draw in the top of the head and the beak of each bird with the ballpoint pen. Use a dressmaker's tracing wheel to mark the dotted lines on the body, tail, neck and crown, following the guidelines on the templates.

3 Draw the eye and the large dots on the wing and neck using the pen. Cut out the birds, cutting just outside the indented outline. Make the hole for the eye with a 5mm/¹⁄₅in hole punch, then use a small punch to make a hole in the bird's back for hanging.

There's more than one way to recycle empty cans: these light-hearted designs turn tin cans into insects to decorate the garden. Use cans that have the same logos so that your insects are symmetrical.

Tin Can Insects

you will need
tracing paper
pencil
strong scissors with small points
large steel beer can, top and
bottom removed
adhesive tape
large paintbrush with a tapered handle
small long-nosed pliers

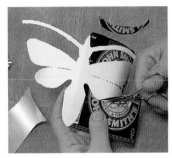

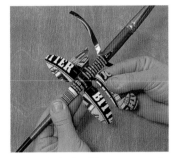

1 Trace the template from the back of the book and cut it out. Cut up the side of the beer can opposite the bar code and open it out. Place the template in position and secure with adhesive tape. Cut all around the template carefully with sharp scissors.

2 Place the body of the insect over the handle of a paintbrush, with the fat part near the head. Bend the body around the handle. Fold the lower wings slightly under the body and the upper wings forwards, folding them slightly over the top of the body.

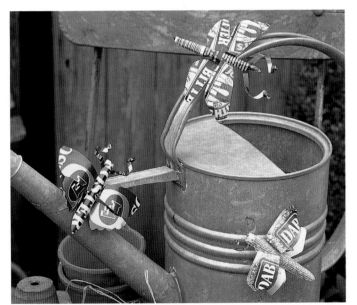

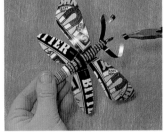

3 Using long-nosed pliers, twist the antennae back on themselves and curl the ends.

Aluminium cans are easy to recycle into attractive and useful objects such as this candle sconce. The shiny interior of the can makes a most effective reflector for the candle flame.

Beer-can Candle Sconce

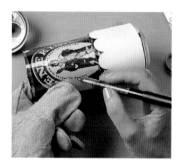

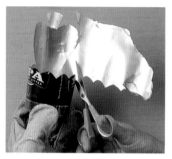

1 To cut off the can top, make a slit in the metal using a craft knife and wearing protective gloves, then cut through the slit with scissors. Enlarge the template at the back of the book to fit your can, and cut it out of paper. Wrap it around the can and secure with adhesive tape. Draw around the shape using a marker pen.

2 Remove the paper template and cut around the design using small, pointed scissors. Make a short slit between each scallop.

3 Use the larger hole punch to make a hanging hole at the top, a hole on either side of the heart shape, and one in each scallop. Use the smaller punch to make a border all round the heart shape. Fold over each punched scallop shape to form a decorative rim for the candle sconce.

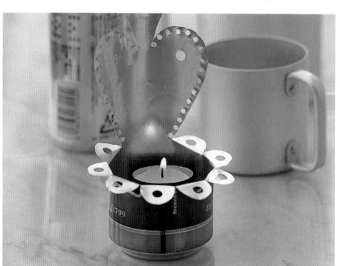

These plant markers will lend an air of elegant order to any flower garden. They are simple to construct and will hold together without any glue. Punch the plant name into each marker.

Plant Markers

you will need
tracing paper
soft pencil
thin cardboard
scissors
sheet of copper foil, 36 gauge
(0.1mm/^{1}/$_{250}$in thick)
permanent marker pen
sheet of chipboard
bradawl (awl)
pliers

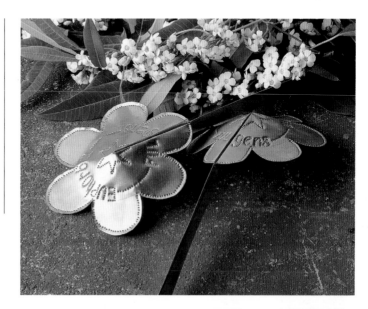

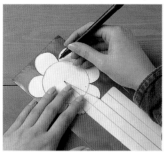

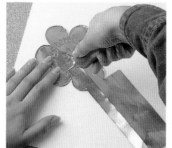

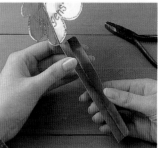

1 Trace the template at the back of the book. Transfer to thin cardboard. Cut out the template and draw around it on the copper foil with a permanent marker pen. Cut the plant marker from the foil using a pair of scissors.

2 Place the copper marker on the cardboard on top of the chipboard. Punch the design and plant name into the front of the marker using a bradawl (awl). Cut all the way up the stem directly under the flowerhead. Using pliers, pleat the middle sections of the plant marker.

3 Hold the cut strips of the stem together so that the two halves of the bottom petal are joined. Make a fold along the two outer lines of the stem. Wrap the stem around the cut section to hold the marker together.

Tin is a soft metal that can be decorated easily using a centre punch or a blunt chisel to create dots and lines. Keep your punched design graphic and uncluttered as too much fine detail will get lost.

Punched Tin Leaf Frame

you will need

wooden frame

thin cardboard

felt-tipped pen

scissors

adhesive tape

sheet of tin

centre punch

hammer

tin snips

protective gloves (optional)

chisel

ridged paint scraper

copper nails

metal polish & soft cloth (optional)

clear varnish & paintbrush (optional)

paper towels & salt water (optional)

wax & soft cloth (optional)

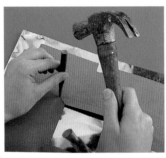

1 Place the wooden frame on a piece of thin card and draw around the outline with a felt-tipped pen. Add extra length at the outside edges and around the centre to allow for turnings, and cut out the template with scissors. Tape the template on to a sheet of tin. Mark the corners using a centre punch and hammer, and mark the straight lines with a felt-tipped pen.

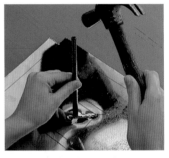

2 Cut out the shape with tin snips. (You may want to wear protective gloves to protect your hands from the tin's sharp edges.) Using a hammer and chisel, cut through the centre of the frame in a diagonal line, then use tin snips to cut along the remaining sides, to leave you with a cut-out square, a little smaller than the centre of the frames.

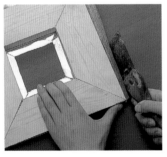

3 Place the wooden frame on the tin and use a ridged paint scraper to coax the metal up the sides of the frame.

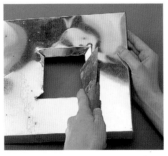

4 Turn the frame over and push down the metal edges in the centre, again using the ridged paint scraper.

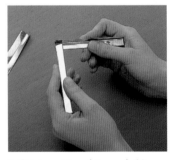

5 Cut two strips of tin, each 20cm × 18mm/8 × ¾in. Snip at the halfway mark and fold at a 90° angle. Nail the strips to the inner edge of the frame, using copper nails.

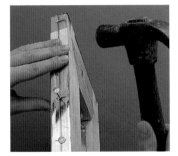

6 Carefully hammer copper nails along the outer edges of the frame so that the tin is firmly secured in place.

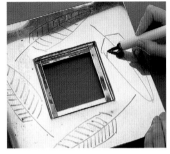

7 Draw a freehand leaf design on the tin frame with a felt-tipped pen. Any errors can be easily wiped away. You can vary the design according to your preference for motif, remembering to keep it simple.

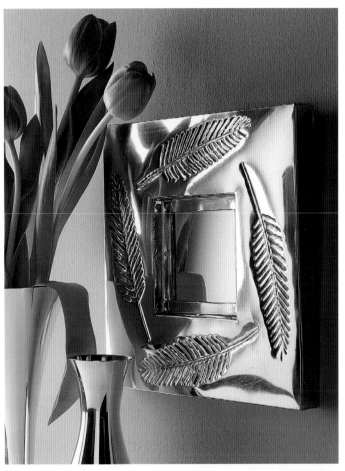

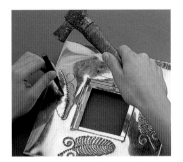

8 Press the leaf design on to the tin in dots, using a hammer and centre punch. Alternatively, a blunt chisel and hammer can be used to press the design on to the tin in straight lines.

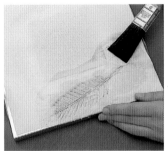

9 There are two ways to finish the frame. Clean the tin with metal polish and a soft cloth, removing any traces of marker pen. To preserve the finish, seal with clear varnish.

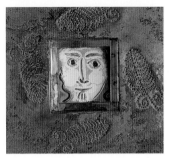

10 To rust the tin, cover with a paper towel and dampen with salt water. Keep the paper damp until the frame has rusted – 2–7 days. Remove the paper, leave to dry and seal with wax.

Two small cake tins have been turned into a delightful wall decoration by the clever use of a metal angle bracket. The metal heart will reflect the flickering flame of a small candle or night-light.

Heart Candle Sconce

you will need
6-holed angle bracket
heart-shaped cake tin (pan), 7.5cm/3in
circular cake tin (pan), 7.5cm/3in
permanent marker pen
clamp and masking tape
drill
2 nuts and bolts
spanner (wrench)
wall plugs (plastic anchors)
screwdriver and screw
candle or night-light

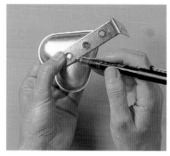

1 Place the angle bracket against the back of the heart tin (pan) and one edge of the circle tin. Mark through the holes in the bracket with a pen.

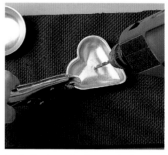

2 Drill through the marked holes. The photograph is styled for clarity – the drill would be perpendicular to the taped and clamped tin.

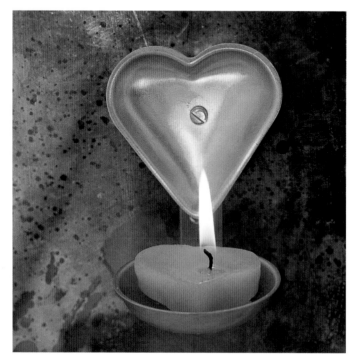

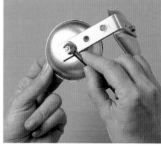

3 Use nuts and bolts to join the round tin to the bracket. Pre-drill and plug the wall, and then screw through the hole in the heart and the bracket into the wall behind. Add the candle to complete the project.

Metallic candle crowns surround and protect the flames and make pinprick patterns of light through punched holes as the candles burn down inside them.

Filigree Candle Crowns

you will need

pencil

ruler

28 x 16cm/11 x 6½in piece of copper foil, 36 gauge (0.1mm/¹⁄₂₅₀in thick)

coin for template

pile of newspapers

bradawl (awl)

scissors

hole punch

brass paper fasteners

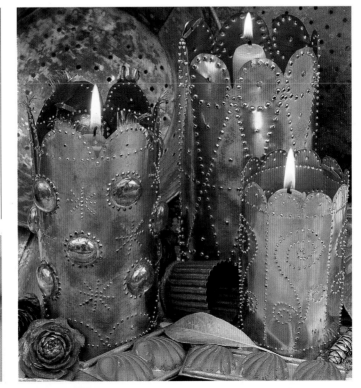

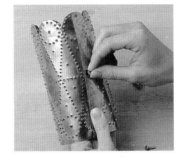

1 Use a sharp pencil and ruler to draw a line across the length of the foil, dividing it in half. Draw diagonal lines across the width of the foil to make a lattice, then draw circles between the parallel lines along the top and bottom edges, using a coin. Protect the work surface with a pile of newspapers. Punch regularly spaced holes along the lines with a bradawl (awl). Punch a hole in the centre of each circle and triangle.

◄ **2** Cut along the top edge with scissors to leave a small border around the punched holes and make a scalloped rim. Bend the foil so that the ends overlap, to form a cylindrical candle crown. Punch through both pieces of foil three times at the overlap. Push a paper fastener through each set of holes to hold the foil in place. Open out the clip ends inside the crown.

This lightweight blind is constructed from bold floral shapes and has a geometric precision that is reminiscent of Islamic decorative motifs. It is easy to hang and can be made to fit any size of window.

Moorish Flower Blind

you will need
protective gloves
scissors
heavy-duty aluminium foil pie dishes
paper
pencil
scrap wood
bradawl (awl)
round-nosed (snug-nosed) pliers
jewellery jump rings (wires)

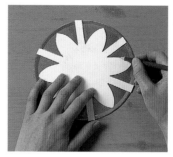

1 Wearing protective gloves, cut the rim from a heavy-duty aluminium foil pie dish. Enlarge the template to the same diameter as the foil disc. Cut it out, then centre it on the disc and trace around it. Cut out the shape. Make as many as you need for your blind design.

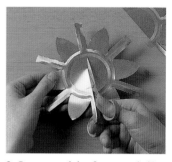

2 Cut some of the flowers in half to make straight-sided pieces for the edges of the blind. Cut one flower shape into quarters to form the four corners of the blind.

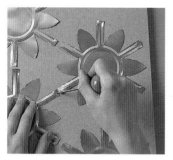

3 Arrange the flowers on a piece of wood. Using a bradawl (awl), pierce a hole about 3mm/⅛in from the end of each strut between the flower petals.

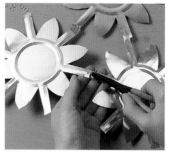

4 Using round-nosed (snug-nosed) pliers, open as many jump rings (wires) as you need to join the flowers. Hook a ring through the hole in one strut, and join to an adjacent flower. Close the ring. Repeat with all the flower shapes.

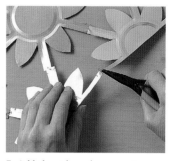

5 Add the side and corner pieces to complete the blind. Add a row of jump rings along the top of the blind from which to hang it.

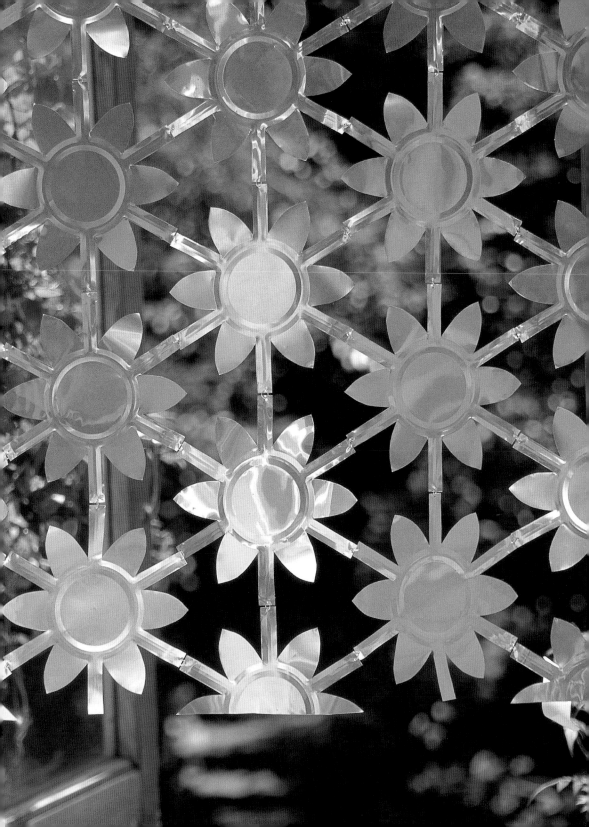

A good way to use up small scraps of tin is to make brooches. These can be simple in construction and made special with some painted decoration. Enamel paints are opaque and look stunning.

Painted Tin Brooches

you will need
scrap of tin, 30 gauge
(0.3mm/¹⁄₈₃in thick)
permanent marker pen
work shirt and protective gloves
tin snips
bench vice
file
silicon carbide (wet and dry) paper
chinagraph pencil
enamel paints
fine paintbrushes
clear gloss polyurethane varnish
epoxy resin glue
brooch fastener

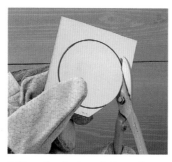

1 To make the brooch front, draw a circle 5cm/2in in diameter on a piece of tin with a marker pen. Wearing a protective shirt and gloves, cut out the circle using tin snips.

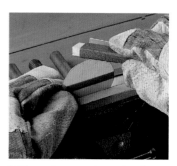

2 Clamp the tin circle in a bench vice and file the edges. Finish off the edges with damp silicon carbide (wet and dry) paper so that they are smooth.

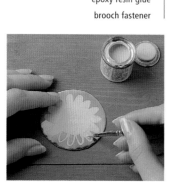

3 Draw your choice of motif on to one side of the brooch using a chinagraph pencil. Paint around the outline with enamel paint, then fill in the design. Leave the brooch to dry thoroughly.

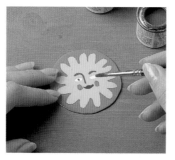

4 Paint in the background, then add any features on top of the first coat of paint. Use a fine paintbrush and enamel paint. Leave to dry. Seal the surface with two coats of clear gloss polyurethane varnish. Leave to dry thoroughly between coats.

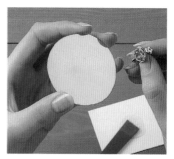

5 Mix some epoxy resin glue and use it to stick a brooch fastener on to the back. Let the glue dry thoroughly before wearing the brooch.

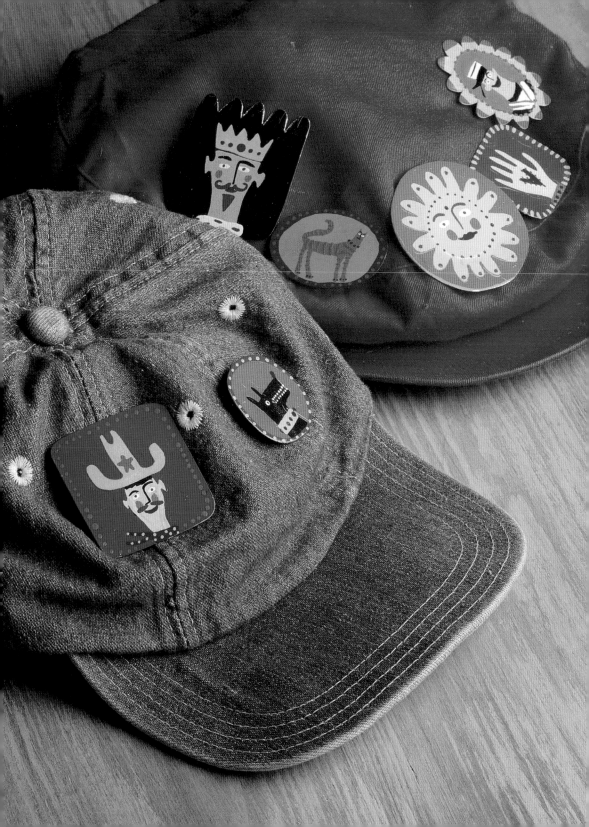

The appearance of a special book can be dramatically enhanced with an embossed metal panel. The panel covering this book imitates the ornate leather and metal bindings adorning early prayer books.

Embossed Book Jacket

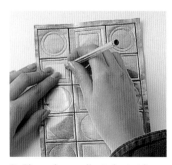

1 Cut a piece of aluminium foil the same size as the front of the book. Using a marker pen and a ruler, draw a 6mm/¼in border all the way around the edge of the foil. Divide the area within the border into squares. Draw over the lines to emboss the foil using a dry ballpoint pen. This is the back of the design.

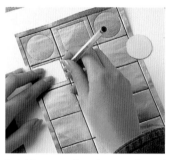

2 Make a cardboard rectangle and circle template. Make them small enough to fit into the grid. Make another circle and rectangle, slightly smaller. Cut out the shapes. Place the large circle in the centre of the first square. Draw around it using a dry ballpoint pen. Repeat with the large rectangle in the next square. Repeat over the whole jacket.

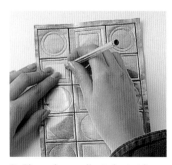

3 Place the small circle inside an embossed circle and draw around it. Place the small rectangle inside a large rectangle and emboss all the shapes in the same way.

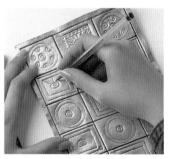

4 Draw small double circles and also double semi-circles in each circle. Draw a double oval and radiating lines inside each rectangle. Emboss a dotted line around each rectangle and around the edge of the jacket.

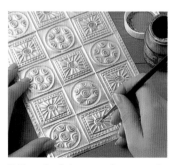

5 Turn the foil over so that it is right side up. Using a fine brush, highlight small areas of the design with the gold lacquer paint. When it is dry, glue the jacket to the front of the book.

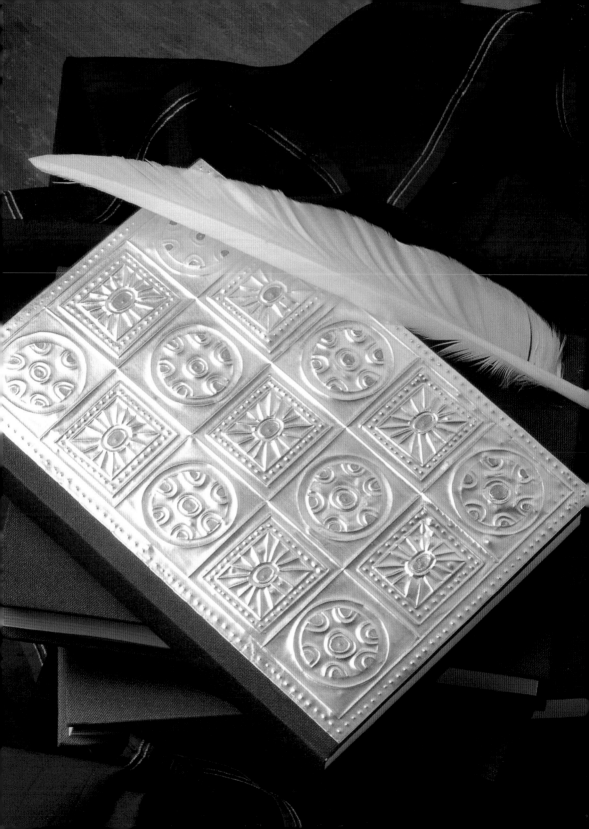

Barquette and petit four tins come in delicate, fluted shapes that are too pretty just to bake with. Using them in a mosaic will make you look at them in a new light and make an attractive decoration.

Metal Mosaic

you will need
8 barquette tins, 6cm/2½ in long
fluted petit four tin, 3cm/1¼ in
diameter
biscuit (cookie) tin lid
spatula or small trowel
ready-mixed tile adhesive
diamond-shaped and circular mirror
mosaic pieces
cloth or cotton buds (swabs)
strong glue
coloured glass pebble

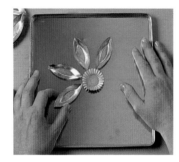

1 Arrange small barquette and petit four tins inside the lid of a biscuit (cookie) tin until you have a design.

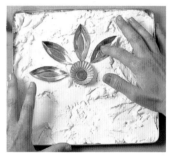

2 Remove the small tins and use a spatula or small trowel to spread an even layer of tile adhesive in the lid. Press the tins into place. Leave to dry.

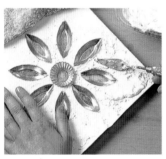

3 Add a second layer of tile adhesive, filling the lid to the level of the tin rims, and smooth the surface (it may help to wet the surface slightly).

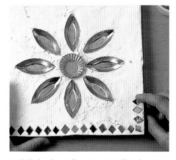

4 While the adhesive is still soft, press mirror mosaic pieces all round the edge of the piece to make a decorative border. Then add small circular mirror pieces between each of the flower petals to complete the mosaic.

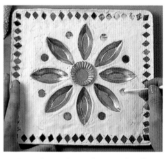

5 Wipe the surfaces clean with a damp cloth or damp cotton buds (swabs). Leave to harden. Glue a coloured glass pebble into the tin in the centre to add focus to the design.

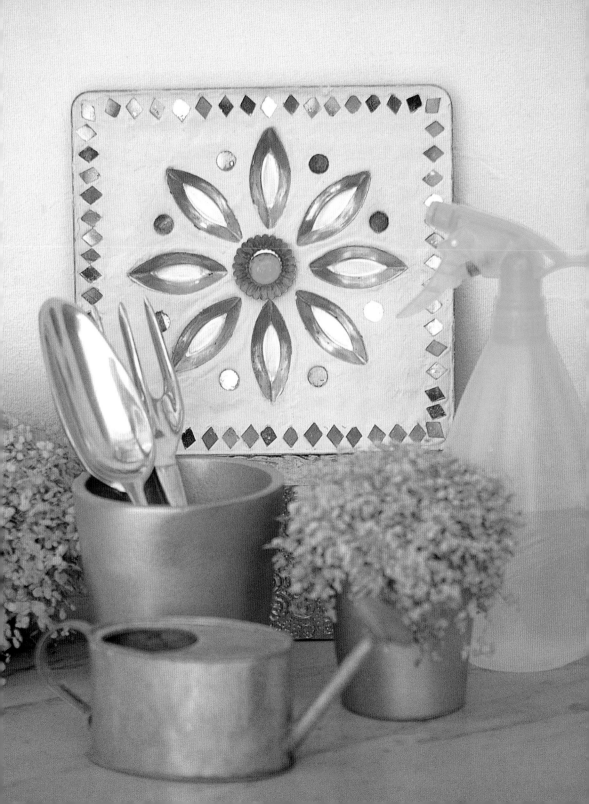

Painted tinware is a popular art form in many countries, particularly India and Latin America, where fine-gauge tin is stamped with highly decorative patterns and often highlighted with translucent paints.

Painted Mirror

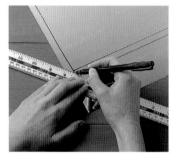

1 To make the frame, draw a 30cm/ 12in square on a sheet of tin. Draw a 1cm/⅖in border inside the square. Measure 2cm/⅘in from the outer corners along each side. Connect these points by drawing diagonal lines, as shown. Wearing protective clothes, cut out the square with tin shears. Cut along the diagonal lines.

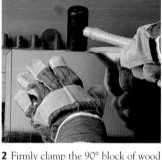

2 Firmly clamp the 90° block of wood in a bench vice. Place the mirror frame on the wooden block with the ruled edge of the tin square resting on the edge. Using a hide hammer, tap along the edge of the tin to turn it over to an angle of 90°.

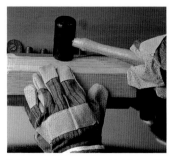

3 Turn the frame over. Hold the 45° block of wood inside the turned edge and hammer the edge over. Remove the block and hammer the edge flat. File the corners of the mirror frame to remove any sharp edges. Cut a piece of graph paper the same size as the frame.

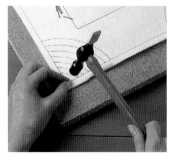

4 Draw the decorative corner lines on to the paper, drawing around the saucer. Draw the centre square slightly larger than the mirror tile. Tape the pattern to the back of the frame, place it face down on the chipboard and secure with panel pins (tacks).

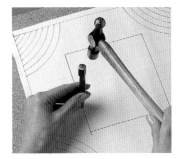

5 Place the point of the centre punch on a line of the inside square and tap it with the ball hammer to make an indentation. Move the punch about 3mm/⅛in along the line and tap it to make the next mark. Continue punching along all the lines until the design is completed.

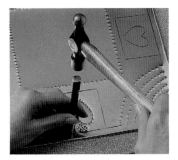

6 Unpin the frame from the board and remove the pattern. Turn the frame over, so the raised side faces up. Using a chinagraph pencil, draw a square halfway along each side. Draw a heart in each square. Pin the frame to the board again and punch an outline around each square and heart. Punch the area between the heart and the square to make a densely pitted surface. Remove the frame from the board. Wipe over the surface of the metal with a clean, soft cloth to remove any grease.

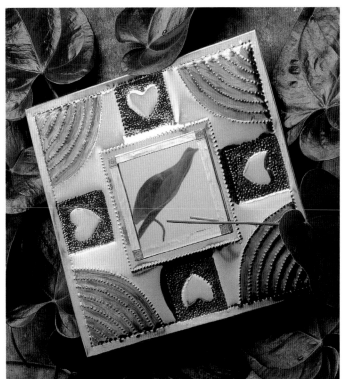

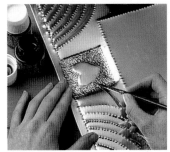

7 Paint the embossed areas and the border. Leave to dry and apply a second coat if the first is patchy. Place the mirror tile on aluminium foil and draw around it, then draw a 1.5cm/⅗in border around that. Cut out the foil. Clip the corners to make folding the edges over easier. Glue the mirror to the centre of the foil. Glue the edges of the foil over the tile.

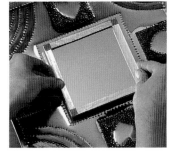

8 Cut four small squares of copper foil, mark your choice of design on each, then glue one square in each corner of the tile. Glue the mirror to the centre of the frame. Glue the hanger to the back of the frame. Allow the glue to dry thoroughly.

Because of its softness, fine-gauge aluminium foil is just perfect for cladding frames. Coloured and clear glass nuggets combine with the subdued tones of the foil to give this frame a Celtic air.

Photograph Frame

you will need
photograph frame
ruler
aluminium foil, 36 gauge
(0.1mm/¹⁄₂₅₀in thick)
scissors
epoxy resin glue
pencil
thin cardboard
marker pen
dry ballpoint pen
coloured and clear glass nuggets

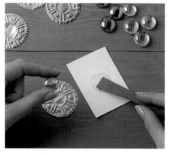

1 Carefully remove the glass and the backing from the frame. Cut foil strips to cover. Make the foil long enough to wrap around to the back of the frame. Mould the foil strips around and glue them in place.

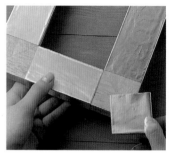

2 Cut pieces of foil to cover the four corners. Mould to the contours of the frame and glue them in place.

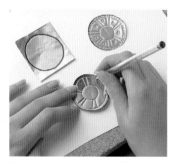

3 Draw a circle on to cardboard and cut out to make a template. Draw around the cardboard on to the foil using a marker pen. Cut out the foil circles. Draw a design on to one side of each circle using a dry ballpoint pen. This is now the back of the circle.

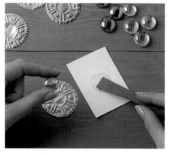

4 Turn the foil circles over so that the raised side of the embossing is face up. Glue coloured glass nuggets to the centre fronts of half of the foil circles. Glue clear glass nuggets to the centres of the other half.

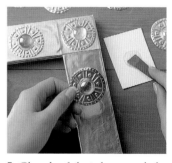

5 Glue the foil circles around the frame, spacing them evenly. Alternate the circles so a coloured glass centre follows one with clear glass. When the glue is thoroughly dry, replace the glass and backing in the frame.

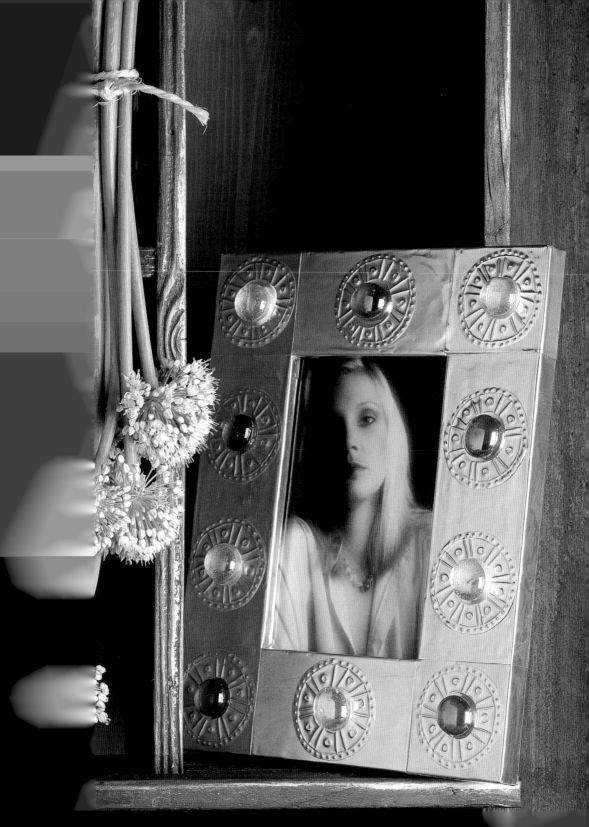

This aluminium candlestick has a cartoon-like appearance that is very appealing. The small sections are constructed first and then joined together. Each section is attached to the next using pop rivets.

Rocket Candlestick

you will need

tracing paper

soft pencil

thin cardboard

glue

scissors

thin aluminium sheet

work shirt and protective leather gloves

tin snips

file

drill

pliers

90° wooden block

hammer

pop riveter and rivets

black oven-hardening clay

epoxy resin glue

1 Trace the rocket templates from the back of the book. Enlarge the pieces if required using a photocopier. Stick the tracings on to thin cardboard, allow to dry, then accurately cut out each shape.

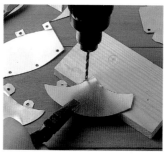

3 Mark the drilling points on each piece and drill the holes. Hold the metal with a pair of pliers to stop it spinning around while you drill.

◀ **5** Place the side sections on the edge of the wooden block and hammer over the edges. Hold each section and gently curve it outwards.

6 Hold two side sections together with the tabs to the inside. Join the sections with pop rivets at the middle and the bottom holes. Join two more pairs.

2 Cut out the templates and draw around them on to the aluminium. Draw six side sections, three fins and one top shelf. Wearing protective clothes, cut out all the pieces using tin snips and file the edges smooth.

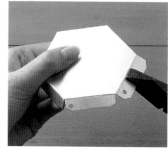

4 Using a pair of pliers, carefully fold down all the sides of the top shelf to make an angle of 90°. Bend the metal over a right-angle object.

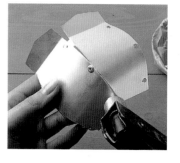

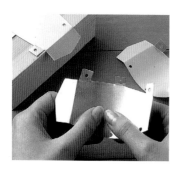

7 Place a fin between two separate side pairs and pop rivet all three layers together at the middle and bottom holes. Pop rivet the remaining side pairs together, with a fin in-between.

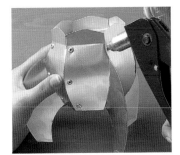

8 Position the shelf at the top of the candlestick with the sides pointing downwards. Join the shelf to the base with pop rivets through the top holes.

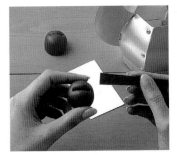

9 To make the feet, roll three balls of black clay. Flatten the base of each and make an indentation in the ball top. Bake the clay according to the manufacturer's instructions. When cool, glue a foot to each fin.

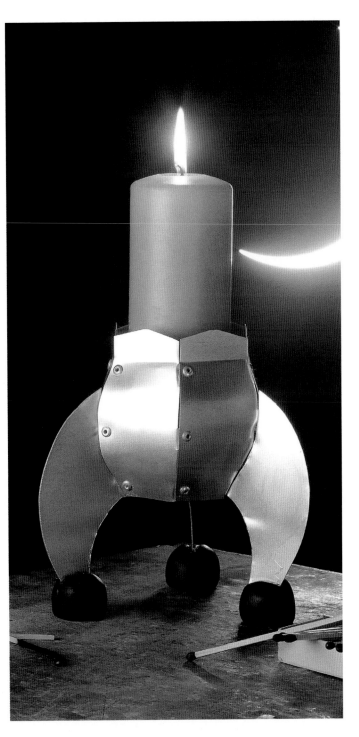

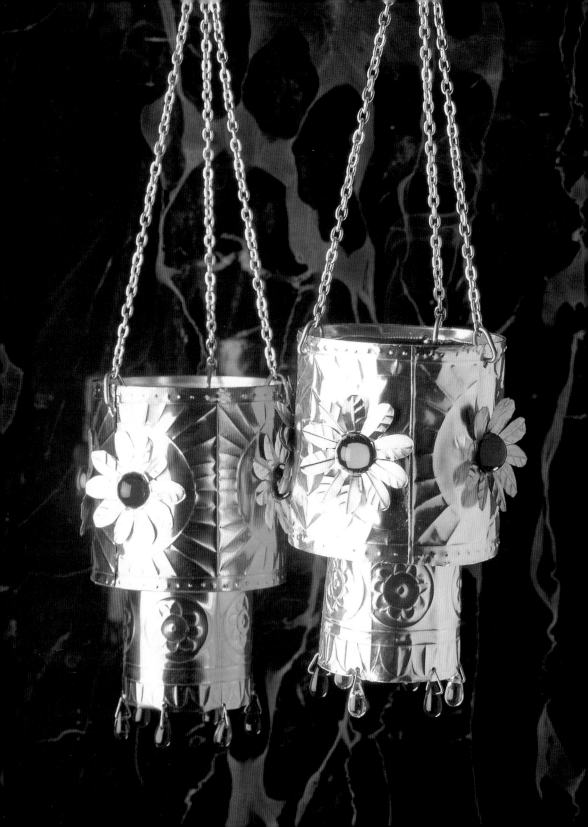

This ornate incense holder is reminiscent of ecclesiastical censers, which are used in religious services and processions. Here, two colours of metal foil are heavily embossed and used to encase a humble tin can.

Incense Holder

you will need

can opener

small tin can

file

aluminium foil, 36 gauge

(0.1mm/¹⁄₂₅₀in thick)

scissors

pencil

graph paper

masking tape

thin cardboard

dry ballpoint pen

copper foil, 40 gauge

(0.08mm/¹⁄₃₀₀in thick)

epoxy resin glue

wooden pole

bench vice

bradawl (awl)

thin metal chain

wire cutters

3 chain triangles

pliers

key ring

glass droplets and nuggets

cardboard tube

metal bottle cap

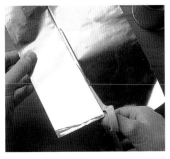

1 Using a can opener, remove one end of the tin can. Carefully file around the inside top edge of the can to remove any rough edges. To make the covering for the can, cut a rectangle of aluminium foil as wide as the can, and long enough to fit around it with 1cm/²⁄₅in to spare.

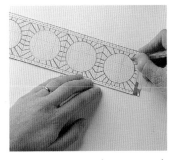

2 Draw a repeating design on graph paper to fit the rectangle. Cut it out. Tape the aluminium foil to a sheet of cardboard, then tape the pattern over the top and draw over the lines using a dry ballpoint pen. Press hard so the pattern will be embossed on the foil.

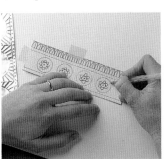

3 Cut a shorter, narrower rectangle of aluminium foil for the lower section. Draw out the decorative pattern for this section on to graph paper. Cut out the paper pattern and transfer it to the narrower strip of aluminium foil as before, using a dry ballpoint pen.

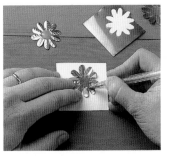

4 Draw a flower on thin cardboard and cut it out to make a template. Transfer the template to copper foil and cut out. Cut as many flowers as you need to fit around the can. Place the flowers on thin cardboard and draw decoration on to the petals.

▶

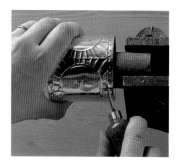

5 Glue the covering around the can using epoxy resin glue. When the glue is dry, firmly clamp a short length of wooden pole in a bench vice. Rest the can on the pole and make three holes at equal distances in the top edge using a bradawl (awl).

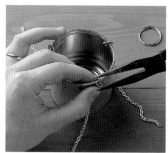

6 Cut three lengths of chain, each 12.5cm/5in. Fix a chain triangle through each hole in the top of the can and, using pliers, attach a length of chain to each. Attach the other ends of the chains to a key ring.

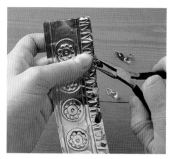

7 Make six evenly spaced holes along the bottom edge of the lower section of the burner using a bradawl. Carefully attach a small glass droplet to each hole, alternating the colours, and tightening the wires of the droplets with pliers.

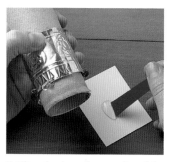

8 Clip tabs along the top edge of the lower section of the aluminium foil. Wrap around a cardboard tube and glue the edges together. Leave to dry and remove from the tube. Bend out the tabs and glue to the underside of the can.

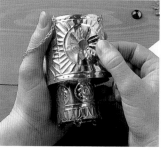

9 Glue the copper flowers around the can with their raised surfaces facing outwards. Glue a glass nugget in the centre of each flower, alternating the colours of the nuggets.

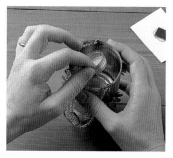

10 To make a holder for the incense cone, glue a metal bottle cap to the inside centre of the can.

This flamboyant chandelier has been created using baking accessories and tins, which come in a wide range of interesting shapes and sizes to inspire you.

Fiesta Chandelier

you will need
fluted flan ring, 30cm/12in diameter, 2.5cm/1in deep
permanent marker pen
galvanized wire
wire cutters
round-nosed (snug-nosed) pliers
blue glass paint
paintbrush
permanent felt-tipped pens: turquoise, green, orange, yellow and pink
9 fluted petit four tins
self-healing cutting mat
hammer
galvanized nails, 2.5cm/1in long
centre punch (optional)
paper
pencil
scissors
aluminium sheet
protective gloves
tin snips
chisel-ended bradawl (awl)
brass paper fasteners
strong glue
glass nuggets
3 wired glass bead necklaces or plug chains

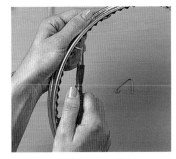

1 Count the flutings on the inner flan ring and mark off three equal sections. Cut three short pieces of wire and then thread them through the fluting at the marked points. Make a loop at the top of each wire using pliers and bend the other end up inside the fluting to secure the loop.

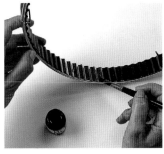

2 Paint the inside of the ring, and the wire loops, with blue glass paint. Leave to dry.

3 Colour the outside of the ring with turquoise and green permanent felt-tipped pens.

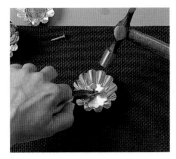

4 Place the petit four tins on a self-healing cutting mat and use a hammer and nail or centre punch to drive a hole through the centre of each tin. Colour the outside of the tins orange with a felt-tipped pen.

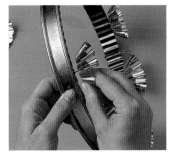

5 Mark nine equally spaced points on the ring for the candleholders. Press a nail through the centre of each of the petit four tins and insert in the flutes of the ring.

▶

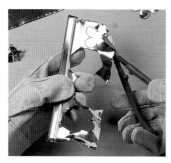

6 Draw a flower 5cm/2in in diameter on paper and use this template to draw nine flowers on the aluminium sheet. Cut out using tin snips and wearing protective gloves.

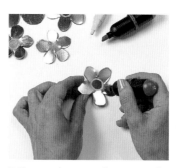

7 Cut one aluminium flower twice the size of the others for the crown at the top of the chandelier. Colour all the flowers using felt-tipped pens.

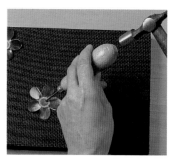

8 Using a chisel-ended bradawl (awl), cut a slit in the centre of each of the aluminium flowers.

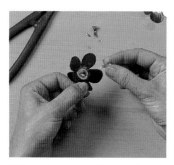

9 Slot a brass paper fastener through the centre of each coloured flower. (Check the size of an opened fastener against the depth of the flan ring – you may need to trim the tips.)

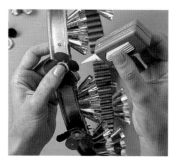

10 Fix on the flowers by sliding the open tips of the paper fasteners under the rolled rims of the flan ring in between the candleholders. Add a spot of strong glue to hold securely. Glue the glass nuggets to the ring midway between the flowers.

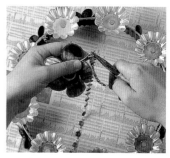

11 Thread a length of wire through the large flower and bend it into a hanging loop at the top and a hook beneath the flower. Attach three necklaces or chains to the loops on the ring and suspend them from the hook under the flower.

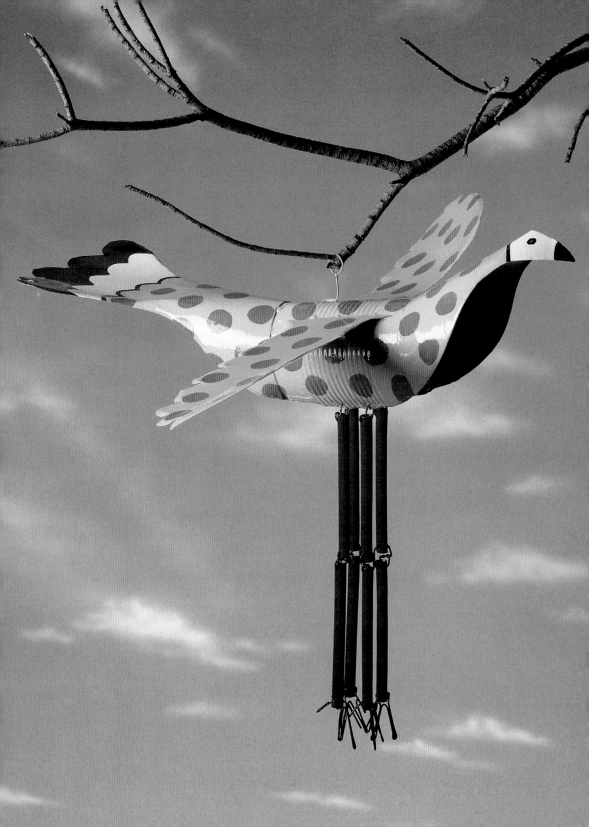

This wonderfully eccentric four-legged bird floats in the air and the passing breeze moves its chiming legs. Its body is a tin can and thin tin plate has been used to make its wings, head and tail.

Bird Chimes

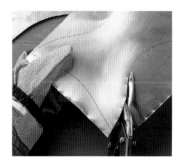

1 Remove both ends of the tin can. File the inside of each rim to remove the rough edges. Trace the templates from the back of the book, enlarging them as necessary, and transfer them to thin cardboard. Cut out. Place on the tin plate and draw around them. Wearing protective clothes, cut out all the shapes using tin shears. File each piece to remove the rough edges.

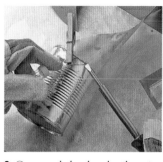

2 Curve each head and tail section inside the tin can. Hold them in place on the tin using wooden pegs (pins). Place the tin can on a soldering mat and, wearing a protective mask and goggles, apply flux and solder along the joins. Curve the two halves of the bird's head together and keep them in place with wooden pegs. Solder along the join. When the metal is cool, file around the beak.

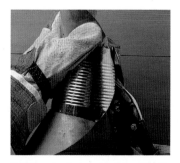

3 Using tin shears, cut the underside of the body. Leave a gap of about 2cm/⅘in between the two curves at the narrowest point, for hanging the legs. File the edges smooth.

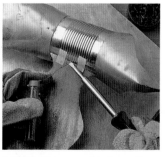

4 Using a hammer and nail, punch two holes near the edge of each side of the body for the legs, and one in the top for the hanger. File the rough edges. Attach the wings with masking tape, then solder. ▶

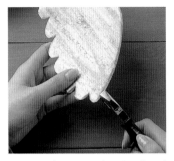

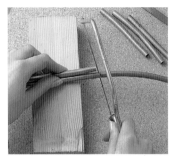

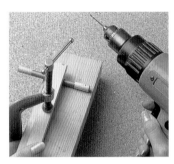

5 Using pliers, turn the unscalloped edges of the wings over and squeeze them flat. Carefully file away any remaining rough edges on the wings, then repeat this process to finish the tail.

6 To make the legs, cut four lengths of copper tubing each 20cm/8in using a hacksaw. Cut each piece in half again and file away the rough edges.

7 Wrap strips of masking tape around the ends of the tubing. Clamp the tubing and drill a hole in each end. The tape will stop the drill bit from slipping. Join both halves of each leg together using lengths of fine wire.

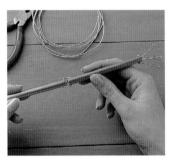

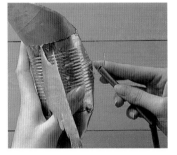

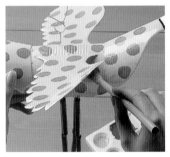

8 Cut four lengths of fine wire and use pliers to shape each piece into a foot. To join the feet to the bird's legs, push the ends of each foot into the holes in the end of the legs and apply a dot of solder.

9 Pass a length of wire through one of the holes in the side of the bird's body. Attach a leg to the wire and twist the ends together to keep it in place. Attach the other three legs to the bird's body in the same way. Using pliers, make a hook from fine wire and push it through the hole in the top of the bird's body. Bend the wire to hold it in place. Attach a split ring to the hook to make a hanger.

10 Apply one coat of metal primer to the bird, leave to dry, then apply a coat of bright yellow enamel paint. When the paint has dried, add orange dots. Paint all the legs red and the feet black. Use black, white and blue paint to add detail to the tail and head.

This scarecrow will bring a note of whimsy to your vegetable garden, and she will also protect your crops from marauding birds by rattling and jingling in the breeze.

Musical Scarecrow

you will need
assorted aluminium drinks (soda) cans
scissors
tracing paper
pencil
adhesive tape
ruler or tape measure
madeleine mould
centre punch
hammer
brass paper fasteners
galvanized wire
wire cutters
pliers
6 copper pipe connectors,
15mm/³⁄₅in wide
rectangular can
fine wire

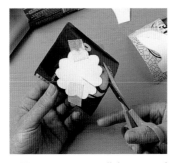

1 Using scissors, cut off the tops and bottoms of the cans. Cut along the side seams and open them out flat. Trace the templates from the back of the book and cut them out. Attach to the metal sheets with adhesive tape and cut around the shapes. Reverse one hand and one shoe to make pairs. Cut out a small flower shape for the scarecrow's knees.

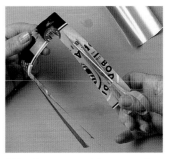

2 For the scarecrow's hair, cut a long rectangle from a can to the same width and twice as long as the top section of the madeleine mould. Cut out the centre of the rectangle, leaving a 2cm/ ⅚in strip at the top and down each side. Cut each side piece into two strips, as shown.

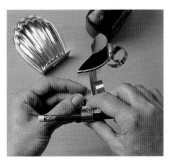

3 Curl each long side strip around a pencil. Make three holes around the top edge of the madeleine mould with a centre punch and hammer.

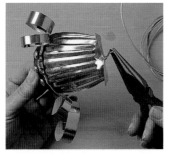

4 Fasten the hair to the madeleine mould using paper fasteners. Pierce a hole in the foot of the mould and thread with a short galvanized wire loop, which will fasten the head to the body.

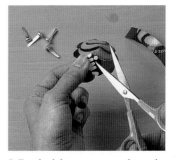

5 For the bikini top, cut a slit to the centre of each flower. Bend into a cone and fix by piercing both layers with the scissors and inserting a paper fastener. Thread the fastener ends through the strip to join the top. ▶

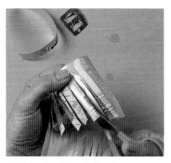

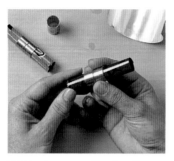

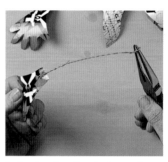

6 Make the fringed skirt by cutting a rectangle of metal into a fringe. Cut a strip for the belt and cut a buckle shape in a contrasting colour. Slot the belt through the buckle.

7 Make the arms and legs by rolling up six rectangles of can. Slot each one through a 15mm/⅜in copper pipe connector to keep it rolled up.

8 Cut four lengths of galvanized wire slightly longer than the arms and legs and make a hook in one end. Pierce the hands and the feet and thread one of the hooks through each hole. Twist with pliers. Slide a tube on to each wire and then bend the straight end of the wire into a loop.

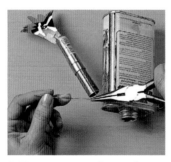

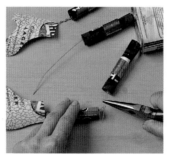

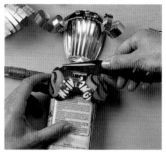

9 Use a centre punch to make one hole in each side and two holes in the base of the rectangular can, which will form the body. Thread a length of wire through the two shoulder holes, so that it protrudes from each side. Thread each end into the loops at the top of the arms, then bend into a loop and twist to secure. Cut off the excess.

10 Fold another length of wire in half and thread through the body so it protrudes through the holes in the base. Thread the last two tubes on to these, then thread the wire through the loops on each lower leg section. Twist the wire to secure it and trim away any excess.

11 Pierce the kneecap flowers with a paper fastener and secure through the wire loop on each leg. Using fine wire, attach the clothing and fix the body to the wire loop on the head.

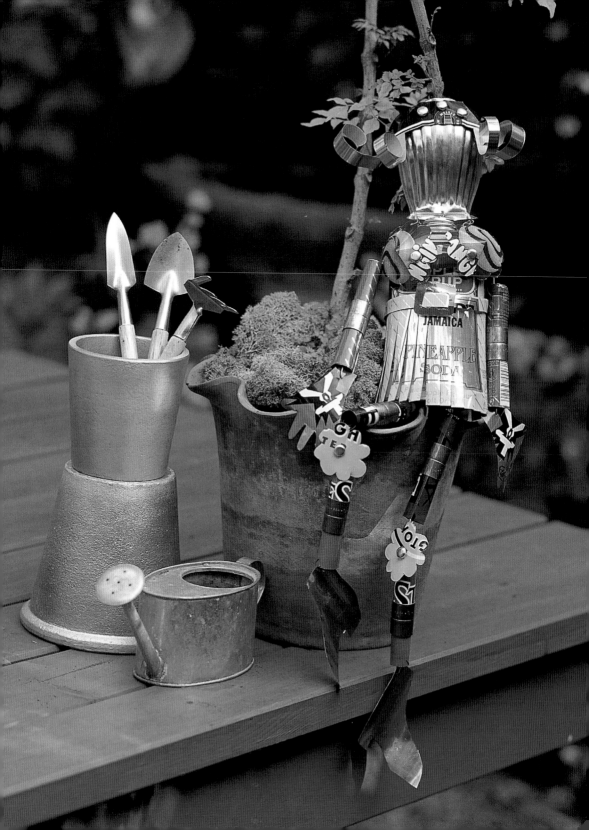

This charming reindeer is made from zinc plate that is thin enough to curve and manipulate easily. Zinc plate is steel that has been coated with a thin layer of zinc to protect it from corrosion.

Metal Reindeer

you will need

tracing paper

soft pencil

thin cardboard

scissors

thin zinc plate

marker pen

work shirt and protective leather gloves

tin snips

file

paintbrushes

small hammer

soldering mat

flux

protective mask and goggles

soldering iron and solder

masking tape

fine wire

wire cutters

pliers

enamel paints: red, blue, yellow and black

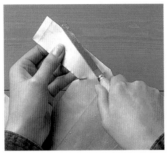

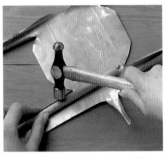

1 Trace the head and body from the back of the book, enlarging them if necessary. Transfer to thin cardboard and cut out. Draw around each on to a sheet of thin zinc plate using a marker pen. Wearing protective clothes, cut out the head and body using tin snips. File all the edges smooth. Draw and cut out two ears.

2 Place a paintbrush in the middle of each leg and the tail and gently tap the metal with a small hammer to curve it into a cylinder. Curve the reindeer's body. The reindeer will now stand upright. Place the reindeer on a soldering mat and apply flux to the joins. Wearing a protective mask and goggles, spot solder along the inside of each leg and the body.

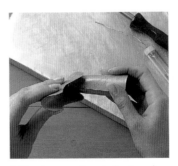

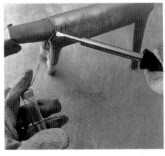

3 Gently curve the reindeer's neck to make a cylinder. Hold the edges together with masking tape while you spot solder along the join. Gently bend the head downwards and curve the sides to make it cylindrical.

4 Place the head inside the body. Wrap a strip of tape around the front legs to pull tightly together so that the head fits snugly inside the body section. Solder along the join where the neck meets the body.

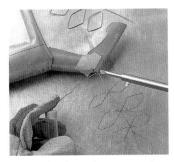

5 To make the antlers, cut two long and 14 short pieces of wire. Bend the short pieces into diamonds, and then solder to the two long pieces. Tape the antlers to the head and solder.

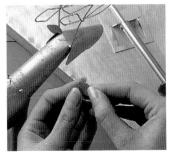

6 Curve the ears, tape in place and solder them next to the antlers.

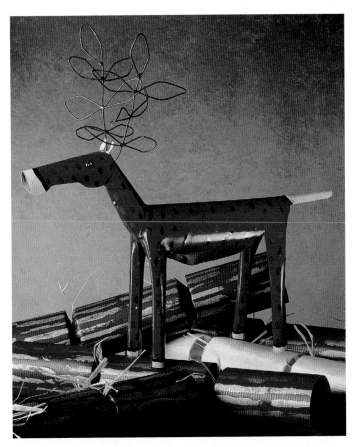

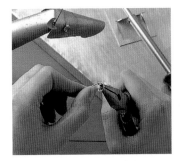

7 To make eyes, cut two short pieces of wire and twist around the end of the pliers to make spirals. Solder the eyes to the sides of the head.

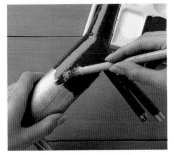

8 Paint the reindeer, except for its antlers, with two coats of red enamel paint, allowing the first coat to dry before adding the second.

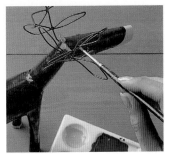

9 When the red paint is dry, paint blue spots on the body. Paint its ears, hooves and nose yellow. Paint a black line around the nose and the hooves and paint the antlers blue.

This chandelier is made from eight small tin cans and a tin flan ring. The chandelier is suspended from strong beaded chain; buy the kind with forged links that can withstand the weight of the chandelier.

Tin Can Chandelier

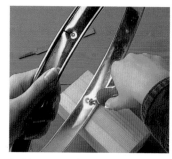

1 Measure and mark eight evenly spaced points around the flan ring. Rest the ring on a block of wood and pierce a hole at each point using a bradawl (awl). File away the rough edges at the back of the holes.

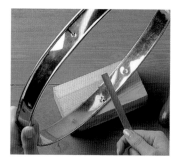

2 Mark three equally spaced points near the top edge of the ring. These holes will be used to suspend the chandelier from the beaded chain for hanging. Pierce them with a bradawl as before and file away the rough edges.

3 Remove the top from each can and file the edges smooth. Mark a point halfway down each can (avoiding the seam). Clamp a length of wooden pole in a bench vice. Support each can on the pole and pierce a hole in the side at the marked point using a bradawl. File any rough edges at the back of the holes.

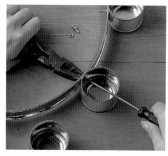

4 Place each can against a hole in the flan ring. Join the cans to the ring using short bolts. Screw the nuts on to the bolts as tightly as they will go so the cans are kept firmly in position.

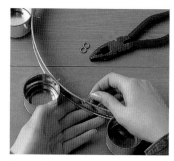

5 Attach an S-joiner through each of the three holes in the top of the flan ring. Using pliers, close the joiners as tightly as they will go.

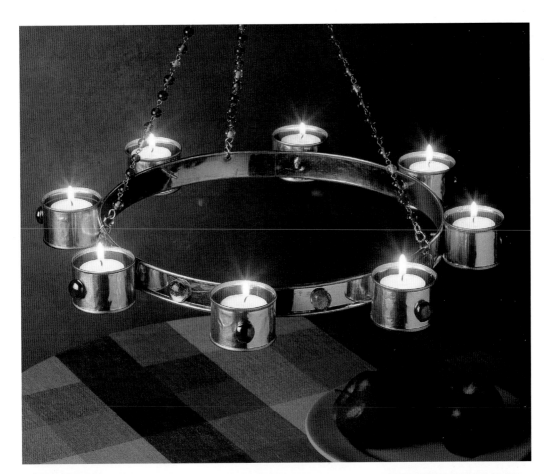

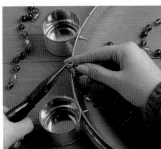

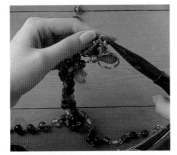

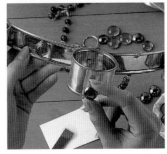

6 Cut three lengths of beaded chain each 30cm/12in. Attach a jump ring (wire) to the end of each length of chain. Attach a length to each S-joiner. Tightly close the jump rings with pliers.

7 Hold the free ends of the chains together and join them using a jump ring. Join the jump ring to an S-joiner and close the ring very tightly. Attach a key ring to the top of the S-joiner to make a hanger.

8 Glue green glass nuggets around the outside of the chandelier. Glue a red glass nugget to the outside of each can.

A Hindu temple was the inspiration for this charming little ornamental shrine assembled from an assortment of tins. Hang it among the branches of a tree in your garden.

Shimmering Temple

you will need
tin cans in assorted sizes
can opener
protective gloves
tin shears or snips
mallet
pencil
hole punch
scrap wood and wooden block
drill
pop riveter and rivets
pliers
scrap of metal lawn-edging (optional)
galvanized wire
wire cutters
self-healing cutting mat
centre punch
hammer
3 fluted petit four tins in different sizes

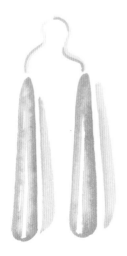

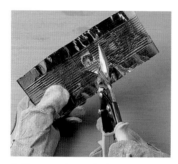

1 Remove the ends from two cans, including the reinforced rims. Wash and dry the cans thoroughly. Wearing protective gloves, cut the cans open with tin shears or snips and flatten with a mallet. Mark windows and a door on one can with a pencil. Pierce with a hole punch, working on a piece of scrap wood. Cut out the shapes with tin shears or snips.

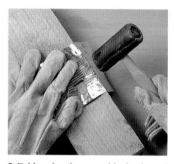

2 Fold each side over a block of wood and hammer with a mallet. The centre panel needs to be wider than the diameter of the can that will stand on top of the box you are making. Repeat with the second can, omitting the doors and the windows. Drill holes through the side panels of both of the sections and pop rivet them together to form the lower box section.

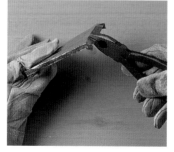

3 Cut a tin rectangle from another flattened can, slightly larger than the box you have made. Turn down all four sides with pliers, clipping the corners to form a lid.

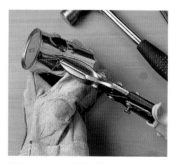

4 Remove the lids, although not the bottoms, from two smaller cans (use two with different proportions). Mark out windows, pierce and cut, making sure the closed end is at the top.

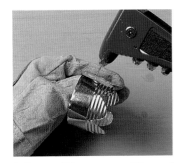

5 Cut a cuff from a piece of flattened can and scallop the edge. Bend into a circle slightly larger than one of the small tins and pop rivet together.

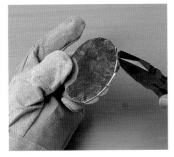

6 Cut a circle from a flattened can or large lid. Scallop the edge all round using tin shears or snips. Fold down each scallop with pliers.

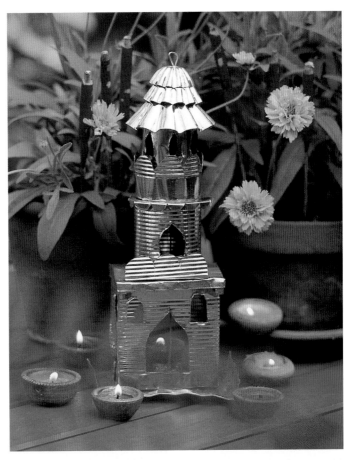

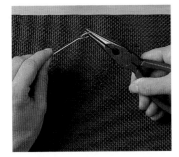

7 Make a base from a scrap of lawn-edging or a large flattened can. Fold up the side edges with pliers. Cut a long piece of galvanized wire and bend the end into a loop.

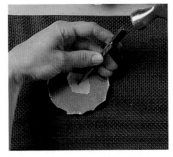

8 Cut a rectangle of ridged tin to sit on top of the lid of the bottom section. Scallop the edge. Bend the front edge up at 90°. Centre punch a hole through all the components, including the petit four tins.

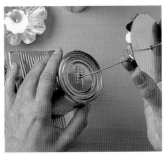

9 To assemble the house, start with the base and thread the wire through all the sections. At the top, trim away any excess wire and bend the top into a hook for hanging.

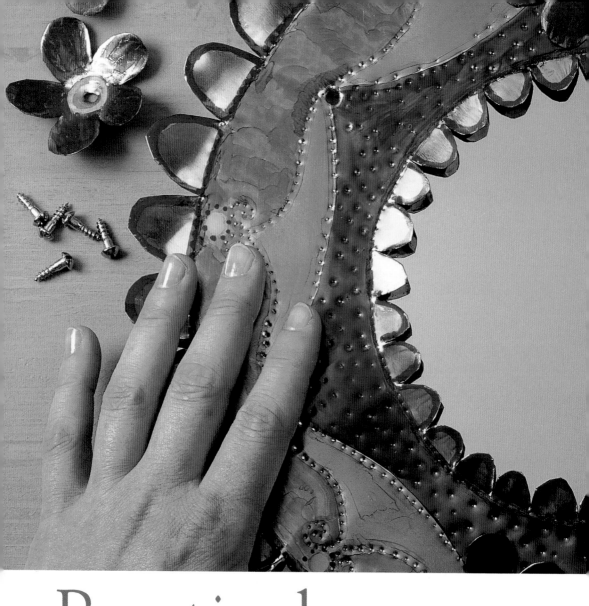

Practical

Tinwork

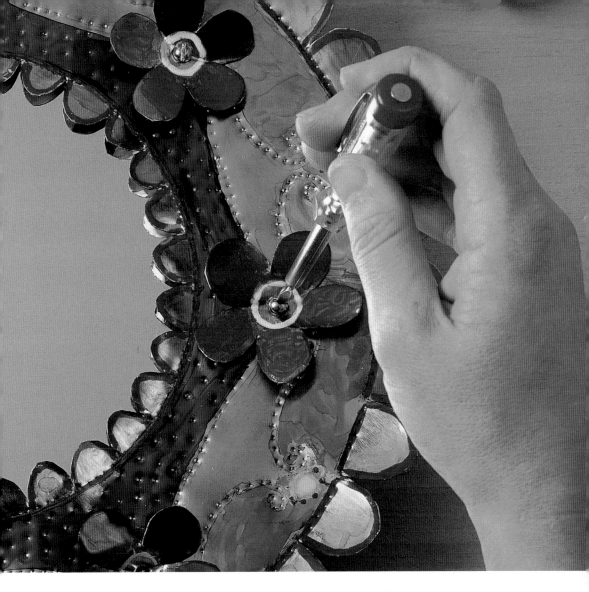

Tin is hardwearing, strong and durable, and ideal for using to create a variety of essential items around the home. You can make an enormous range of exciting projects, from cutlery boxes, lunchboxes and mailboxes, to coat racks and spice racks, clocks and cabinets, and even a hammered weathervane to attach to your roof. This extremely versatile and attractive material can be used to meet many of your domestic requirements.

Steely Surfaces

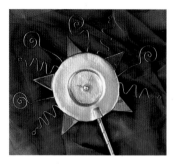

Tin is an ideal material to use around the home. It is strong, sturdy, easy to clean and also looks good. Choose from the bright shine of aluminium, the soft glow of copper, or the hammered look of pewter. Alternatively, you can paint or burnish metal to achieve a different effect altogether. Working with metal is not too difficult,

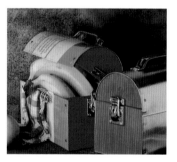

but you may need to practise on spare pieces of metal before you launch straight into a project. Creating a pewter-effect shelf, for example, may sound easy, but to achieve a professional-looking finish requires considerable dexterity. Likewise, creating a punched tin cabinet front may simply appear to be a case of tracing around a stencil, then punching a line of dots around the traced line. However, ensuring that all the punched dots look regular and even does

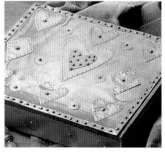

require a certain amount of skill with a centre punch. Nevertheless, if you take your time and are prepared to practise, you will achieve wonderful results and enjoy the great sense of satisfaction that comes with acquiring a new skill.

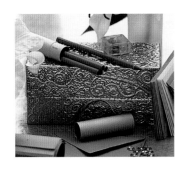

In this chapter you can learn how to make a wide variety of functional metal boxes for your home, ranging from jewellery boxes and cutlery boxes to mailboxes, in addition to clocks, doorstops, number plaques, birdbaths, suitcases, buckets and even a barbecue. The projects range from simple to more complex, so make sure that you choose a project suitable for your skill level.

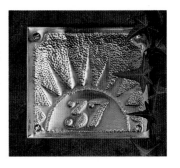

The metals used in this chapter range from thin zinc sheet to recycled oil drums and anything in between. When cutting metal, you need to wear goggles and thick protective gloves as the cut edges of metal can be very sharp. All the projects involve

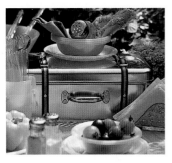

the use of special tools, such as tin snips, hide hammers and pop riveters. If you have never used any of these tools before, don't be put off by them; once you have experimented with them, you will find they are easy to manipulate. Using the right tool for the right job will ensure your projects are made accurately and with as good a finish as you would want.

You will have endless pleasure watching birds preening and cleaning themselves in this beautiful beaten copper birdbath. Keep a fresh water supply to ensure the health and happiness of the birds.

Copper Birdbath

you will need
chinagraph pencil
string
copper sheet, 0.9mm/¹/₂₇in thick
protective gloves
tin shears
file
blanket
hammer
medium copper wire, 4m/13ft long
bench vice
cup hook
drill and 3mm/¹/₈in bit

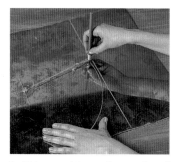

1 Using a chinagraph pencil and looped string, mark a 45cm/17¾in circle on the copper. Wearing gloves, cut out the circle with tin shears. File the sharp edges smooth.

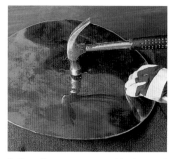

2 Put the copper on a blanket and hammer it lightly from the centre. Spread the dips out to the rim. Repeat, starting from the centre each time, to get the required shape.

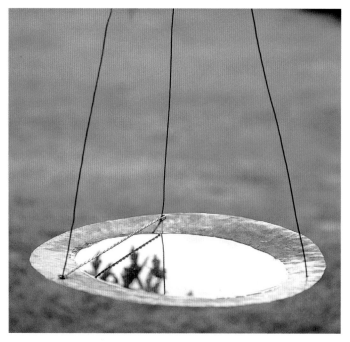

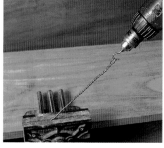

3 To make the perch, double a 1m/40in length of wire and hold the ends in a vice. Fasten a cup hook into the chuck of a hand drill and loop it through the wire. Twist the wire with the drill, then drill three 3mm/¹/₈in holes around the rim of the birdbath. Bend a knot into one end of three 1m/40in lengths of wire. Thread the wires up through the holes. Slip the perch over two of the straight wires.

This project fuses the clarity of high-tech design with the quirkiness of surrealist sculpture – and it provides an ideal place to keep your cutlery at the same time!

Cutlery Box

you will need

small silver-plated knife, fork and
spoon, polished

3 metal boxes with lids

permanent marker pen

coarse-grade sandpaper (glasspaper)

file

metal-bonding compound

craft knife

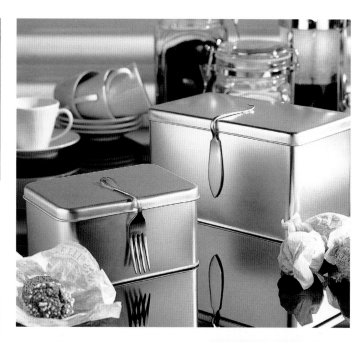

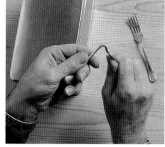

1 Bend the knife to a right angle halfway along the handle. It should bend easily, but if not, do it over the edge of a table. Place the knife on one of the boxes and mark its position. Roughen the contact point on the knife with sandpaper. Rub the part of the lid that will make contact with the knife handle with a file.

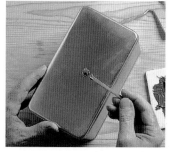

2 Mix the metal-bonding compound, following the instructions supplied. Apply the bonding to the area on the lid that has been roughened. The knife is fixed only at this point, so the bond needs to be strong.

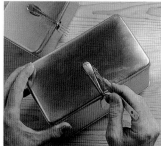

3 Press the knife handle firmly into position on the bonding. Use a fine instrument, such as a craft knife, to remove any surrounding bonding compound. Repeat to add the fork and spoon to the other boxes.

If you want to jazz up an old piece of furniture, corrugated metal lawn edging is perfect for the job. Simply find the most suitable width of edging, cut it to size and screw it to the drawer fronts.

Metal-faced Drawers

you will need

ruler or tape measure

set of drawers

permanent marker pen

protective gloves

metal lawn edging strip

tin snips or shears

clamp

scrap board

drill

screws

screwdriver

drawer handles or knobs

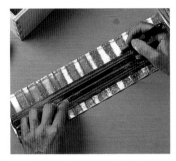

1 Measure the fronts of the drawers. Transfer these dimensions to the lawn edging with a marker pen. Wearing protective gloves, cut the metal lawn edging to size using tin snips or shears.

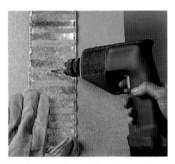

2 Clamp each metal strip to a piece of scrap board and drill a hole in all four corners of the metal strips and in the centre for the drawer handles or knobs.

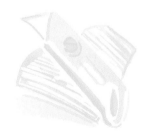

3 Place the metal on the front of the drawer and then mark the positions of the holes with a marker pen.

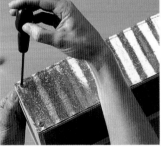

4 Drill holes in the four corners of the drawer front. Screw the metal strip to the drawer at each drilled hole.

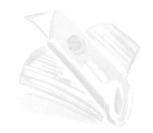

5 Finally, screw a decorative handle to the centre front of each drawer.

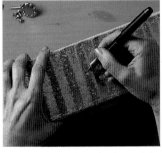

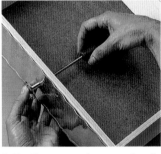

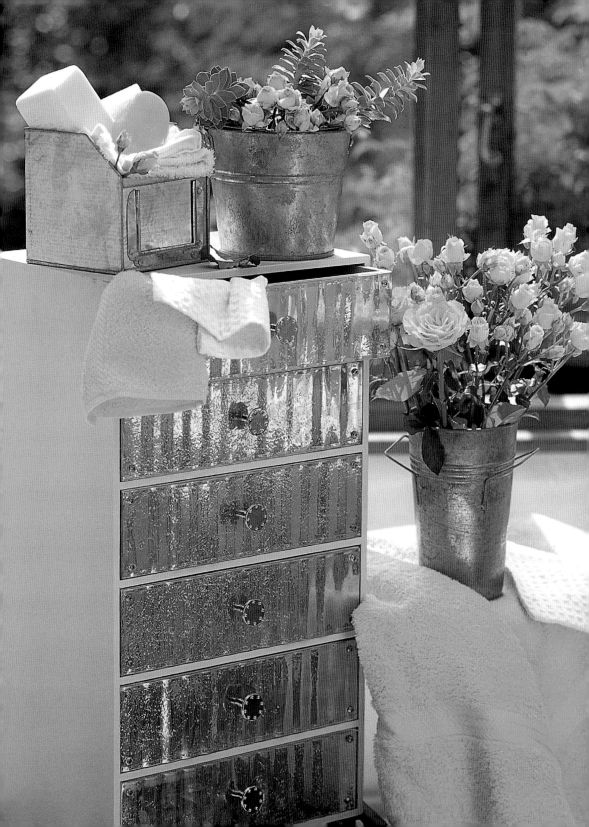

Minimalist detail and smooth contours give this clock a sophisticated look of industrial chic. It would look ideal in a chrome kitchen where the shiny aluminium would add a reflective quality.

Contemporary Clock

you will need
2 aluminium ring moulds
drill
clock mechanism with extra long shank
screwdriver
paper
pencil
scissors
strong glue
4 square nuts, 1cm/²⁄₅in wide
double-sided adhesive pads

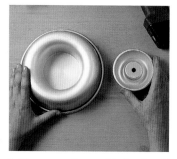

1 Choose two ring moulds that fit well together. Drill a hole in the centre of the smaller mould to take the shank for the clock hands.

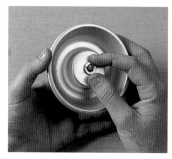

2 Insert the clock mechanism and screw in place. Make sure the hands will fit inside the rim of the small ring mould.

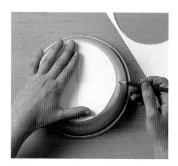

3 Draw around the smallest end of the large mould and cut out the paper circle. Fold it carefully into quarters, unfold it and lay on top of the mould. Make a light pencil mark on the mould at each quarter line.

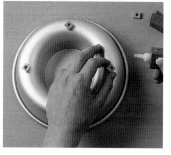

4 Using strong glue, carefully fix a square nut at each quarter mark on the larger mould.

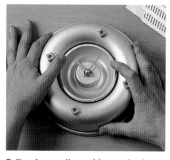

5 Fix the small mould into the larger one using adhesive pads. Mount the clock on the wall.

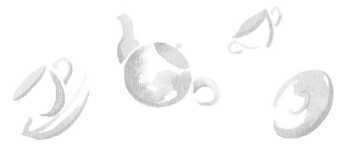

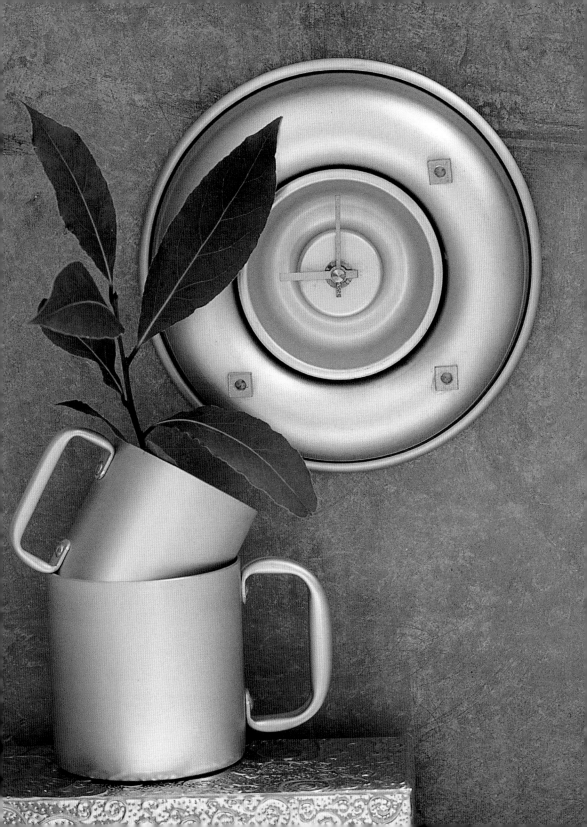

This jewel box is made from a combination of thin zinc sheet, which has a subtle sheen rather like pewter, and brass shim, which is a fairly soft metal used mostly by sculptors.

Jewel Box

you will need
work shirt and protective
leather gloves
tin shears and snips
thin zinc plate
old cigar box
file
pencil
thin cardboard
scissors
brass shim
sheet of chipboard
hammer and nail
soldering mat
protective mask and goggles
soldering iron and solder
strong glue

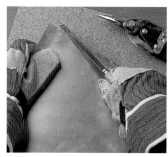

1 Wearing a work shirt and protective gloves, use tin shears to cut a piece of zinc to cover the lid of the cigar box. The zinc should be slightly larger than the box lid, to allow for a rim to cover the edges of the lid. File any rough edges. Draw a diamond and two different-sized hearts on a sheet of thin cardboard and cut them out.

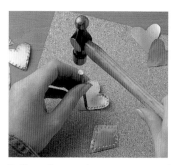

2 Place the templates on a piece of brass shim and draw around them – six small hearts, one large heart and two diamonds. Draw some small circles freehand. Draw one small heart on a scrap of zinc. Cut out all the shapes and file the edges smooth. Place them on the chipboard and stamp a line of dots around the edge of each using a hammer and nail. Do not stamp the circles and zinc heart.

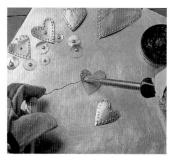

◀ **3** Cut four strips of shim to make a border around the zinc lid cover. Place all the pieces on a soldering mat and, wearing a protective mask and goggles, drop a blob of liquid solder in the centre of the circles, small hearts and diamonds. Cover the zinc heart with solder blobs. Add a line of blobs to each piece of the shim border.

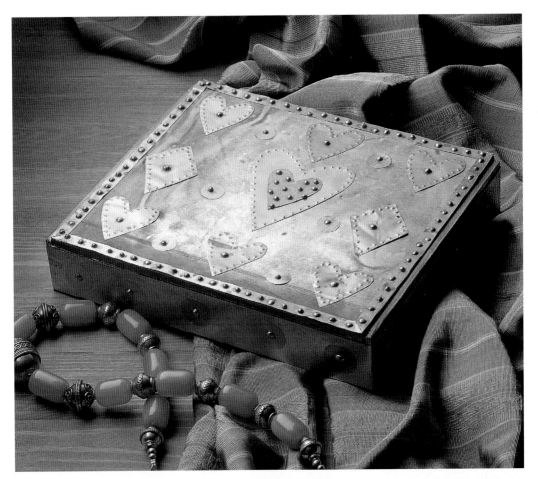

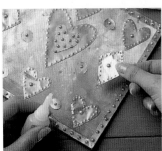

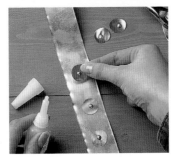

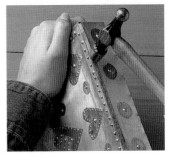

4 Turn down a narrow rim around the zinc panel at 90° to turn down over the sides of the lid. Glue all the shapes and the borders to the panel.

5 Cut a strip of zinc the width of the box side and long enough to fit all around. File the edges smooth. Cut circles of shim, decorate each with a blob of solder and glue in place.

6 Glue the zinc strip around the sides of the box. Glue the zinc panel to the top of the lid. Gently tap the edges of the panel to make them flush with the sides of the lid.

Aluminium flashing, traditionally used in roofing, takes on an unusual, pitted appearance that resembles pewter when it is hammered. It can be used to cover simple shapes such as this shelf.

Pewter-look Shelf

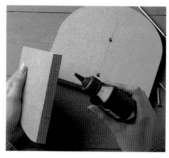

1 Mark the two shelf pieces on MDF, (medium density fiberboard) using the template. Cut them out with a hand saw. Draw a line down the centre and mark two points for the drill holes. Mark corresponding points on the long edge of the stand. Drill holes at these points, then glue and screw the shelf and stand together.

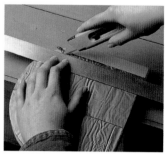

2 Cut lengths of aluminium flashing roughly to size using a craft knife. Peel away the backing and stick them to the shelf top, trimming the rough edges at the side with a craft knife and ruler as you go. Join each new length of flashing very closely to the last, so that no MDF is visible beneath the covering.

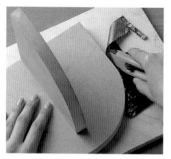

3 When the top is covered, place the shelf face down on a large piece of scrap MDF and trim away the excess flashing using a craft knife.

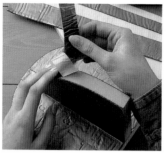

4 Cut lengths of flashing to cover the back and sides of the shelf, and stick them in place.

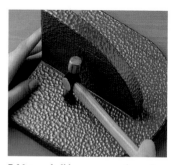

5 Using a ball hammer, tap the surface of the flashing to make indentations close together. Vary the force with which you strike the flashing, to make an interesting and irregular pattern.

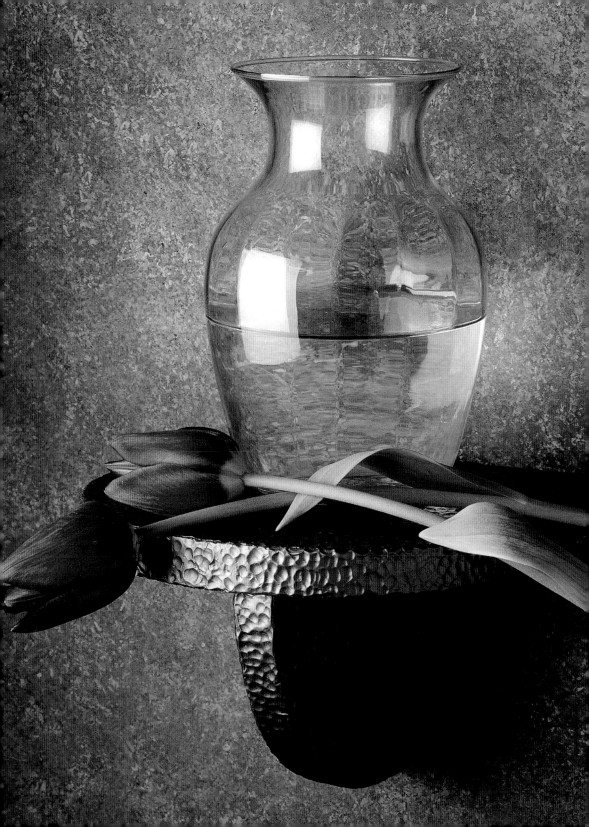

This punched tin cabinet is based on those of the American settlers, who produced a wide range of household artefacts using tin plate and in doing so, raised the decorative punching process to an art form.

Punched Panel Cabinet

you will need

small wooden cabinet with a recess in the door

ruler

sheet of tin plate, 30 gauge (0.3mm/¹⁄₈₃in thick)

permanent marker pen

work shirt and protective leather gloves

tin shears

90° and 45° wooden blocks

bench vice

hide hammer

file

pair of compasses (compass)

pencil

graph paper

scissors

sheet of chipboard

panel pins (tacks)

tack hammer

masking tape

centre punch

ball hammer

small chisel

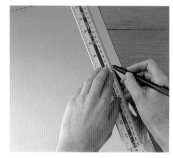

1 Measure the recess in the door of the cabinet. Mark out the dimensions of the recess on the tin using a marker pen. Draw a 1cm/⅖in border inside the rectangle. Mark points along the sides 2cm/⅘in from each corner of the outer rectangle. Draw diagonal lines from these points to the corners of the inner rectangle.

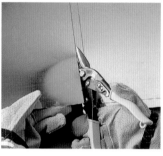

2 Wearing a work shirt and protective leather gloves, cut the panel from the sheet of tin using tin shears. Cut along the diagonal lines at the corners. This will allow the border to be folded behind the panel to give it a smooth edge.

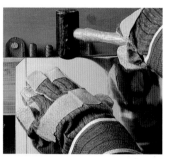

3 Firmly clamp the 90° block of wood in the bench vice. Place the panel on the wooden block with the ruled edge of the tin resting on the edge of the block. Using a hide hammer, tap along the edge of the panel to turn it over to an angle of 90°.

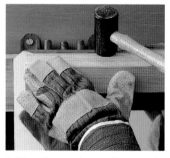

4 Turn the panel over. Position the 45° wooden block inside the turned edge and hammer the edge over it. Remove the block and hammer the edge flat. Finish the remaining sides of the panel in the same way. File the corners to remove any sharp edges.

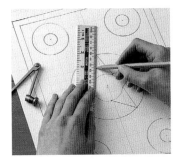

5 Using a pair of compasses (compass) and a ruler, measure out and draw the panel design on graph paper. Cut the paper to the same size as the panel.

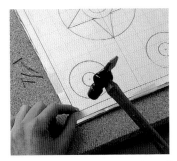

6 Place the panel face up on a sheet of chipboard and secure each corner to the board with a panel pin (tack). Tape the paper pattern to the front of the panel.

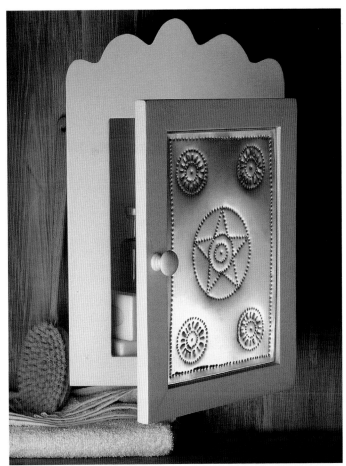

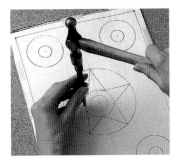

7 Place the centre punch on one of the lines. Tap it with the hammer to indent the tin. Move the punch along the line and tap it to make the next mark. Complete the design.

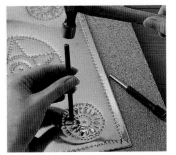

8 Remove the paper pattern and add extra decoration to the front of the panel using a small chisel. Unpin the panel from the board.

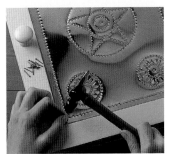

9 Place the decorated panel in the recess on the front of the cabinet. Use panel pins at each corner to attach the panel securely to the cabinet.

Pewter shim is simple to emboss. For this project, a wooden block is wrapped like a parcel with the embossed pewter to make an attractive doorstop – you could also use it as an unusual bookend.

Scrollwork Doorstop

you will need
pewter shim, 38 x 39cm/15 x 15½in
self-healing cutting mat
permanent marker pen
ruler
dry ballpoint pen
embossing stylus
lollipop (popsicle) stick
pencil
wooden block, 19 x 9 x 9cm/
7½ x 3½ x 3½in
2 metal washers, 4cm/1½in diameter
hammer
2 roofing nails

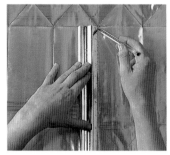

1 Place the pewter shim on a cutting mat. Following the template at the back of the book, use a marker pen and ruler to draw the foldlines on to the metal. Using a dry ballpoint pen, score a line 3mm/⅛in from one end and fold over. Score along all the solid marked lines. Turn the pewter over and score the remaining dotted lines.

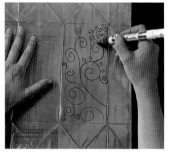

2 Turn the sheet back again and use a permanent marker pen to draw the pattern in freehand on the areas shown on the template. Vary the design according to your personal taste. If you are using a more formal design than these freestyle curlicues, plan it on paper first. This is the back of the design.

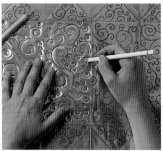

3 Score the pattern on the pewter with a stylus. Use a lollipop (popsicle) stick end for thick lines and a pencil for fine ones.

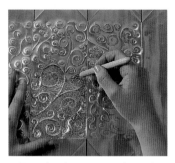

4 Turn the sheet over and complete the design by indenting dots around the lines using the stylus or pencil.

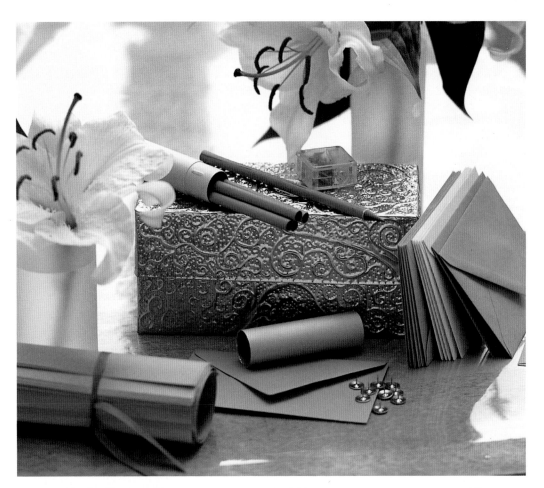

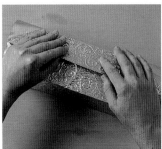

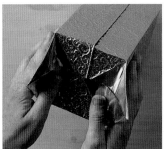

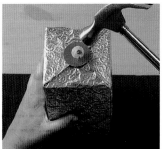

5 Wrap the shim around the wooden block, allowing the neatened, folded edge to overlap the other edge. Make sure you place the block centrally, with equal amounts for folding.

6 Fold along the scored lines and wrap up the block as if it were a present.

7 Place a metal washer centrally on the end of the block and hammer a roofing nail through it to secure the pewter and give it interesting detail. Repeat at the other end of the block.

The rising sun has been incorporated into the design of this number plaque. Small indentations are punched into the front of the plaque to create a densely pitted surface and to raise the unpunched areas.

Number Plaque

ɤɤɤ

you will need

sheet of tin plate, 30 gauge
(0.3mm/⅓₃in thick)

permanent marker pen

ruler

work shirt and protective
leather gloves

tin shears

90° and 45° wooden blocks

bench vice

hide hammer

file

graph paper

scissors

pencil

masking tape

sheet of chipboard

panel pins (tacks)

tack hammer

centre punch

ball hammer

wire (steel) wool

clear polyurethane varnish

varnish brush

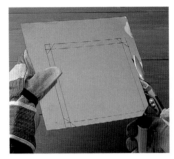

1 Draw a rectangle on a sheet of tin. Draw a 1cm/⅖in border around the inside of the rectangle. Measure a point 2.5cm/1in from each corner of the outer rectangle. Draw diagonal lines across all the corners. Wearing protective clothing, cut out the plaque with tin shears.

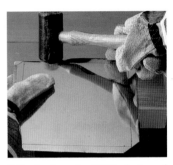

2 Firmly clamp the 90° block of wood in a bench vice. Place the plaque on the wooden block with the ruled edge of the tin resting on the edge of the block. Using a hide hammer, tap along the edge of the plaque to turn over all the marked border areas to an angle of 90°.

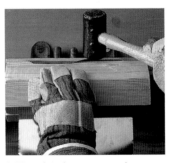

3 Turn the plaque over and position the 45° wooden block inside the turned edge. Hammer the edge over it, remove the block and then hammer the edge completely flat. Finish the remaining three sides of the plaque in the same way. Carefully file the four corners to make them smooth.

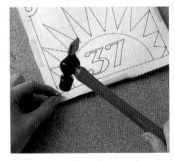

4 Cut a piece of graph paper the same size as the plaque. Draw your pattern and desired numbers, then tape the pattern to the front of the plaque. Secure it to the chipboard with a panel pin (tack) in each corner.

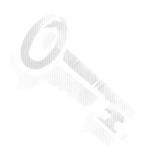

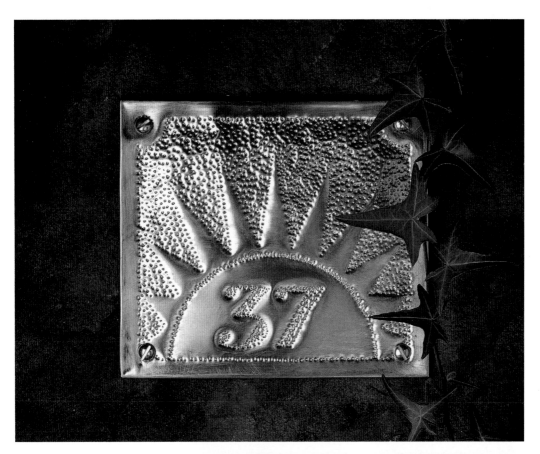

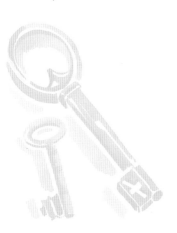

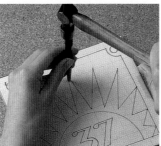

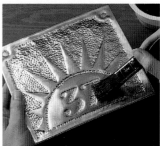

5 Place the centre punch on a line and tap it with a ball hammer to make an indentation. Move the punch about 3mm/⅛in along the line and tap it again to make the next mark. Continue to punch along the lines until the design is completed.

6 Remove the paper pattern, then randomly punch the surface around the sunburst and inside the numbers. Scour the surface of the panel with wire (steel) wool before sealing the plaque with varnish. Allow to dry before screwing in place.

The gently sloping sides of a dustbin (garbage can) lid allow smaller birds to paddle in the shallow water, while larger birds can splash in the middle without emptying the water.

Chrome Birdbath

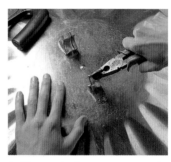

1 Using a hacksaw, saw across the middle of the dustbin (garbage can) lid's handle. Bend back both sides of the severed handle using pliers.

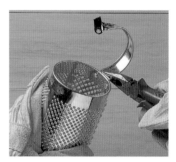

2 Wearing protective gloves, remove the handle from the top of the metal cheese grater (shredder) using the pliers.

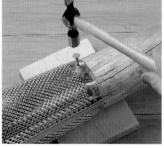

3 Push the narrow end of the cheese grater on to the fence post and secure it with galvanized nails through the holes left by the handle rivets.

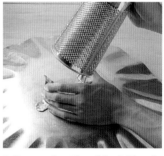

4 Squeeze the sides of the lid handle together to insert them in the wide end of the grater. Place a night-light inside the grater to stop the water in the birdbath from freezing.

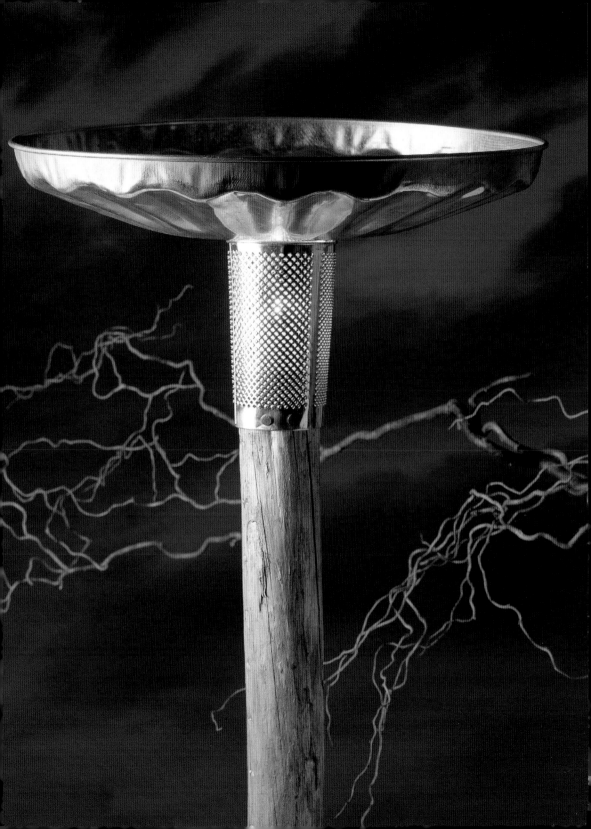

Punched tin designs are a staple technique of folk-art interiors, but they are often kept to quite small areas. However, used over a larger area, punched tin will look much more dramatic.

Punched Tin Folk-Art Wall

you will need
scrap paper
pencil
thin tin sheet
tin shears
protective gloves
file
chinagraph pencil
long metal ruler
metal punch
tack hammer
wood offcut
drill, with metal and masonry bits
carpenter's spirit level
straight edge
wall plugs (plastic anchors)
dome-headed screws
screwdriver
clear varnish or lacquer
varnish brush

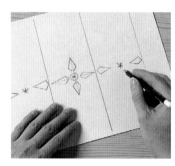

1 Design and draw the pattern for the punched tin wall to scale on paper. Cut a piece of tin sheet to size using tin shears and wearing protective gloves. Using a metal file, smooth any rough edges.

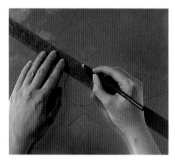

2 Using the paper pattern as a guide, draw the design to the correct size on the reverse side of the metal sheet using a chinagraph pencil and long metal ruler. Make sure any repeated straight lines are parallel.

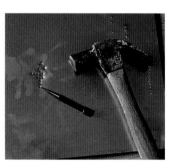

3 Using a metal punch and a tack hammer, practise punching on a spare scrap of metal to get a feel for how hard you need to punch.

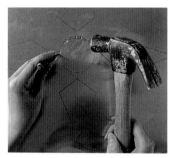

4 Place an offcut of wood behind the tin to protect your work surface. Then punch out the pattern. Drill holes in the corners of the metal sheet.

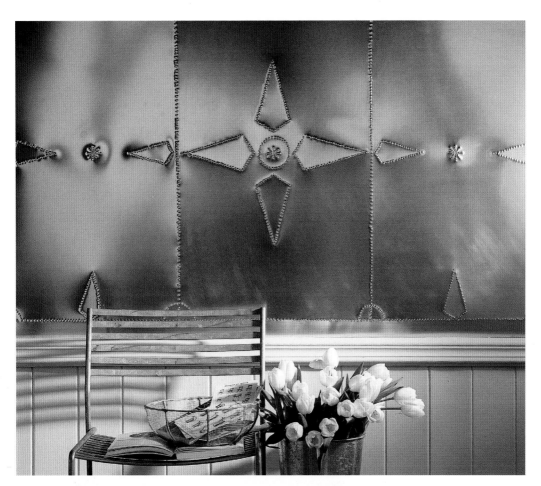

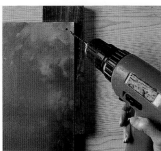

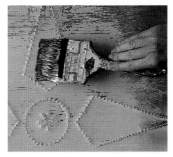

5 Using a carpenter's spirit level and straight edge, draw lines on the wall to show the position of the sheet. Drill holes for the corners. Insert wall plugs (plastic anchors).

6 Screw the metal sheet in position on the wall. Coat the metal sheet with a protective layer of varnish or lacquer to protect it against rust.

This ingenious workshop accessory efficiently dispenses different kinds of string from its three funnels. Its brilliant patchwork background is made from a collection of colourful printed tin cans.

String Dispenser

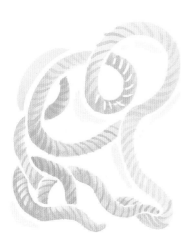

you will need
assorted printed tin cans
can opener
protective gloves
tin shears
mallet
length of wood, 10 x 2cm/4 x ⅘in
self-healing cutting mat
nails
hammer
ruler
3 metal funnels
permanent marker pen
drill
2 mirror fixing plates
screws
screwdriver
3 balls of string

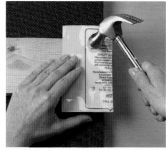

◀ **1** Remove the lids and bottoms from the cans including the reinforced rims. Wash them and leave to dry. Wearing protective gloves, cut the cans open with tin shears and flatten them using a mallet. Select two cans slightly wider than the length of wood. Working on a cutting mat, nail them to each end of the wood so that they overlap the edges, as shown.

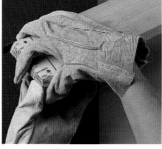

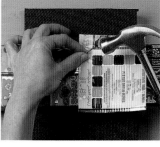

2 Clip the corners of the cans diagonally with tin shears. Fold them neatly over the edges of the wood. Hammer the edges down flat with the mallet, then nail in place.

3 Arrange the other cans along the wood until you are satisfied with the arrangement. Nail in place to cover the wood, overlapping them slightly. Fold over the edges as before and nail to secure.

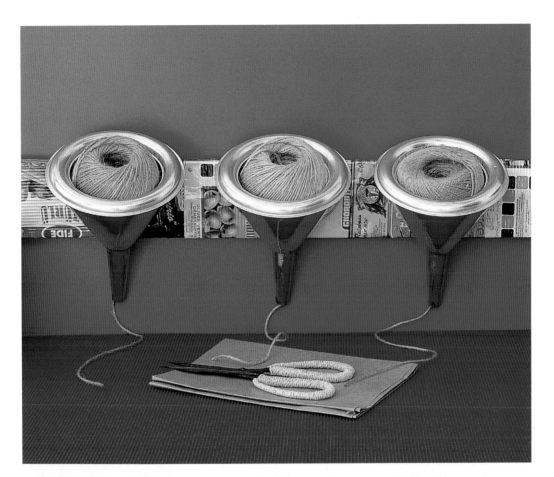

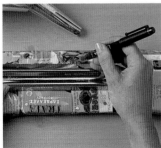

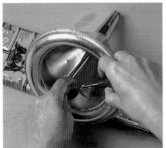

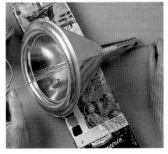

4 Measure the finished panel to work out the position of each funnel. Mark with a marker pen. Drill a guide hole at each marked point. Turn the panel over and attach two mirror fixing plates at the back for hanging.

5 Drill a hole in identical positions in each of the funnels, so that the top edges align. Screw the funnels into the guide holes on the panel.

6 Put a ball of string into each funnel and thread the end (taken from the centre of the ball) through the spout. Attach the string dispenser to the wall as required.

Turn an ordinary tin into a stylish suitcase with webbing straps and a smart handle. Embellish the case by attaching a foil plaque embossed with your name or initials.

Stylish Suitcase

you will need
metal drawer or cupboard handle
rectangular metal tin with hinged lid
ruler
permanent marker pen
clamp
drill
nuts and bolts (or rivets)
screwdriver (or pop riveter)
narrow luggage webbing straps
scissors
hole punch or bradawl (awl)

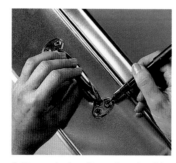

1 Centre the handle on the side of the tin opposite the hinges and mark the fixing positions using a permanent marker pen.

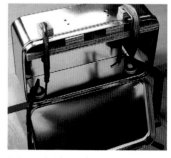

2 Securely clamp the case to the work surface in preparation for drilling the holes for the handle. Use wooden supports as shown.

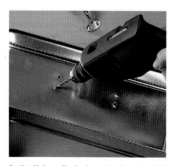

3 Drill handle holes. Mark and drill two strap holes midway between the box sides and the handle fixings. Drill two holes in corresponding positions on the hinge side of the tin case.

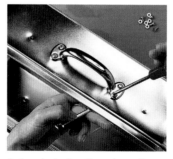

4 Attach the handle with small nuts and bolts (or you could use rivets).

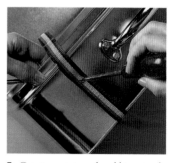

5 Cut two strips of webbing to fit around the box and mark them with the positions of the drilled holes. Punch a small hole at each marked point and attach the straps in the same way as the handle.

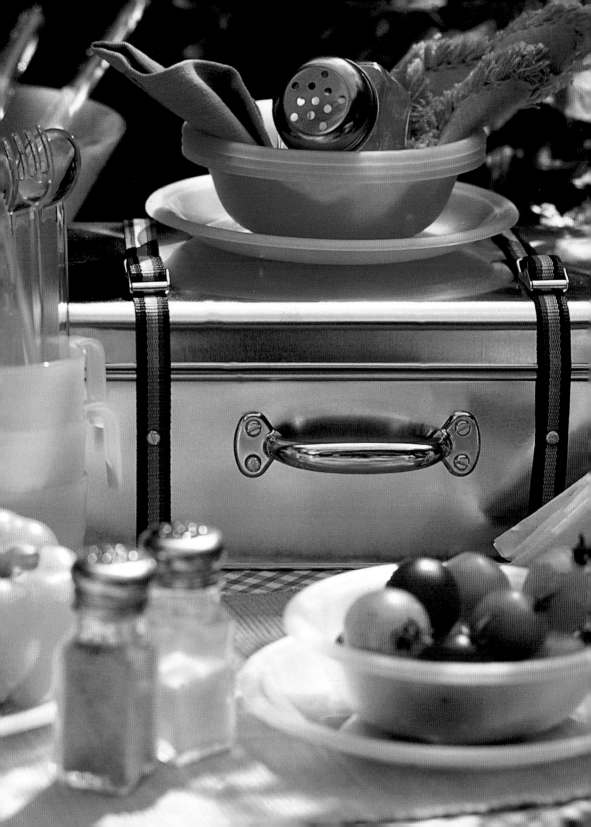

Unwanted food containers are a good source of tin and are perfect for making items such as this handsome spice rack, as they are already partly formed into the right shape.

Spice Rack

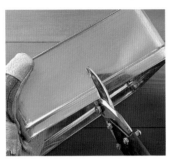

1 Wearing protective clothes, cut the base of the biscuit (cookie) tin in half carefully using tin shears. File all the cut edges of the tin smooth. You will only need one half of the tin for this project. Dispose of the other half safely.

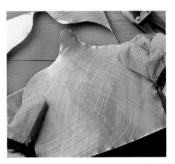

2 Draw the curved shape of the back panel of the spice rack on to the lid of the tin. Cut out using tin shears and file all the cut edges smooth. Place the curved back panel against the cut edge of one half of the biscuit tin. Hold the two together with masking tape.

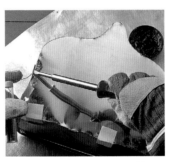

3 Place the spice rack on a soldering mat. Wearing a protective mask and goggles, apply flux to the join, then solder the two parts together. Using pliers, fold in the filed edges of the back panel and the base to flatten them completely. File any remaining rough edges smooth.

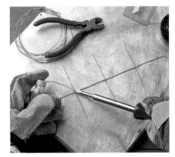

4 Measure the dimensions of the inside of the spice rack. Cut lengths of fine wire and solder them together to make a grid to form compartments for the spices. Place the grid inside the spice rack and solder it in place.

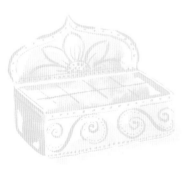

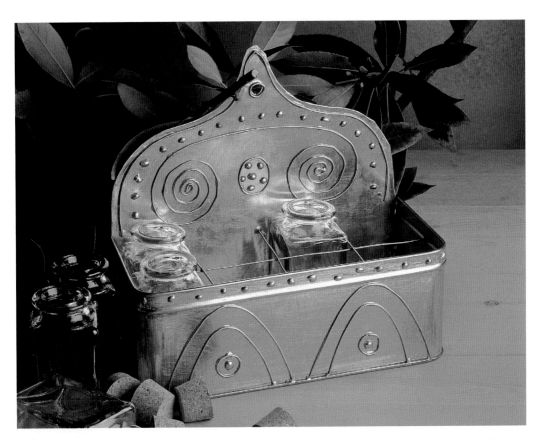

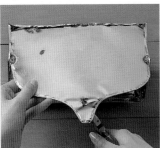

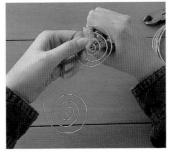

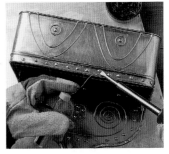

5 Place the top edge of the rack on a block of wood and pierce a hole in it using a bradawl (awl). Open the hole slightly using a pair of pliers. File the rough edges from the inside hole. Turn over the edges around the hole and squeeze them flat with pliers.

6 Cut a length of fine wire and form a spiral at each end. Cut six lengths of wire and form two large and two small curves and two small circles. Solder the spiral to the back of the rack and the curves to the front. Shape a wire to fit around the edges of the back of the rack and solder in place.

7 Cut a small circle of brass shim and glue it to the centre back of the rack. Apply decorative blobs of solder to the shim circle, along the edge of the rack, around the spiral and in the small circles. Make a wire circle to go around the shim and solder in place.

You don't need metal-working skills to make this cheerful weathervane, as the shapes are cut out of rigid plastic sheet and covered with strips of roof-flashing, which is given a densely pitted texture.

Hammered Weathervane

you will need

paper
pencil
ruler
scissors
permanent marker pen
rigid plastic sheet (Plexiglas)
coping saw, jigsaw or band saw
scrap wood
drill
craft knife
small paint roller
galvanized wire
aluminium flashing
metal straight edge
hacksaw
file
brass screw
screwdriver
metal rod or broom handle
newspaper
small hammer
blue glass paint
paintbrush

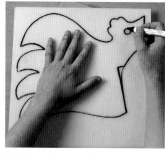

1 Scale up the template at the back of the book and cut out paper patterns for the rooster and an arrow 24cm/9½ in long. Draw around these shapes on to the plastic sheet.

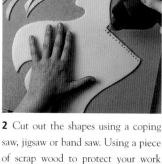

2 Cut out the shapes using a coping saw, jigsaw or band saw. Using a piece of scrap wood to protect your work surface, drill a row of small holes as shown. Drill the rooster's eye.

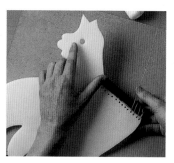

3 Use a craft knife to cut the central plastic tube from a small paint roller and use galvanized wire to attach it to the rooster.

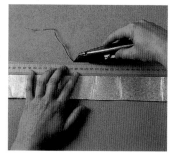

4 Cut strips of aluminium flashing long enough to cover the plastic shapes. Trim the edges of the strips using a craft knife and straight edge, so that you can make neat joints.

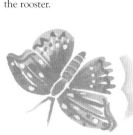

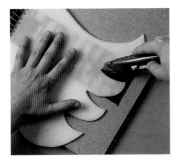

5 Apply the strips of flashing to both sides of the rooster, trimming the edges with a craft knife as you stick them on. Wrap the lower strips on the rooster around the roller.

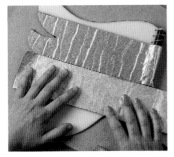

6 As you apply further strips, join the long edges together carefully. Cut out the eye of the rooster. Cover the arrow with flashing, then drill a small hole for the screw.

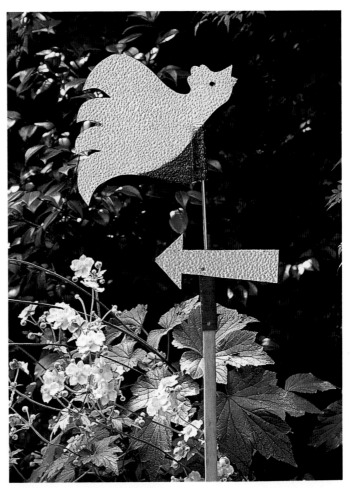

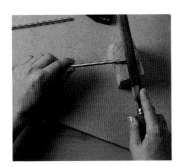

7 Using a hacksaw, remove the bent section of the paint roller handle. File the sawn edges smooth.

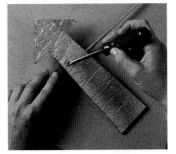

8 Screw the arrow to the plastic roller handle. Fit the roller handle to the metal rod or broom handle to make a mount for the weathervane.

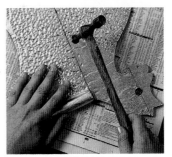

9 Working on newspaper, tap gently all over the bird to give it texture. Colour the section marked on the template blue. Attach the rooster.

A coat rack will keep coats, umbrellas and hats tidy, avoiding clutter in halls. The rich purple background and the slightly matt tones of the metal foils give this rack a touch of splendour.

Regal Coat Rack

you will need

pencil

graph paper

ruler or tape measure

scissors

sheet of MDF (medium-density fiberboard), 5mm/¼in thick

hand saw or jigsaw

fine-grade sandpaper (glasspaper)

wood primer

paintbrush

satin-finish wood paint

tracing paper

soft pencil

thin cardboard

copper foil, 40 gauge (0.08mm/⅟₃₀₀in thick)

dry ballpoint pen

aluminium foil, 36 gauge (0.1mm/⅟₂₅₀in thick)

centre punch

epoxy resin glue

drill

3 ball end hooks

2 mirror plates

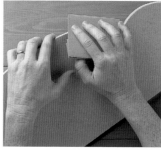

1 Draw the basic shape for the coat rack on to graph paper to make a pattern. This rack is 60cm/23½in wide by 20cm/8in high at its highest point. Cut out and draw around it on to the MDF (medium-density fiberboard). Saw out the shape with a hand saw or jigsaw. Smooth the edges with sandpaper (glasspaper).

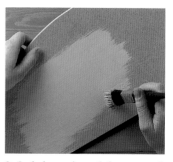

2 Seal the surface of the coat rack with one coat of wood primer. When it is dry, lightly sand the surface, then paint it with satin-finish wood paint. Allow to dry thoroughly. Trace the crown, fleur-de-lys and star templates from the back of the book. Transfer them on to a sheet of thin cardboard. Cut out the shapes to make templates.

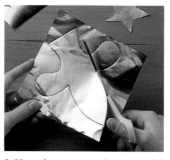

3 Place the crown on the copper foil and draw around it using a dry ballpoint pen. Repeat. Draw around the fleur-de-lys and stars on aluminium foil. Draw two stars. Cut out all of the shapes using scissors.

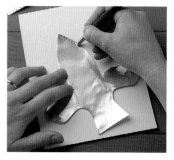

4 Rest each shape on a piece of thin cardboard. Make a line of dots around the edge of all the shapes by pressing into the foil using a centre punch.

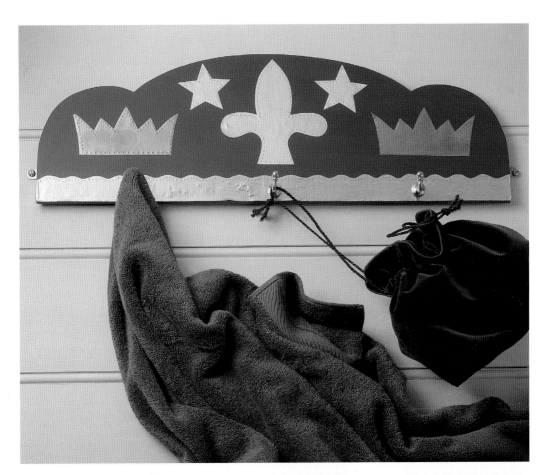

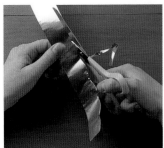

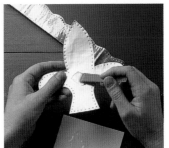

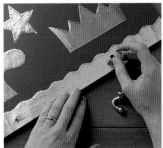

5 Cut a 5cm/2in-wide strip of the aluminium foil the same length as the bottom edge of the rack. Cut a wavy line along the top edge of the strip and then mark a row of dots along it with the punch.

6 Place the wavy edging and the stars, crowns and fleur-de-lys on the front of the rack with the raised side of the dots facing upwards. Use epoxy resin glue to stick the pieces in place.

7 When the glue is thoroughly dry, drill three holes at equal distances 2.5cm/1in from the bottom edge of the coat rack. Screw a hook into each hole. Attach a mirror plate to both sides of the coat rack for hanging.

This delightful clock is made from copper sheet and wire on a base of self-hardening clay and is decorated with paint and gold pigment. This novel timepiece is designed to be kept on display.

Magic Wand Clock

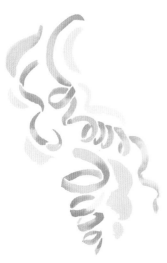

you will need

tin shears or snips

copper wire

copper sheet

pair of compasses (compass)

thin cardboard

pliers

fretsaw (scroll saw)

aluminium tube, 1cm/²⁄₅in diameter, 40cm/15³⁄₄in long

self-hardening clay

rolling pin

sharp modelling tool

terracotta-coloured acrylic paint

paintbrushes

clear acrylic varnish

gold powder pigment

clock movement and hands

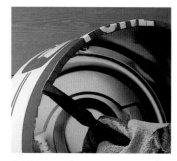

1 Using tin shears or snips, cut five 20cm/8in lengths of copper wire and four 18cm/7in lengths. Cut out five triangles and one heart shape from the copper sheet. Draw a circle 11.5cm/4½ in in diameter on cardboard and cut out. Draw a second circle inside with a diameter of 6cm/2½in and cut out the centre.

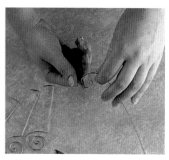

2 Using pliers, bend the shorter pieces of wire into zigzag shapes with looped ends and four of the longer ones into spirals. Bend the top ends of the wire over slightly. Using a fretsaw (scroll saw), cut the aluminium tube into two pieces, one piece measuring 10cm/4in, the other measuring 30cm/12in.

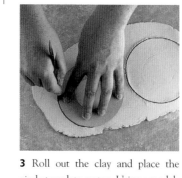

3 Roll out the clay and place the circle template on top. Using a modelling tool, cut two clay discs, one using the outer edge only, the other including the inner circle as well. While the clay is wet, embed the copper triangles around the edge of the solid circle.

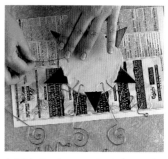

4 Stick the zigzags and spirals into the clay, alternating them between the triangles. Place the short aluminium tube at the bottom of the circle. Place the hollow disc on top so that it fits flush with the solid one. Press them together and remove the tube.

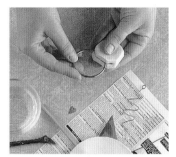

5 Roll out the leftover clay and cut out two hexagons. Bend a length of copper wire into a loop and insert between the two hexagons. Insert one end of the longer aluminium tube between the hexagons and press them together. Fit the other end of the tube into the moulded hole made by the shorter tube in the head of the clock. Press the metal heart into the centre of the top hexagon. Make a hole in the circle for the clock movement and leave all parts of the clock to dry for two to three days.

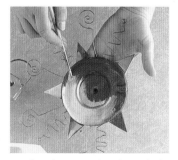

6 When dry, prime the clay with the terracotta-coloured paint. Leave it to dry. Mix clear acrylic varnish with gold powder pigment and paint over the terracotta-coloured areas and the tube. Fit the clock movement and hands and, to finish, wind copper wire up around the aluminium tube.

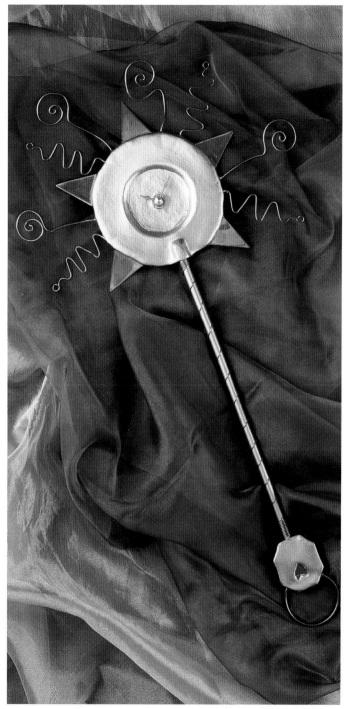

Add a touch of fairy-tale romance to your garden with this whimsical tower. Secure it to a tray on top of a tree stump or post, and sprinkle bird food all around.

Rapunzel's Tower

you will need

paper

pencil

garden twine

ruler or tape measure

scissors

metal tubing, 15cm/6in diameter

45 x 45cm/18 x 18in copper sheet, 0.9mm/¹⁄₂₇in thick

chinagraph pencil

protective gloves

tin shears and snips

file

drill, 3mm/¹⁄₈in bit

blind rivet gun and 3mm/¹⁄₈in rivets

glue gun and glue stick

2.5 x 5cm/1 x 2in copper foil, 0.2mm/¹⁄₁₂₅in thick

nail or wire, 6.5cm/2½in long

twigs

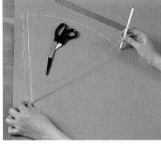

1 Make a pattern for the cone-shaped roof to fit around the metal tubing; add a 2cm/⅘in overlap for joining the edges. Transfer on to the copper sheet with a chinagraph pencil. Wearing protective gloves, cut out the shape using tin shears. File off any sharp edges. Bend the copper into a cone shape with an overlap. Check the fit on the tubing.

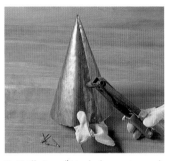

2 Drill 3mm/⅛in holes at intervals through both layers of copper along the overlap and fasten the overlap using blind rivets. Squeeze the handle of the rivet gun until the rivet shaft snaps off, securing the overlap firmly. Use a glue gun to glue the cone-shaped roof in place on top of the metal tubing. Allow the glue to dry.

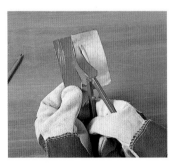

3 Cut a wavy flag for the roof from copper foil. Cut a sideways "V" in one end of the flag and bend the other end around a nail or short piece of wire as a flagpole. Glue to the tip of the roof.

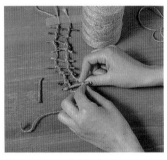

4 Make a rope ladder by knotting cut lengths of small twigs between two lengths of twine. Cut an entrance hole in the tubing with tin snips and glue the ladder in place.

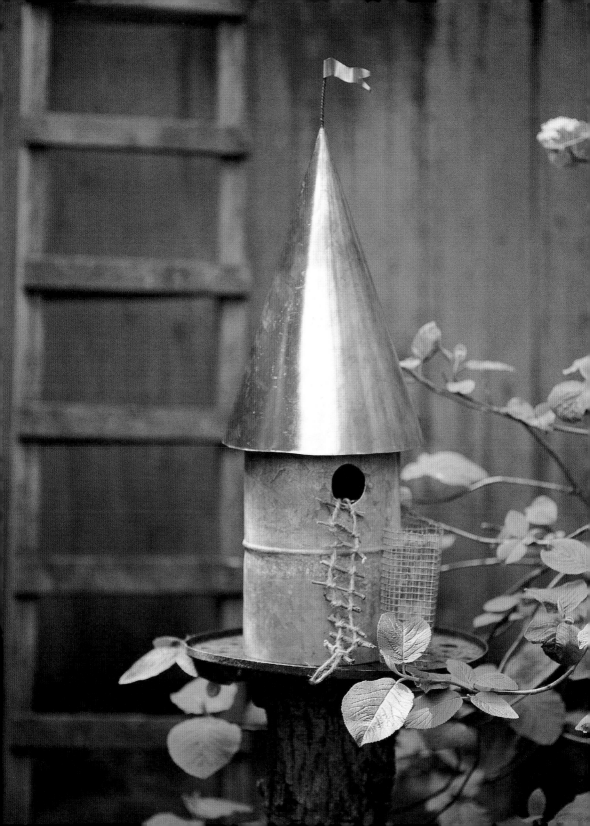

The idea of decorating metal objects with raised punched patterns has been around ever since sheet metal was invented about 300 years ago. Bare metal buckets are ideal for this sort of pattern-making.

Punched Metal Bucket

you will need
permanent marker pen
bare metal bucket
piece of wood
blunt nail or centre punch
hammer
rag
lighter fuel (or similar solvent)

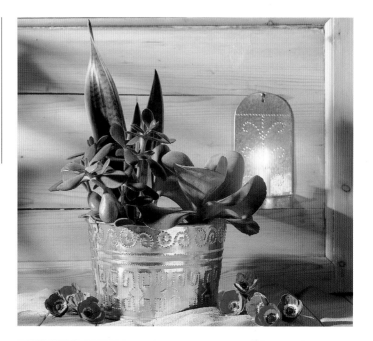

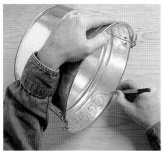

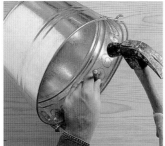

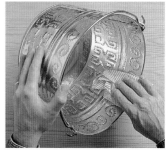

1 Using a permanent marker pen, draw your pattern on the inside of the bucket. Any repeated curves or shapes are suitable.

2 Rest the bucket on a piece of wood to protect the work surface. Following the pattern, tap the nail or centre punch with a hammer, keeping the dents about 1cm/⅜in apart. Hammer the pattern all over the inside.

3 Use a rag and lighter fuel to clean off the marker pen pattern that is left between the punched marks.

Inspired by Mexican folk art, this brilliantly painted and punched mirror frame will give your room a touch of exotic colour and warmth. Use the brightest paints or pens you can find.

Mexican Mirror

you will need

paper

permanent marker pen

scissors

aluminium sheet

glue gun and glue stick

self-healing cutting mat

hammer

small and large centre punches

tin snips

protective gloves

chisel

blue glass paint

paintbrush

permanent felt-tipped pens or

glass paints: turquoise, green,

orange and pink

circular mirror, 15cm/6in diameter

circular cake board, 25cm/10in

diameter

double-sided adhesive pads

nail or fine drill bit

galvanized wire

wire cutters

pliers

7 short screws

screwdriver

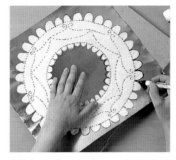

1 Enlarge the template at the back of the book to a diameter of 30cm/12in and then cut it out. Stick the paper pattern to the aluminium sheet using a glue gun, and trace around this with a permanent marker pen.

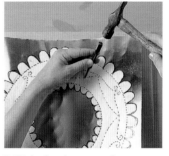

2 With the aluminium sheet resting on a cutting mat, make indentations along the lines of the pattern using a hammer and small centre punch. Just two taps of the hammer at each point should be sufficient.

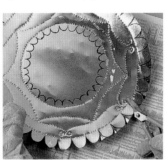

3 Cut out the shape with tin snips, wearing gloves to protect your hands. To cut out the central area, first punch a hole through the centre using a chisel, and cut from there.

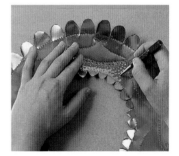

4 Using the small centre punch, hammer indentations at random all over the inner section of the frame to give it an overall texture.

▶

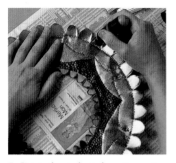

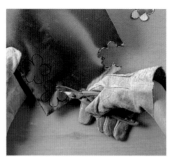

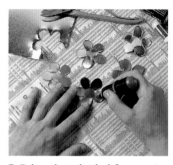

5 Paint the indented section using translucent blue glass paint. Leave to dry. Colour the rest of the frame as shown using permanent felt-tipped pens or glass paints.

6 Draw and cut out a five-petalled flower template with a diameter of 5cm/2in. Trace all around it on to an aluminium sheet using a permanent marker pen to make seven flowers. Cut them out using tin snips.

7 Colour the individual flowers using permanent felt-tipped pens or glass paints in bright colours.

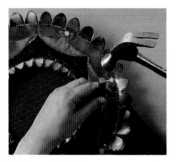

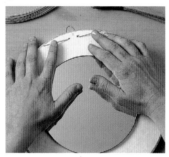

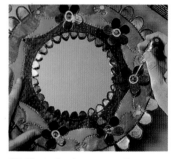

8 Place all the flowers on a cutting mat and use a large centre punch to hammer a hole through the centre of each, big enough for a screw to pass through. If the flowers buckle, bend them back into shape. Make similar holes at all the points on the frame, following the template.

9 Attach the mirror to the bottom of the cake board using double-sided adhesive pads. Pierce two holes near the edge of the board using a nail or fine drill bit. Cut a piece of galvanized wire and bend into a hanging loop. Thread the ends through the holes and bend them flat against the board.

10 Place the frame over the mirror and backing board. Place the flowers in position so that holes correspond with those in the frame and screw them on through the frame into the backing board. Colour the screws to match the flower centres.

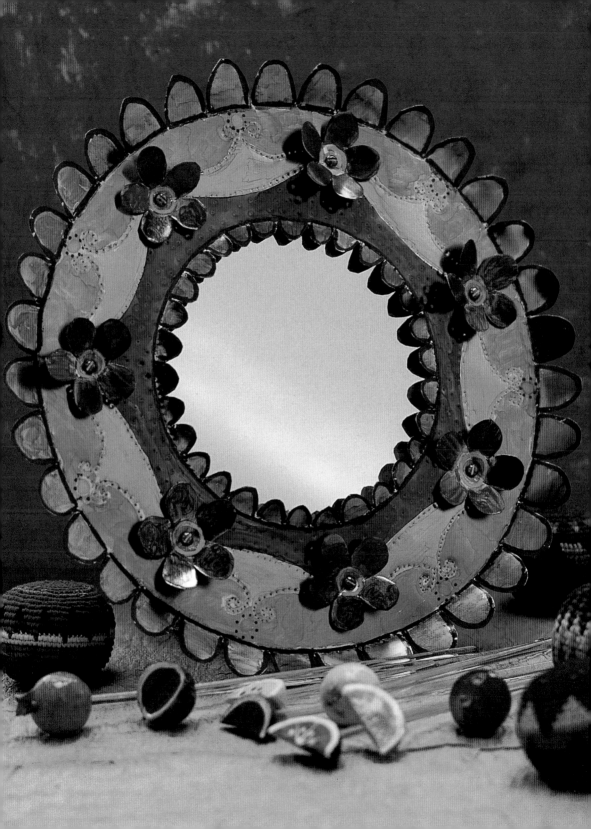

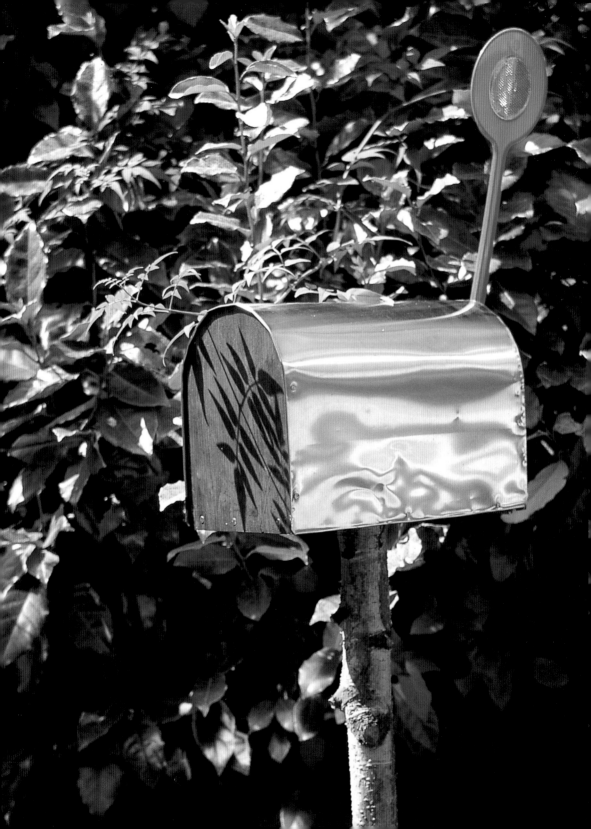

Fix this traditionally styled mailbox to your garden gate with its door open. The reflective indicator will tell you at a glance when the door is closed and your post has arrived.

Classic Mailbox

you will need
pencil and ruler
exterior plywood, 18mm/¾in thick
tenon saw
saucer
coping saw, jigsaw or band saw
sandpaper (glasspaper)
tinted exterior varnish (or polyurethane)
varnish brush
nails
hammer
screws
2 brass screw hinges (spring hinges)
tin shears
protective gloves
cooking-oil drum
metal straight edge
scrap wood
mallet
drill
bicycle reflective indicator
bolt
spanner (wrench)

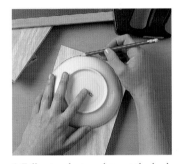

1 Following the templates at the back of the book, mark the dimensions of the base, back and door on to the plywood surface. Cut out with a tenon saw. Mark the curves by drawing around a saucer.

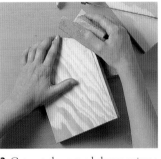

2 Cut out the curved shapes using a coping saw, jigsaw or band saw. Smooth the edges with sandpaper (glasspaper). Paint all the wooden pieces with tinted exterior varnish (or polyurethane) and leave to dry.

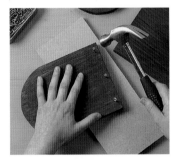

3 Partly hammer nails in the back then hammer the back to the base.

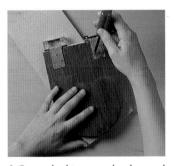

4 Screw the hinges to the door and attach to the front of the wooden base. ▶

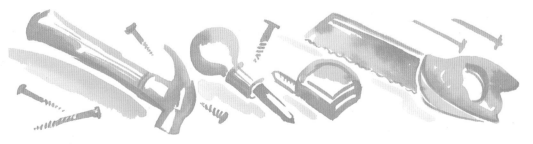

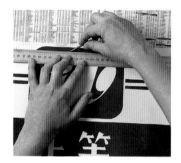

5 Use tin shears to cut off the top and bottom of the oil drum, wearing gloves for protection. Discard carefully. Cut down the seam and flatten the drum. Using the template measurements, mark the metal using a straight edge and a nail, as shown.

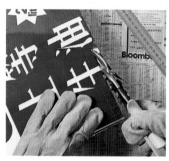

6 Cut out the metal sheet using tin shears, wearing gloves to protect your hands. Leave a border all around for turning, as marked on the template.

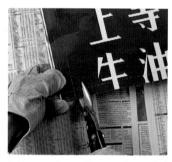

7 Cut out the small rectangle marked at each of the corners. This enables the edges of the tin to be folded in neatly, without any overlap.

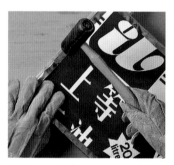

8 Protecting the work surface with some scrap wood, turn in the edges of the metal to eliminate the sharp edges. Tap them flat with a mallet.

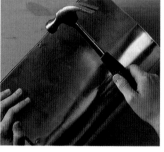

9 Pull the metal cover over the base, aligning the edges. Nail the metal to the mailbox base and back, starting at the centre of each side and working outwards. Ensure the door is free.

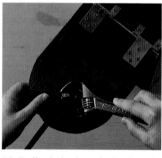

10 Drill a hole through the door for the indicator and fix it securely in place with a bolt.

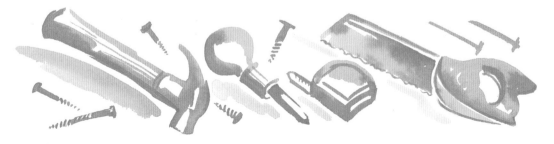

With its distinctive curved lid, this lunch box is based on traditional American designs. The extra space under the box lid makes a handy compartment for storing drinks flasks, which lie on top of the food.

Lunch Box

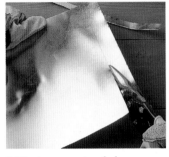

1 Wearing protective clothes, cut one end from an oil drum using a hacksaw. Using tin shears, cut open the drum and remove the other end to leave a metal panel. Wipe any excess oil from the panel.

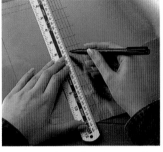

2 Using a ruler and marker pen, draw the cover following the template. Using tin shears, cut out the cover.

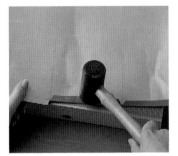

3 Clamp the 90° block of wood in the vice. Place the cover on it and turn over one edge using a hide hammer. Turn the cover over. Position the 45° wooden block inside the turned edge and hammer the edge over it. Remove the block and hammer the edge flat. Repeat on the other two edges. File all corners smooth. Repeat with the lid.

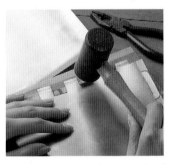

4 Using pliers, turn alternate tabs of the hinges over. Turn the tabs on each of the two covers so that each folded tab is opposite an unfolded tab. Flatten the tabs using a hide hammer.

▶

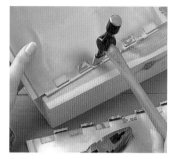

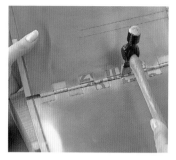

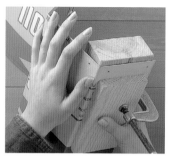

5 Bend half of each unflattened tab back using pliers. Cut a piece of fine wire the same length as the hinge and insert it through the tabs of one of the covers. Hammer the edges of the tabs on this cover firmly under the wire to secure them.

6 Carefully line up the edges of the hinge and slot the remaining tabs under the wire. Fold the tabs around the wire and hammer the ends under as before to finish off the hinge.

7 Place the cover on a wooden block. Hold the edge with pliers and drill a small hole 9mm/⅜in in from the side edges, and about 2.5cm/1in from the ends, folds and hinge. Drill another hole halfway along the edge of the lid. Place the 90° block inside along a foldline and clamp in place. Bend the cover over. Bend all the folds.

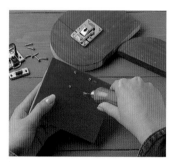

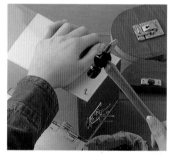

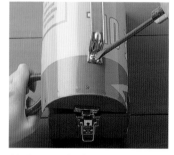

8 Cut two end blocks from MDF (medium-density fiberboard) using the template as a guide. Cut across each block, as indicated by the dotted line, to create two semi-circles. Stain the wood red. Fit the case locks.

9 Separate the blocks and semi-circles and place the blocks inside the cover. Using a bradawl (awl), mark the nail positions on the blocks through the holes. Nail the cover to the blocks. Place the semi-circles of MDF on top of the blocks and close the catches to hold them. Press the lid around the semi-circles and then nail it securely to the semi-circles.

10 Remove the handle from the oil drum. Place it on a wooden block and drill a hole in each end of the handle. File the holes smooth. Place on top of the lunch box. Using a permanent marker pen, transfer the position of the holes in the handle to the top of the lunch box and drill through. File the holes smooth, then bolt the handle in place.

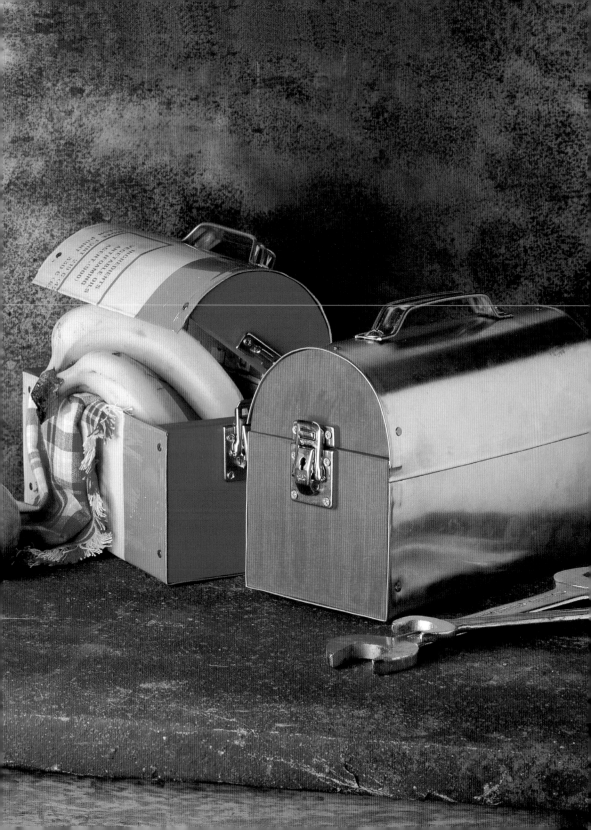

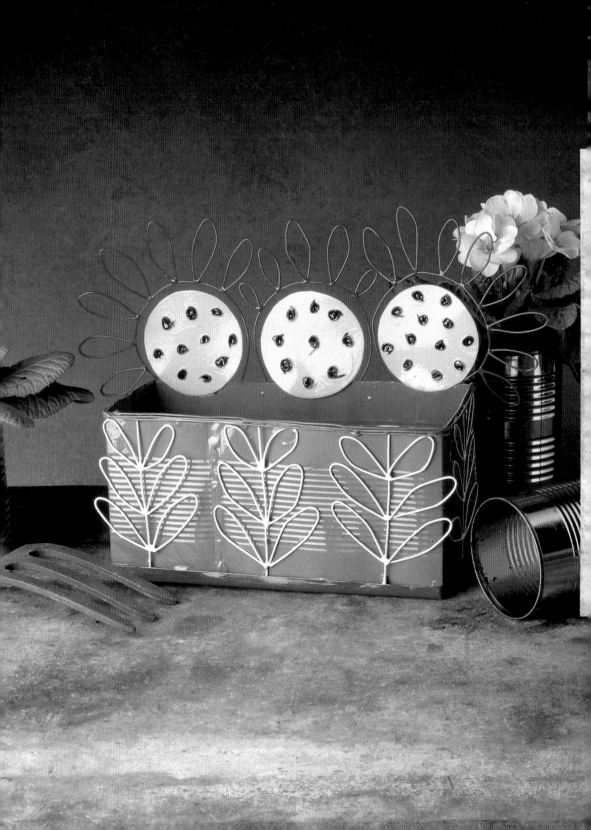

This brightly painted herb container has an appealing folk-art charm. It is made from recycled tin cans that are hammered flat and soldered together to make a box. The top edges are bound with fine wire.

Herb Container

you will need
can opener
4 tin cans
work shirt and protective
leather gloves
tin shears
sheet of chipboard
hide hammer
file
masking tape
protective mask and goggles
soldering mat
flux
soldering iron and solder
thin tin plate
block of wood
small hammer
bradawl (awl)
fine wire
wire cutters
pliers
wooden pegs (pins)
enamel paints: blue, white, red, yellow
and black
paintbrush

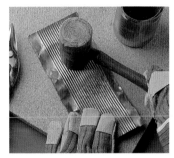

1 Using a can opener, remove the tops and bottoms from four tin cans. Wearing a work shirt and protective gloves, cut the cans open down one side using tin shears. Place the tin panels on a sheet of chipboard and flatten them using a hide hammer. File all the edges of the tin to make them completely smooth.

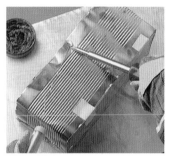

2 Use one flattened piece of tin to make the base. Bend the other three cans around the base to make a box shape. Hold all the sections together with strips of masking tape. Wearing a protective mask and goggles, put the box on a soldering mat, apply flux to the join and solder the sections of the box together.

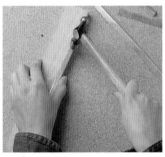

3 Cut two long and two short strips of thin tin plate the same lengths as the sides of the box base and file smooth. Arrange each strip along the edge of a long block of wood and hammer it over the wood to make a right angle along its length.

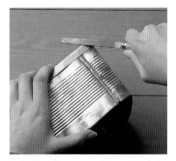

4 Solder the strips of tin around the base of the box and then carefully file all the corners to remove any sharp edges. Using a bradawl (awl), punch two holes in the bottom of the box for drainage and file around the holes to remove the rough edges. ▶

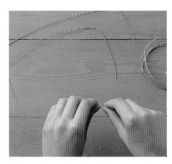

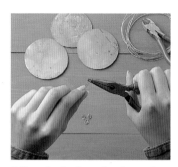

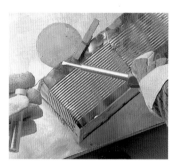

5 Cut three lengths of fine wire long enough to fit around the sides and front of the top of the box. Bend the pieces of wire to the shape of the box and solder together along their lengths. Solder the wire around the side and front edges of the top of the box.

6 To make the flower heads, cut three circles of thin tin about the same size as the tops of the cans. File all the edges smooth. Cut short lengths of wire and twist around the end of a pair of pliers to make seed shapes. Place several seeds on each flower head. Drop a solder dot in the centre of each seed to join it to the head.

7 Solder the flower heads to the back of the box. Hold them in position using wooden pegs (pins) as you work. Cut three lengths of wire long enough to fit around the flower heads. Using your fingers, make long loops of wire for petals. Solder the petals at equal distances along each length of wire.

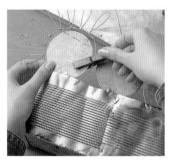

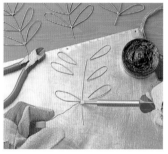

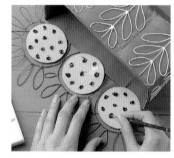

8 Bend the wire petals around the flower heads and solder to the back edge of the box. Use pegs to keep the petals in position while you work.

9 To make the flower stems, cut five lengths of wire the same height as the front and sides of the container. Use your fingers to make six wire leaf shapes for each stem. Solder the leaves to the stems. Solder the stems to the front and sides of the box.

10 Paint the box using blue enamel paint. When the blue paint has dried, paint the stems white and the petals red. Paint the flower heads yellow and paint the seeds black. Paint the strip around the base of the box red.

Oil drums are a great source of metal and this one has been cleverly recycled into a barbecue. Every part of the drum has been used and a tin can has been transformed into a crazily angled chimney stack.

Rocket Barbecue

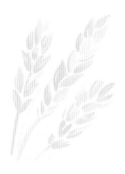

you will need
work shirt and protective
leather gloves
oil drum and oil drum scraps
hacksaw
tin shears
permanent marker pen
ruler
grill (broiler)
pliers
file
length of dowel, 2.5cm/1in-diameter
hand saw
wooden block
bradawl (awl)
annular ring nails
hammer
drill
pop riveter and rivets
tin can, open at one end

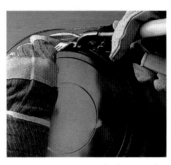

1 Wearing protective clothes, cut the oil drum in half using a hacksaw blade and tin shears. Draw two lines around the cut rim of the lower part of the drum, the first about 5mm/⅕in down and the second 2.5cm/1in down. Place the grill (broiler) on top of the drum and mark a point on each side where each bar of the grill touches the drum.

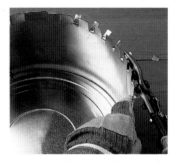

2 Using tin shears, cut down to the lower line from each of these grill points to make thin tabs, leaving wider tabs in-between. Using pliers, bend the thin tabs outwards. Clip them shorter using tin shears and then bend them inwards and down to the inside of the oil drum.

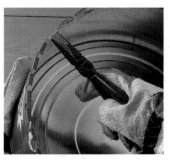

3 Using pliers, grip the edge of each of the wider tabs where the upper line is drawn. Bend the edges over and squeeze them firmly to flatten them.

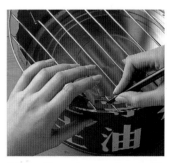

4 The grill rests between the tabs. To make it sit securely, cut tabs near the unmarked side sections on a diagonal. Place the grill on top of the drum and check its position. ▶

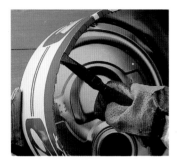

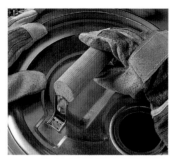

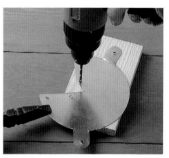

5 To make the lid of the barbecue, draw a line around the other half of the drum, 1cm/⅖in down from the cut edge. Cut equally spaced tabs all around the rim as far as the line, using tin shears. Using pliers, bend over the tabs to the inside of the drum and flatten them.

6 Remove the stopper from the top of the drum. Cut the handle in half using tin shears. Using pliers, bend both halves of the handle up at an angle of 90°. File the edges of the halves smooth. Cut a length of dowel to fit between the halves. Hold a wooden block against the side of each handle half and make a hole in each using a bradawl (awl). File the rough edges around the holes. Nail the handle halves to the dowel through the holes.

7 Draw the chimney roof pattern on to a spare piece of oil drum metal as shown here. The diameter should be about 12cm/4¾in. Cut out the roof using tin shears and file the edges smooth. Place the roof on a block of wood and drill holes as shown. Hold the metal with a pair of pliers to stop it spinning round as you drill. Gently curve the roof around so that the holes match and pop rivet the sides together.

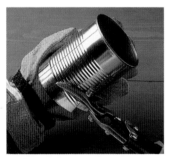

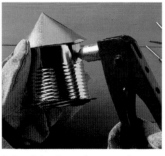

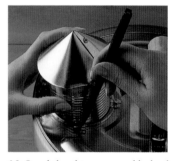

8 Bend the roof tabs under. Place the can on the tabs and mark where the edges of the can touch them. Bend the tabs back along the lines with pliers. To make the chimney, draw a line all the way around the base of the can to give the chimney a slanting base. Draw a second line parallel to the first, 1cm/⅖in above it. Draw four tabs at equal distances around the can between the lines. Cut around the upper line, leaving the tabs in place.

9 Bend the four tabs outwards, using the pliers. Place the roof on the chimney. Transfer the position of the holes in the tabs to the sides of the chimney. Drill holes in the chimney to match and file away the rough edges. Pop rivet the roof to the chimney.

10 Stand the chimney on a block of wood and drill a hole in each tab. Place the chimney on the top of the lid. Transfer the position of the holes in the tabs to the lid. Drill and file the holes. Pop rivet the chimney to the lid. Drill a hole every 5cm/2in around the base of the barbecue to allow air to circulate when it is in use. File the rough edges around the holes.

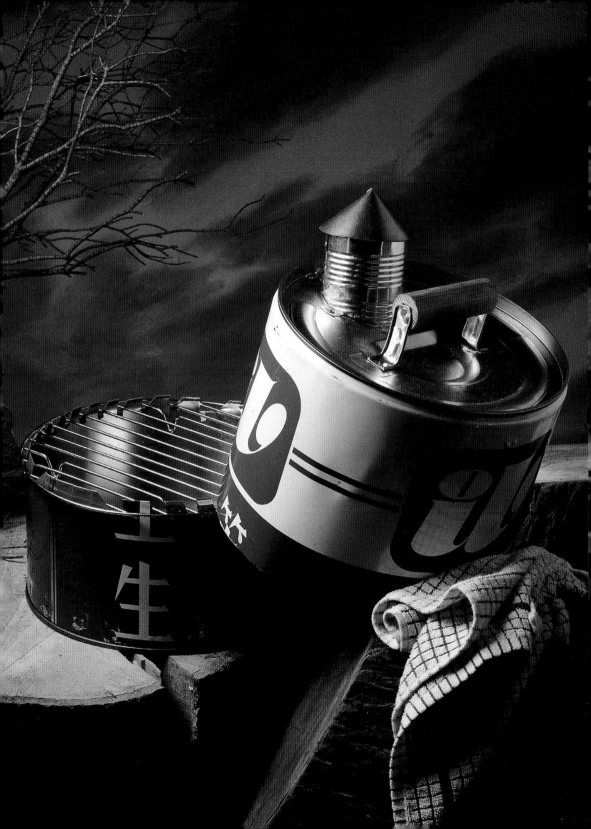

Templates

Enlarge the templates on a photocopier. Alternatively, trace the design and draw a grid of evenly spaced squares over your tracing. Draw a larger grid on to another piece of paper and copy the outline square by square. Finally, draw over the lines to make sure they are continuous.

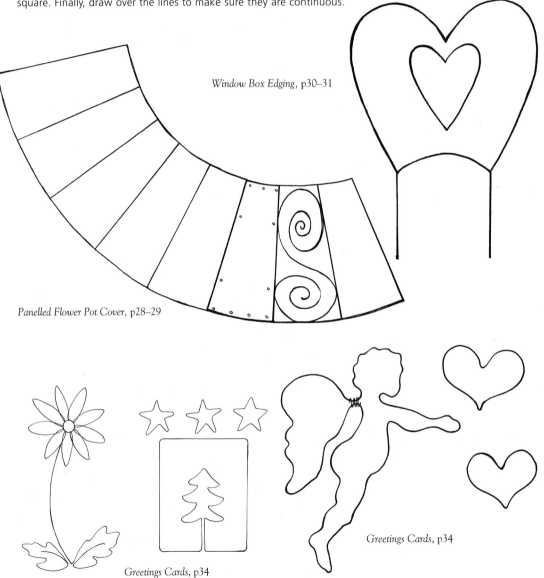

Window Box Edging, p30–31

Panelled Flower Pot Cover, p28–29

Greetings Cards, p34

Greetings Cards, p34

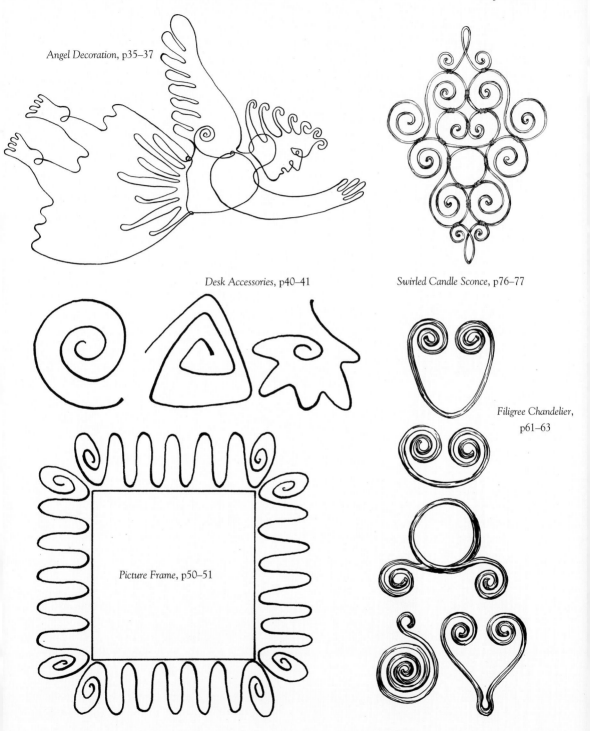

Angel Decoration, p35–37

Swirled Candle Sconce, p76–77

Desk Accessories, p40–41

Filigree Chandelier,
p61–63

Picture Frame, p50–51

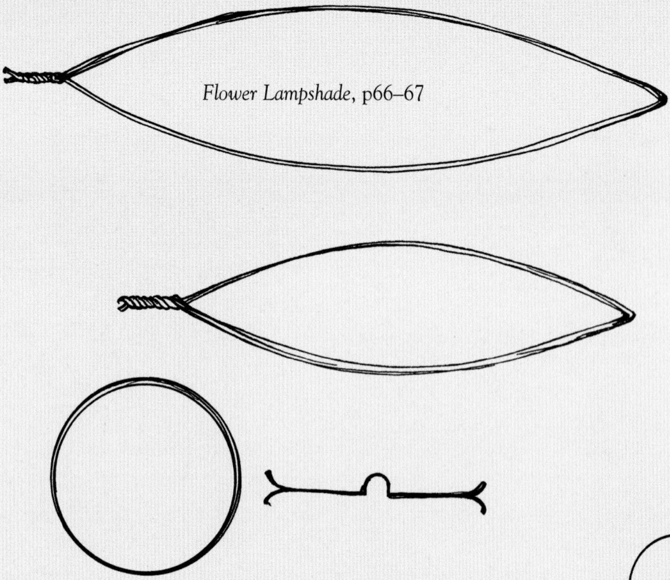

Flower Lampshade, p66–67

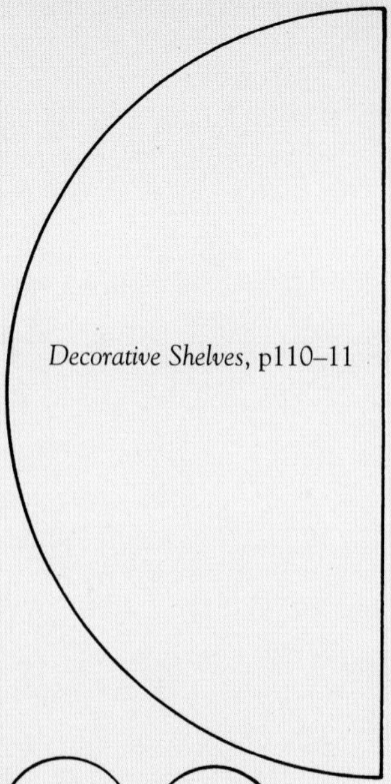

Decorative Shelves, p110–11

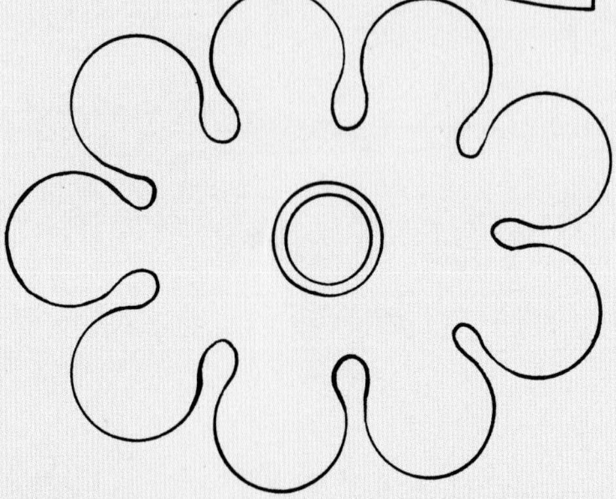

Monogrammed Clothes Hanger, p86–87

Flower Fly Swatter, p90

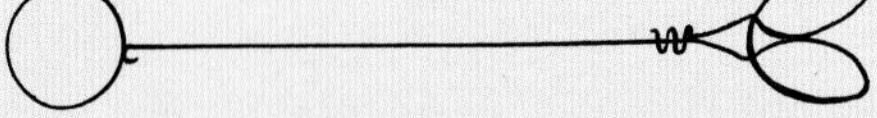

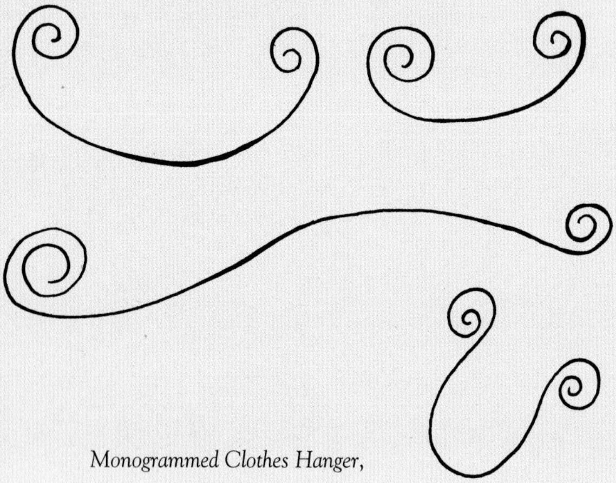

Monogrammed Clothes Hanger, p86–87

A B C D E F G H I J K L M

N O P Q R S T U V W X Y Z

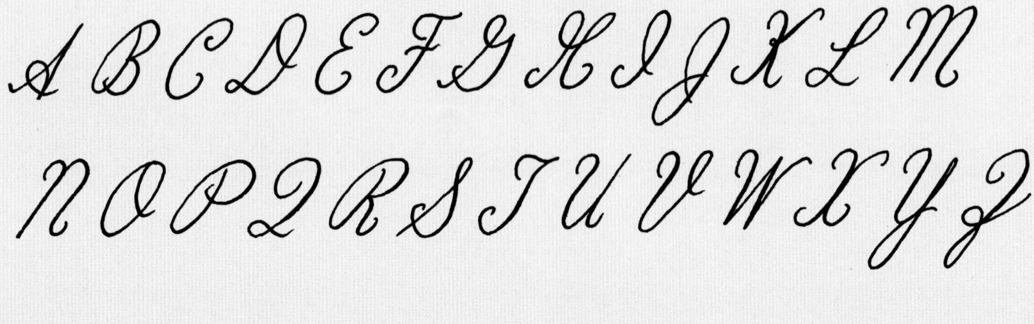

Embossed Greetings Cards, p141

Lacy Silver Gloves, p142

Repoussé Frame, p143

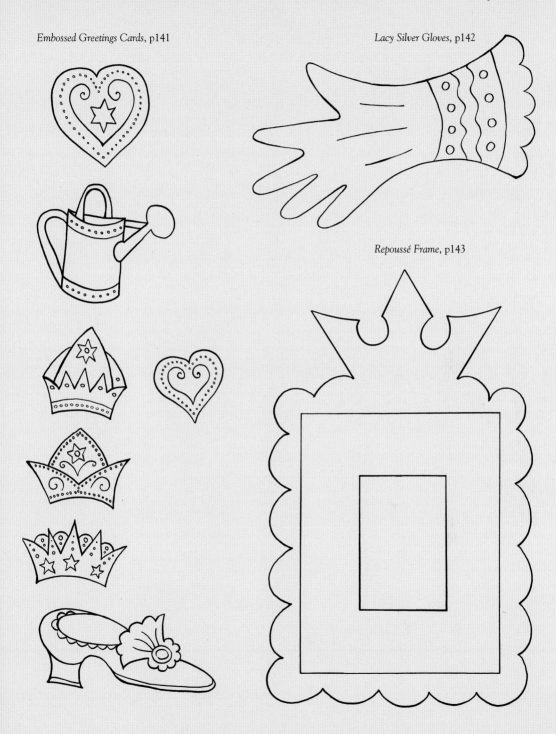

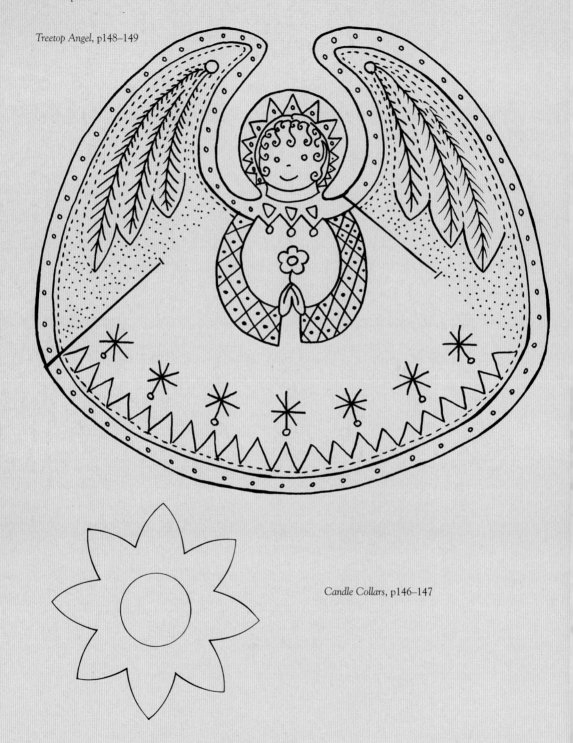

Treetop Angel, p148–149

Candle Collars, p146–147

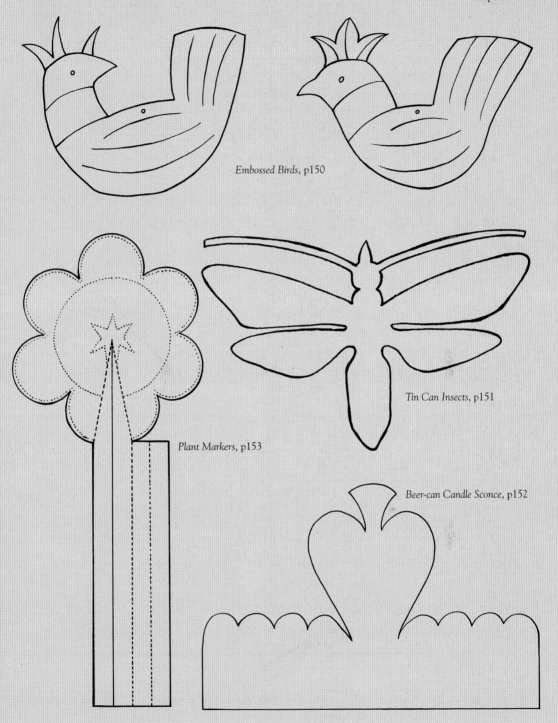

Embossed Birds, p150

Tin Can Insects, p151

Plant Markers, p153

Beer-can Candle Sconce, p152

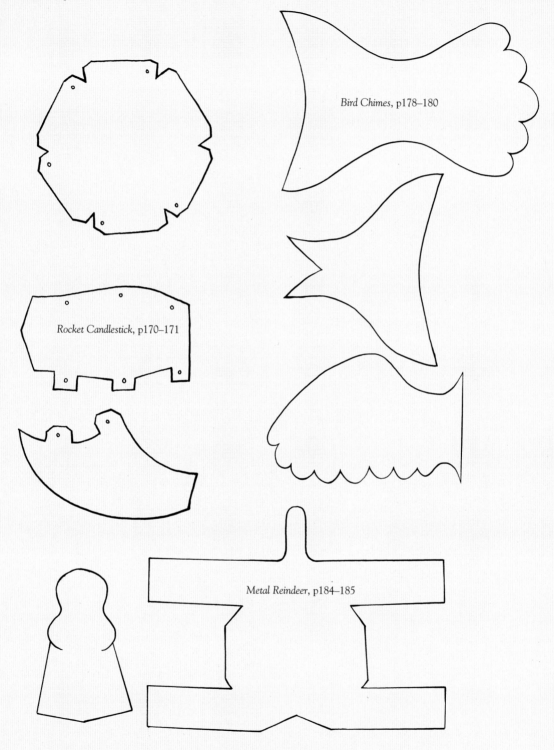

Bird Chimes, p178–180

Rocket Candlestick, p170–171

Metal Reindeer, p184–185

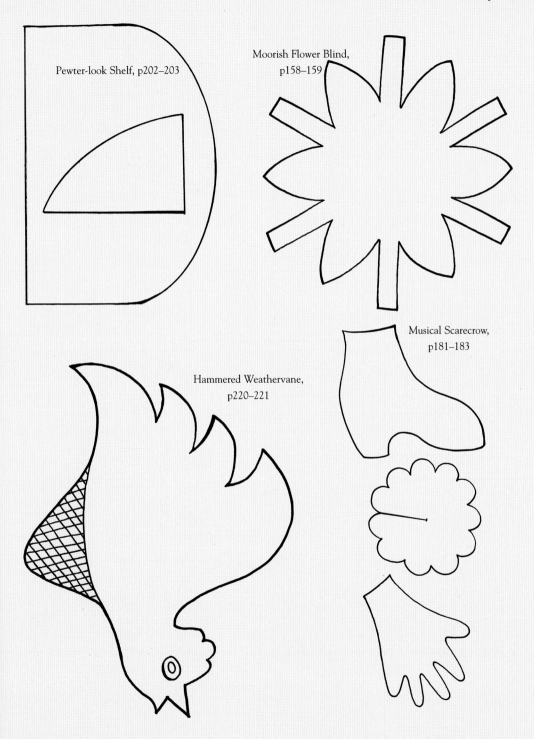

Pewter-look Shelf, p202–203

Moorish Flower Blind,
p158–159

Musical Scarecrow,
p181–183

Hammered Weathervane,
p220–221

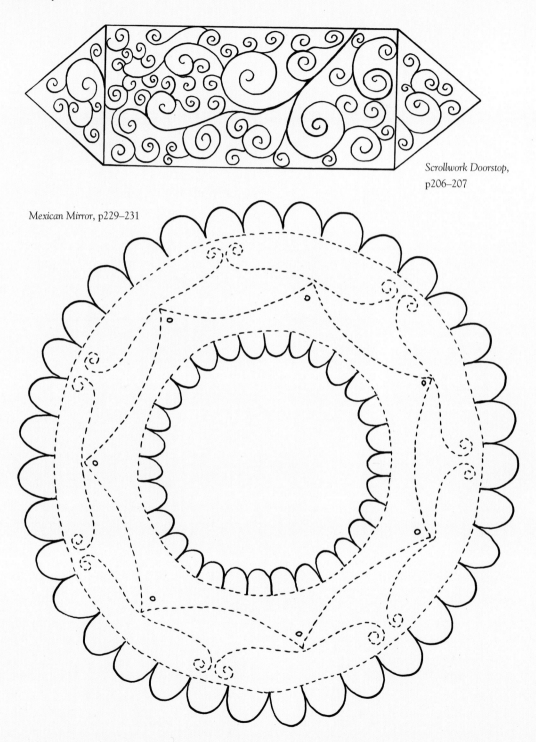

Scrollwork Doorstop,
p206–207

Mexican Mirror, p229–231

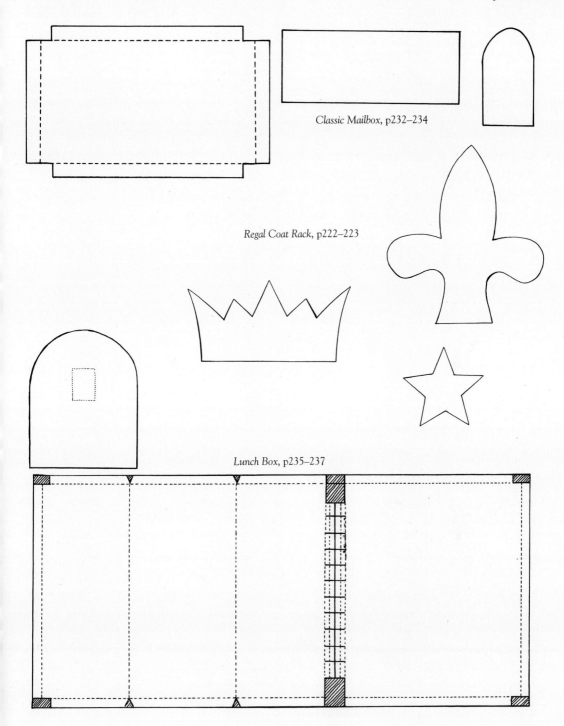

Classic Mailbox, p232–234

Regal Coat Rack, p222–223

Lunch Box, p235–237

Index

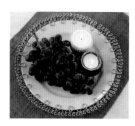

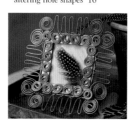
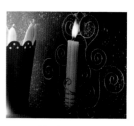

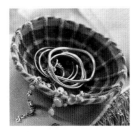
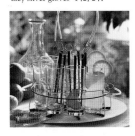

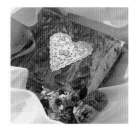

Acknowledgements

The publisher would like to thank the following people for designing projects in this book:

Evelyn Bennett for the Photograph Frame p168–169, Bird Chimes p178–180, Metal Reindeer p184–185, Jewel Box p200–201 and Spice Rack p218–219 and Herb Container p238–240.

Penny Boylan for the Embossed Greetings Cards p141, Musical Scarecrow p181–183, Shimmering Temple p188–189 and String Dispenser p214–215.

Marion Elliot for the Moorish Flower Blind p158–159, Painted Tin Brooches p160–161, Embossed Book Jacket p162–163, Painted Mirror p166–167, Incense Holder p172–174, Tin Can Chandelier p186–187, Punched Panel Cabinet p204–205, Number Plaque p208–209 and Regal Coat Rack p222–223.

Andrew Gilmore for the Festive Light Bush p38–39, Toasting Fork p48–49, Flower Fly Swatter p90, Toilet Tissue Holder p94–95, Bottle Carrier p96–97, Egg Tree p99–101, Hanging String Dispenser p106–107, Spoon Rack p112–113, Garden Drinks Carrier p126–127, Plant Markers p153, Rocket Candlestick p170–171, Metal-faced Drawers p196–197, Pewter-look Shelf p202–203, Hammered Weathervane p220–221, Classic Mailbox p232–234, Lunch Box p235–237 and Rocket Barbecue p241.

Dawn Giullas for the Pocket Clips p33 and Greetings Cards p34.

Karin Hossack for the Window Box Edging p30–31, Mesh Place Mat p44–45, Pretty Plate Edging p46–47, Woven Pipe Cleaner Basket p102–103 and main image on cover and Decorative Shelves p110–111.

Alison Jenkins for the Panelled Flower Pot Cover p28–29, Desk Accessories p40–41, Picture Frame p50–51 and Fabric-covered Baskets p104–105.

Mary Maguire for the Happy Hippy Necklace p32, Angel Decoration p35–37, Decorative Candle Sconce p52–53, Filigree Chandelier p61–63, Bicycle Toy p79–81, Wire Vegetable Basket p108–109, Toast Rack p116–118, Copper Bowl p122–123, Garden Lantern p124–125, Spice Rack p128–129, Garden Tray p130–131, Utility Rack p134–135, Embossed Heart p140, Treetop Angel p148–149, Heart Candle Sconce p156, Metal Mosaic p164–165, Fiesta Chandelier p175–177, Contemporary Clock p198–199, Scrollwork Doorstop p206–207, Stylish Suitcase p216–217 and Mexican Mirror p229–231.

Sue Radcliffe for the Flower Lampshade p66–67, Jewel Nightlight p70–71. Classic Candlesticks p74–75 and Monogrammed Clothes Hanger p86–87.

Jennie Russell for the Spiral Napkin Holders p42–43, Flower Holder p64–65, Fiesta Oil Bottle p72–73 and Toothbrush Holder p88–89.

Deborah Schneebeli-Morrell Repoussé Frame p143, Candle Collars p146–147, Embossed Birds p150 and Beer-can Candle Sconce p152

Adele Tipler for the Woven Bottle p54–55, Fused Flowers p68–69 and Woven Chair p119–121.

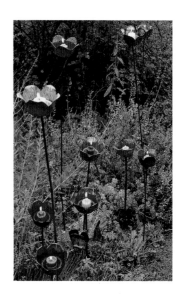

NOTES

NOTES

NOTES

NOTES

NOTES

NOTES

NOTES

NOTES